TRAVELS WITH HARLEY

Trusting in the Unknown Road Ahead

SUSAN DOLLENGER

TRAVELS WITH HARLEY

TRUSTING IN THE UNKNOWN ROAD AHEAD

With many thanks to Irene Wanner, Dede Feldman, Mark Feldman, and Peter Harrington for their help in editing and for their support. And thanks to Erica Kane for her perseverance.

Cover and book design by Erica Kane
photos by Susan Dollenger

CONTENTS: COAST TO COAST

PREFACE

Life doesn't offer security, not really, just the mirage of safety and security. I was never so aware of this truth as while we were on the road. In the wake of the loss of my mother, my fiancé and I had sold our house, quit our jobs, bought a camper and hit the road with our golden retriever, Harley. This is the story of our odyssey, the music we played around campfires from coast to coast, the many people we met and learned from along the way, and the meditation we shared that helped open us to a new way of life in the campgrounds across this country. It's the story of how we came to open our minds, let go, and live in the flow of synchronicity. How we were trained by our dog to live a simple life, free of expectations, satisfied with whatever arose. Sometimes the journey took courage, as we faced loneliness, feelings of vulnerability, releasing the familiar, and embracing the unknown. We were counseled by the *I Ching*, an ancient book of Chinese wisdom, which advised us, "The wanderer remains humble and flexible when in a foreign land. The land that is nowhere, that is your true home." And as we grew to realize, our true home was right there inside ourselves.

This book was written during the pandemic of 2020, a time when many people discovered the value of camping as a safer way to travel, a way to open their lives from "sheltering in place". And the book Nomadland, published in 2017, pointed to those "full-timers" who chose to live in vans or

I

campers as an alternative to the expense of renting or owning. And for a time, we joined this tribe of nomads, some much less fortunate than others. But on the road, we were all pretty much on a level playing field, part of the growing movement of those who had no permanent abode, only the four wheels that carried us along.

*** PART ONE ***

HEADING WEST

"You must make a revolution in your mind!" Peter quoted from his old Korean Zen teacher as we drove along. And we were doing just that. We'd sold our house, quit our jobs, were leaving behind everything we'd known, saying goodbye to friends and family, and hitting the road in our camper. Making a radical change in our lives. We felt so open and free!

My fiancé Peter, our golden retriever Harley, and I were heading west, where the sky was brilliant, blue, expansive. The allure of the West had been calling our names for ages, we'd been planning, and now the day had finally arrived! At 6 a.m. we drove away from our homeland in Maryland, pulling up all our stakes, disengaging from the busy, goal-oriented life we'd lived there, and taking to the freedom of the open road.

In the tradition of ancient Hindu Brahmin priests when beginning a new venture, I'd held a coconut in both hands and waved it three times clockwise in front of the camper, then smashed it on the concrete driveway to consecrate the journey before embarking. Half of the coconut remained on the ground as a treat for some raccoon, the other half was installed on the dashboard altar of our camper, with a daffodil from our yard nestled inside the curve of its white flesh. Like the first spring flower, our outlook was hopeful and full of new possibility, as we three started out.

The wind whistled through the camper's screen windows which were opened for Harley, who was lying on our bed in the back. The truth of it was that Harley had never actually been that keen on traveling, but he loved getting there, since we always made it a priority to find campgrounds nearby a river, stream or lake where he could swim and wash off the miles. He was a great traveling companion, never whining or complaining, just going with whatever was happening. True to his golden retriever genes, he was good natured and friendly to all we met along the way.

Our home had shrunk to the size of the little camper we shared together and that was the only possession we'd be responsible for on this open-ended journey. We felt that understanding and insight would evolve as we traveled, and serendipity would weave itself into the fabric of this magical life on the road. But Peter proposed that there would also be some "gypsy bad luck", as he called it. Things would happen beyond our control that would test our mettle, since any pilgrimage holds both the wondrous and the challenging. Just then, a truck passed us with "Trust in the Lord" scrawled in the dust on its back. Yes, we trusted in the wisdom of the road, and aimed to move with the rhythms of our intuition.

Actually, we'd already had some mettle tested recently. My mother had needed to go into an assisted living facility where I'd visited her frequently. It had been one thing after another, in and out of the hospital, as she went on the downhill path toward the end of life. She finally passed away at the age of 95, only a couple of months ago. It was a blessing and a relief to come to the end of the suffering. But even so, I missed her deeply and was grieving her loss. My mother and I had been spiritual buddies and shared a very special relationship. Yet all that care, love, and concern for her toward the end had taken its toll. I'd become really run down.

On top of that loss, Peter and I had undergone the grueling process of selling our house. There had been an exhausting kind of grand finale after it finally sold, a manic sorting out and triaging of belongings, putting things in order before leaving that chapter of our lives. We had placed what we could on consignment and had given away the rest. And a few precious things went into storage for we knew not how long. One last trip to the dump that morning and we'd said goodbye to Maryland. The reality of it was, we were both completely worn out, our reserve tanks just about used up. We were badly in need of some R and R.

HEADING EAST

And so it was that we began our pilgrimage out west by heading east. We turned around in our tracks and aimed for the beach, Assateague Island National Seashore to be exact. The campground at this barrier island on the Atlantic shores of Maryland had been our haven of rest and recuperation for many years. The ocean air was healing and just what the doctor ordered, so we'd stay in this pristine place as long as it would take to recover our energy. Being at our sanctuary helped me breathe a deep sigh of relief. Wild ponies roamed the beach, creating a magical and special atmosphere, and actually two ponies were grazing peacefully right beside our campsite as we pulled up. Being wild, they could kick or bite, so thankfully, Harley seemed content to let the ponies be, at least for now.

Over the dunes from our camper was the ocean, out of view, yet the ongoing sound of the surf carried across. Dispersed along the dunes were grasses and bayberry bushes, where the red-winged blackbirds gathered to sing in the morning and evening. A glorious sunset at night turned the whole sky a gentle soft pink, and at dusk, the sound of peepers emerged from the marshland nearby. Drinking deeply of this wild ocean refuge was so very comforting, and sleep came easily that night.

But the next morning, I realized I was feeling all cramped up and tense and not even sure how to begin to relax. This tension had been building up for a while, so I guessed it would have to be a gradual letting go, little by little. I headed up to the ocean with my buddy Harley, just a short distance along a boardwalk scattered with dried pony droppings, evidence of their comings and goings.

There were heavy mists and fog as we walked along the beach that morning, imbibing the moist salt air. The sound of the waves was a mantra repeating itself and sinking deep into my bones, like a medicine, just the right medicine. Harley ran back and forth by the water's edge, wagging his entire body with absolute joy, prancing along with his beloved tennis ball in mouth, the wind blowing his ears inside out. He looked back at me occasionally, as if to say thank you, thank you! And I felt the same. The untamed energy of this ocean haven was a potent healing tonic for my exhausted body and spirit, so deeply satisfying.

Later, Harley rested in the camper while Peter and I took our bikes off the rack and found our way to the bay side of the island. Campsites there opened out on the marshes, where herons and egrets stood as still as statues, biding their time until the right unwary fish swam by. Signs by the water instructed how to rake up clams, reminding "Don't Take More Than You Will Use", and how to pull up blue crabs "The Chesapeake Way" by tying a chicken neck to a string and lowering it in the water.

As I got back on my bike, though, I fell off onto the sandy soil and Peter worried over me. Touched by my sweetheart's concern and feeling so thankful we were in this adventure together, I told him "I'm fine".

But he admitted, "Well, I've been aware of how my mind is worried, anxious lately." This kind of mental unrest was unusual for Peter, so I reassured him, "We both just need to rest here at the beach until our energy gets back on track."

In the afternoon, the mists and fog began to lift, the sky cleared, and it morphed into a bright blue sky day. The mood lightened, kids played in their T-shirts and shorts, and families set up tents.

"Shawny, come back", his big sister shouted, running after him. Shawny was running free, discovering a joyous sense of his own independence, stopping briefly to give Harley a pat, and then he was off again, with big sister still trailing after him. She seemed to be charged with the job of corralling him.

Peter and I pulled out the instruments that had been stored under our bed in the camper, a fiddle and guitar for Peter and a guitar and a small harp for me. He practiced a lot and had a natural talent. I played only occasionally and sometimes felt overshadowed by his gift for music. It was an old story where I compared myself and came up short. But on this journey, I aimed to break free of old conditioning, to reroute those mental pathways, to bring about a real shift in my life. As I was focusing on that intention, a group of ponies had gathered and was peacefully grazing right at our campsite.

One little pony approached and Harley barked at him as if to tell him who was boss at this site. But as the pony moved closer to sniff Harley, our brave dog lay back in the submissive position, as if to say "Never mind!" Watching them, I thought, no judgement; just be who you are. Simple.

6

I remembered a book I'd been reading by Natalie Goldberg. She talked about how from the compost heap that had been raked and turned over, a fresh green shoot was gathering force under the surface. What would it be? I imagined a new sense of ease and simplicity, a greater wisdom that would evolve on the road. This was the journey of discovery we'd given ourselves. A time to free ourselves from the roles we'd played, to let go and step of the established, the habitual, to discover a more ex-pansive perspective. Friends would say, "Oh, I've always wanted to do that, to let go of everything and hit the road!" And I'd think, yes, but it's not so easy to disengage from the familiar. It's a little like leaping into a void. We had no home base except our camper, no security except in trusting the open road, no known except the ever-changing moment. And yet, something inside was so happy not to know. So ready to make a revolution in my mind. And it was my intention to do my best to give birth to something worthy and beneficial through it all.

ASSATEAGUE

I first came to Assateague National Seashore when I was 19, when few people seemed to know about it and the campground was pretty empty. With a boyfriend at the time, we wandered the beach alone and didn't see another person all day. I remember taking my clothes off and basking naked in the sun, being so sure that no one would disturb our privacy.

Now, you can no longer arrive and find an open campsite in season. You have to reserve six months in advance to secure your space. And only if you rise early enough might you be just about the only one on the beach to witness the glorious sunrise over the Atlantic.

Coming from the mainland on the Eastern Shore of Maryland and leaving behind the honky tonk beach resort of Ocean City, crossing the Verrazano Bridge over the Sinepuxent Bay, you arrive onto Assateague Island and the atmosphere changes. All becomes peaceful, with just the sounds of breezes moving through the trees, the occasional whinnying of a pony, the distant breaking of the waves. On this pristine barrier island there's a natural purity that has been preserved and respected, and that's what makes this ocean refuge so precious. Sometimes, ponies can be seen grazing along the grasses by the bay, and invariably there are a few cars pulled to the side of the road for picture taking. We once saw what looked like an ancient snapping turtle crossing this road, making his way to the bay. Diverse marine life thrives in the tidal waters, including mussels, clams, and blue crabs, and great blue herons and white egrets feast in the salt marshes when the tides go out.

Loblolly pines, carved by the winds, and holly bushes line the road into the rustic ocean campground at the national seashore. No electric or water hookups here. It's just vault toilets, cold water showers, and a pump providing potable water. Campsites with picnic tables and fire rings are spaced well apart along the sand behind the dunes, and there's also an area where tent campers can walk in and camp right by the beach. Sometimes, small sika deer can be seen grazing quietly among the bayberry bushes nearby, and little swallows and red-winged black-birds sing their songs from the branches in the mornings. Ponies move about the campground, grazing, not seem-ing to mind the people nearby, but we're cautioned not to feed them or try to pat them. They're wild. They travel in groups, often with one male and his band of two or three females and maybe a foal, occasionally just standing still as if meditating and then after a while, all slowly moving on together. Bands of ponies often make their way on the walkway over the dunes to the beach and stand together in the sand gazing out at the ocean, enjoying the cooler breezes there. Sandpipers run in and out with the waves, scouting for tiny crabs to eat along the shore. Gulls call out from above and pelicans fly by in groups patrolling the ocean for their dinner.

The campground hosts, there for the season, came by in their little golf cart to say hi. They reminded us to put food away, as the ponies would try to take whatever they could. Once when Peter and I were camped here some years ago, we were surrounded by a group of ponies, one from each direction, closing in on our picnic table. We'd been playing a game of Scrabble, and while I waited for Peter to take his turn, I was chopping some carrots for dinner on a little cutting board. Surprised to look up and see the ponies drawing near, we backed off as they began to move in and munch away at the carrots. Peter ran in the camper and got a pot to bang on, scaring them away. But not before they'd eaten all the carrots and some of the Scrabble pieces as well!

NATURE RULES

Children on this campground were so dear, I loved them all! There was little Shawny, running everywhere with his hands flapping in the air. "Hi goggy," he'd call to Harley as he raced by.

"He likes to wander," his mother said.

And I responded, "Yes, so do we!"

His big sister, Shannon, always retrieving him, stopped to pat Harley. "You know what?" she asked. "I love dogs because they're so playful!" She handed me a treasure, a clamshell she'd found on the beach. I told her about raking clams on the bay side, and she was immediately up for it. "Mommy, let's go rake up some clams!"

I learned that it was her dad's first camping trip ever. He was wearing a UPS sweatshirt, maybe from where he worked, and somehow didn't appear to be a person who'd take many risks. Yet here he was, inspired to go on this adventure tent camping with his wife and children.

"It was so windy, the tent was flapping all night," he related. "I thought we'd blow away!"

He seemed like some kind of noble hero to me, willing to be in an unfamiliar situation, willing to open up to a new experience with his family, making it up as they went.

And then, there were the little blond angels a couple of campsites over. They loved our guitar and harp and sat right next to us as close as they could get while we played. They squealed with excitement when a pony came over and sniffed Harley's nose. A tender moment, and Harley didn't seem to feel cornered this time, except that he was keeping a close eye on his tennis ball just in case.

It was a sweet but ephemeral community at the campground, which had filled up since the dicey morning of foggy weather when we'd first arrived. The wind was an ever-present force, though, playfully making havoc with all our efforts to create an aesthetic campsite. The tablecloth simply would not stay put on the picnic table and landed in a heap on the sand on top of which Harley contentedly curled up. We tried to weigh down the rug we laid the by the step into the RV, but the wind made light of it and rolled the rug up into a tube and blew it along the sand.

The beach had become a work of art. Constant winds created beautiful rippled effects of various textures, the darker sand marbleizing with lighter sand into all kinds of subtle patterns. Sand swirled on the dunes and furrowed all along the little wooden fence meant to protect the dunes from erosion. Spumes of spray blew off the waves as they crested and crashed in lacy foam onto the shore. A lone kiteboarder was out there tapping into this mighty force, holding onto his sail harness with what probably took all his strength. Surely he must have been surging with life force as he caught hold of the tail of the dragon.

Nature ruled at this remote sandy outpost that civilization had barely touched. Ponies had to endure the harsh conditions of wind, rain, biting flies, strong summer sun, and cold winter snows. The national seashore team looked after them, had each of them catalogued and seen by a vet when necessary. And every year, some of the ponies were released to swim across to Chincoteague, the island to the south, where they were auctioned off. In this way, the population on Assateague was kept to around 100 ponies which was all the limited resources there could support.

At night I felt so at peace in this healing refuge, stretched out on the bed in the camper, Harley curled up all snuggly beside me. Reading, dreaming, listening, I began to gently drift off to sleep while outside Peter sat on top of the picnic table, playing his sweet tunes into the deepening dusk.

MOM

My first impulse as I was waking up was to call Mom, I'd tell her about our adventure! But then realized once again, oh, she's gone. How could it be she was really gone?

I'd love to talk with her as we always used to, and share the challenges, the ups and downs, the wonders of our lives, supporting each other in our growth and self-discovery. She had always been there to listen, and likewise, I to her. We'd called on the highest wisdom we knew, for each other.

She'd had a powerful spiritual awakening when I was only two. She told me she'd danced around the house with me in her arms, and I'd laughed with the same joy. "You know, don't you?", she'd asked me. She later began to teach meditation and spiritual healing to groups, and when I was eleven, she taught me to "sit in the silence" as she'd called it. I had come to her and asked her if she would be my meditation guide on this journey of life.

She became my best spiritual growth buddy as I grew older. Once in 1976 we went together to take the EST training, an experience designed to free the mind of conditioned beliefs. The training was held during two weekends at a hotel in Washington, DC, so we shared a room overnight. I remember coming back to our room on break, and we laughed until we cried, rolling around on our beds, realizing the shtick that we'd been playing with each other. I was rebellious and free-spirited and took joy in doing things that would shock my mother. And she worried about me and even went to a psychiatrist for help. That routine never held the same power over us, once we saw it for what it was.

When I was in my mid 30's, I came in contact with a meditation path, Siddha Yoga, and went to the group's ashram in New York state to discover the practice for myself. When I returned, I called Mom right away to tell her of the transformative experience I had there. I related how I hadn't had enough cash with me to get a room at the ashram, so my little 3 year old son and I went to a nearby campground and slept in the back of my hatchback car. I'd been broken-hearted not to be sleeping right there in the ashram. But during the night, I awakened to see the whole car filled with a scintillating blue light, and an atmosphere of profound love permeated everything. I couldn't believe my son slept through it. The whole car had pulsated with the blue light.

Hearing about my mystical experience, Mom wanted to go, but my father who had Alzheimers was in her care. I offered to keep him safe with me while she went, and from that point on, we shared this spiritual path for the next 20 years. All the meditation and chanting retreats we attended, all the learning and growth we experienced together on this path over the years, I cherished every bit of it. During the 1980's, we traveled twice to visit the group's ashram in India, while my father was being cared for at a facility back home. What wondrous adventures we shared.

No one, no relationship in my life was quite the same as the one I'd been blessed to have with my mother. And toward the end of her life, as she was in and out of the hospital, she looked at me with a question in her eyes. Yes, my mother, I said, I will be here for you. I will see you through. And like so many daughters and sons, I put my desire for freedom and travel on hold while I did so. And I'm so thankful that I did.

The day before she passed on, her essence appeared to me in the middle of the night. The whole bedroom was alive, vibrating with her presence. She was jubilant, free. She let me know that from then on, I could find her in the world of spirit. I was so happy for her, though I still really wanted to be able to call her on the phone!

GOODBYE AGAIN

Our friends, Sandra and Anita, would be coming to visit us at Assateague that day, and I was busy in the camper making shrimp salad and potato salad for our lunch together. It was amazing how much our little fridge in the RV offered up. We could have eaten for a month off of all we had.

There was a bright sky, so totally blue it vibrated, with not a single cloud in sight. The wind had died down, so I rolled up my pants legs and soaked up the sun. In a while, Sandra and Anita drove up to our site number 30, and at first, it was kind of dreamlike being with them. We'd known them for a few years from our meditation group, they knew and loved my mother, and Sandra had been coming to me for massages for a while. We laughed, remembering old times together, ate dessert first (the last of the Linzer torte that Peter's mother had made for us before we'd left), then walked together on the beach.

On this glorious day, my head felt so wide open and deliciously free. Anita said when she once had gone on the road for almost three years, that was what she remembered the most, a feeling of being open and free. They made reference to how they'd have liked to be on the road as we were. But Sandra and Anita both had mothers who they needed to be around for and keep a watch on. I really knew what that was like.

They talked about how a friend's mother had lived to be

103, and Anita remarked, "That'd be 20 more years, I'd be eighty-three before I could get back on the road. Oh, my god, please don't let that happen!"

We daughters who put our lives on hold to care for our mothers, how we longed for our freedom. I had the opportunity now, as much as I missed my mother, to discover a new place in myself, a new self that wasn't daughter or caretaker, not nurse or massage therapist. What would I make of this opportunity? What would emerge? And what a precious gift this time of freedom was. I silently vowed to myself to aim for spiritual growth and greater understanding that would be of benefit to all around me.

After lunch, they gave us two small pieces of obsidian to bring us good fortune on our journey, then we said goodbye. It was so hard and sad to be saying goodbye once again when it seemed I was done with all that after leaving Maryland. But this one caught me off guard, and I was feeling such an ache in my heart. I placed the obsidian stones on our dashboard altar. Then, making a cup of tea, I looked up and who was driving back up but Sandra and Anita!

"Hello again, we forgot to give you a jar of jam we got for you from a Delaware road stand."

I made them cups of tea, we ate some dark chocolate I fished from the cabinet, we looked at maps together, then finally said goodbye again. We all agreed that this time was easier and sweeter than the previous goodbye.

But still, it felt lonely and empty at the campground that night. All the people we'd connected with had pulled up stakes and moved on. Sometimes you realized your fundamental aloneness, especially in the evening when the wind blew cold as it was right then. And you were a long way from your mother and whatever you used to call home. Peter and I held each other close, Harley curled up on the bed by our feet. We were all in this adventure together. We were family. And we came to learn that our true home was right there inside ourselves.

A SURPRISE

It was supposed to be raining the next day or two, so we hatched a plan to move to an oceanfront motel in nearby Dewey, Delaware. One last walk with Harley on the beach before leaving, and my phone rang, a call from Derek, my son, whom I deeply loved, the only child I'd been blessed to give birth to in this lifetime. His father and I had been separated when Derek was only 2, and from then on, except for every other weekend and some holidays with his dad, it was my joy to raise Derek. As a child, he had a playful nature and loved to pretend, so we made up games, like Derek being a dolphin named Flippy and doing tricks in the bathtub, just like during the dolphin show at the aquarium. I took him to Assateague camping when he was around 6. We'd set up a tent and roasted hotdogs on sticks over the campfire. We laughed with delight when a seagull swooped down and stole his hotdog. Now he was a grown man with an innate practical wisdom and great common sense, but still maintaining that quirky sense of humor. Peter said that Derek had "duende", an authenticity and presence, a strong belief in himself that gained others' confidence and attracted them to him. And he'd found a wonderful girlfriend, Kayla, who seemed like a perfect match. She was intelligent, enjoyed an adventure, shared Derek's love of fishing and camping, and was beautiful and friendly too.

So when Derek called to say that he and Kayla would like to meet us at the beach that weekend, I was thrilled. What a fun surprise! They'd come from their home in

Florida to visit his dad in Baltimore, but wanted to see us one last time before we took off west. We decided to stay one night at the motel in case of the predicted rain and then move back to Assateague the next day. They'd meet us at the Atlantic View Motel, the only oceanfront with a vacancy. There was just one caveat. It turned out this motel didn't allow pets, only service dogs, and I had my heart set on being able to see and hear the ocean from our room. Especially knowing that we'd soon be leaving the beach for the Southwest, I wanted to maximize my time by the ocean. Kayla had brought her little dog, so we agreed to try smuggling in our "service dogs". Derek and Kayla were up for the adventure!

We all met first for dinner, leaving Emo, Kayla's dog, and Harley in the camper together. The rain picked up, but it was cozy inside at the Stoney Lonen, a bar and restaurant that had great fried oysters and fish and chips. We enjoyed a fun dinner together, sharing a spirit of anticipation for our upcoming adventure.

Back at the motel, Kayla smuggled in her little dog wrapped up in a beach towel. No problem. We put Harley on a leash, and I did reconnaissance at the front desk while Peter slipped by unseen with Harley. OK. So far, so good. Derek and Kayla joined us for a while in our room, overlooking our beloved ocean which looked so dramatic with huge waves crashing, all stirred up from the wind and rainstorm. They'd brought some Prosecco and strawberries, so we toasted to a wonderful weekend ahead, to no barking from our dogs, and to avoiding being evicted that night!

BUSTED

We were up at 5 a.m. to smuggle Harley back out to the camper before the day staff came on. But, uh-oh. As I passed quickly by, the guy at the front desk looked up and busted me. "Excuse me, ma'am. You do know we don't allow pets here, right? What room are you in?"

Quick on my feet, I answered, "Yes, I do know that, but my boyfriend didn't and just brought his dog up to my room. I told him he couldn't do that, and grabbed the dog to bring it back out as quickly as I could."

The clerk seemed to go for it, and I ran outside to posit our four-legged contraband in the camper. Kayla was able to safely bring her beach towel, which was wriggling slightly, past the front desk and outside. We all breathed a sigh of relief, and the four of us celebrated our coup over breakfast outside at the Sunrise Cafe, the dogs at our feet. Our plan was to regroup at campsite number 30 for the weekend.

Back at Assateague, there was a little residual rain, so we all piled into the RV for a few games of Scattergories, and then it was done. The skies began to clear, and by day's end, it was sunny and a feeling of optimism was in the air. We shared some crab cakes, potato salad, coleslaw and farm stand tomatoes for dinner at the picnic table, all local bounty. Around a crackling campfire, we drank cups of red wine and got into telling ghost stories. We were sere-naded by a rowdy chorus of frogs, whose increasing vol-ume and enthusiasm made it sound like they were coming closer and closer to our campsite. Kayla said, "They'll make great white noise for sleeping tonight. That, and the sound of the waves." We hugged each other goodnight and Derek and Kayla went off to their tent with Emo. Peter and I lingered a little longer by the campfire, lying on our backs, holding hands, and gazing up at the million stars splashed across the sky. I felt so very thankful to share this precious weekend here with Derek and Kayla. What a gift. There was a sense of being fully committed to having every moment with them count, not knowing when or where we'd be together again.

A GOLDEN DAY

Harley and I took a thermos of coffee to Derek who'd
been fishing since 5:30 a.m. He'd caught a little kingfish
and was using it for bait. Derek had loved fishing all his
life, having learned when young from his dad. Together,
they went on many fishing trips throughout the years.

Sand crabs were everywhere, their little tunnels scrolled
in the beach by the scrabbling of their claws. Later in the
day, Derek got the idea to catch one, chased it, and captured it in his T-shirt. Next thing we knew, he was casting
it out on the end of a hook. We were feeling pretty hopeful. This could be the bait that landed a big striper! Derek
did a crazy little crab dance, his knees bent, moving
sideways, arms up, elbows bent with fingers pinching.
The dogs barked and barked with the excitement of our
laughter. Meanwhile, five little girls were doing cartwheels
along the beach, lending a celebratory tone to the scene. I
just loved their fearlessness, their light bodies and spirits.
No one wanted to leave, so Peter tried his hand at fishing,
getting a lesson from Derek, but still no striper.

Finally, pulling ourselves away and regathering back at
site 30, we mixed some margaritas and gave numerous
toasts to sharing this idyllic day. I put out some guacamole and chips to tide us over till dinner. In lieu of that
striper, Derek had a backup plan and put some salmon on
the grill. With corn on the cob, some sliced Maryland

tomatoes, it was simply the best. Food always tastes so great when you're camping. Kayla, not a timid little eater, enjoyed it all. I loved that about her!

Just then, a pony stampede came pounding through the campground and terrorized the band of little cartwheel girls. One nearly got sideswiped by a pony and fell. There was a big hubbub as her father created an even bigger scene, shouting "Yes, I want 911. She's been knocked down by a fuckin' pony!" And even more tears and wailing rippled throughout the pack of girls. One was sobbing near me. I smoothed her hair and she hugged me as her tears flowed. To complete the whole drama, two police-men came by, asking who'd seen what, as if it were a crime scene. There was much ado, but in the end, the girl who'd fallen was fine and playing with the others as though nothing had ever happened. It turned out that one stallion had tried to steal another stallion's mare and that was what had caused the stampede. Derek joked, "That stallion should be voted off the island!"

Around the campfire that evening, the s'mores were re-ally out of control with the humongous marshmallows Kayla had brought, so huge that they splurted out the sides of the graham crackers and got our fingers all sticky. Kayla ended up putting them one by one into the fire, and we watched them convolute like some sci-fi ec-toplasm. Derek wanted to go down to the beach to collect sand crabs for bait in the morning, but then I saw there were actually scads of them skittering about right by us. Derek called out, "Shine the headlamp, Kayla!", and he threw his shirt over two, then captured a third which he loaded into a little cooler we'd put sand into. Then he did his crazy crab dance to the delight of us all. We hugged and said goodnight to the music of the frog orgy and the waves crashing. Though I'd have liked to keep that perfect day forever, it was already slipping away, and all I could do was give a thankful sigh and let it go.

GIVE ONE HUNDRED PERCENT

Derek's surf rod was still in its holder, a sign he and Kayla were sleeping in. I took Harley for a romp on the beach under a dark, cloudy sky. When we returned, Emo, looking through the tent window, saw Harley and barked her greeting, waking up Derek and Kayla. They emerged from the tent, coffee was made, Peter built a morning campfire, and we all gathered around, mugs of the steaming brew in hand. Derek took down their tent while I made breakfast, an omelet with tomato and feta cheese, as well as toast with the strawberry jam that Anita and Sandra had brought for us. Derek did his goofy crab dance, we laughed, the rain started up. And then I felt it…time for them to go. When would we see each other again, on this unknown path Peter and I were on? I was moved to give them some words of advice. "Each of you, give one hundred percent. This life goes by so quickly." There were many hugs and I love you so much's, and then off they drove in Derek's white pickup truck, heading for Ocean City, a game of Skee-Ball, some boardwalk fries, and back home to Florida in a couple of days.

Sadness was in the air, a feeling of emptiness in the wake of their departure. It was so hard to say goodbye. But I reminded myself to be thankful for the very precious time we'd shared together. I reminded myself that everything in this life is uncertain, that we can't hold on to anything. Still, my heart ached and felt so heavy.

Peter and I got busy, cleaning up the RV, shaking out the sand and dog hair from our bed. Peter shaved and took a bath; I cleaned the cabinets and reorganized our stuff. We were ready for a new start. The sun was in and out from a bank of clouds as we went on to do our errands: buy a new set of light-gauge strings for my guitar, get a new screwdriver, some groceries, ending with dinner at the Assateague Crab House.

Back at the campground, the sky looked dark and fore-boding, threatening a major storm. But later it blew over, and a gorgeous rainbow spread its glory out across the sky. Peter and I played our music till after sunset, trying to chase away the blues.

THE WIND CHANGES

So here was our morning routine while on the road. When we woke up, I'd get Harley out for a walk or just hook him up on his tie-out, then put two pots of water on to boil. One for coffee in the French press, the other was for a nice warm washcloth for the face. So civilized! Meanwhile, Peter would smooth out the bedcovers while sitting on them. I called it the art of yogic bed making. We'd drink some coffee, light a stick of incense, I'd ring a bell, and thus would begin our morning meditation sitting on the bed, Harley curled up right by us. He was a good doggy meditator, just quietly falling asleep while we sat for 30 minutes or so. Sometimes there was a lot of thinking. Other times, so still. This little time of spacious awareness set the tone for each new day.

Our energy had picked up, the healing ocean air had brought us around to a higher vibration than when we first arrived. But our dear beach retreat held us close for one last day before we'd part ways. We took Harley down to walk on the beach, and Peter threw the ball for him while I searched for shells with holes to hang for wind chimes. We met Super-Dave, the dog, whose people said, "That's what we need to get for our dog, a tennis ball." We told them to keep it, we had more, and besides, Harley wanted to share. (Hah!) We distracted Harley with a stick, and he seemed to forget all about the ball that was now in Super-Dave's mouth.

Back at site 30, I made some egg salad sandwiches for breakfast. Peter rigged up a colorful striped umbrella to shade the picnic table while we ate, lending a festive look to our table. There was a land breeze, which meant that the flies would be drifting our way in droves from inland. The ponies hung out in groups by the ocean all day, trying to avoid the bothersome flies. I noticed a bunch of dead flies floating in Harley's water bowl, emptied it, and took him to the beach to get some relief, just like the ponies did. He was eager to get away from the irritating insects that had been landing on his wet nose and eyes, and dug himself a cool hole in the sand to nestle into.

Later in the day, the wind changed direction, blowing in from the ocean now, thankfully taking most of the flies back inland. It was a perfect evening, so we built a campfire and I made s'mores in honor of Kayla, and of my mother who'd also loved them. I'd taken Mom here when Derek was a little guy. It had been her first camping trip ever, at age 83. I loved that she was always game for a new adventure! I set up a tent for her. She slept in it on a folding chaise, with a bedpan she'd brought in case she had to go in the middle of the night. Mom particularly enjoyed cooking out, roasting hotdogs on a stick over the the campfire. S'mores were her favorite, but she loved it all! How could it be that she was gone now? I still really couldn't believe it. I'd have loved to tell her about the adventure Peter and I were on at this time in our lives. What a great, enthusiastic spirit she'd had. She would've appreciated it so much, with a fun-loving twinkle in her eyes. Mom was always young at heart, so beautiful from the inside out.

During the night, a big storm blew up, shaking the camper with strong winds. We sleepily glimpsed the sweet family beside us as they dealt with their tent down and shade tarp blowing apart. Their little headlamps moved about in the dark, trying to set things as straight as they could be for the night. Harley crowded a little closer to me on the bed, but I was too drowsy to bother relocating him. And he was probably counting on that.

GOODBYE ASSATEAGUE

I took Harley for a walk on the deserted beach. No foot-
prints yet that morning, only the delicate tracings of a high
tide along the shoreline. A perfect, weird little conch shell
had washed up on the sand and I claimed it as a precious

gift for myself from the ocean.

Feeling moved to make some omelets to share, I invited our neighbors to join us for breakfast. After describing their experience of all the excitement last night with their tent down in the wind, they then warned us of the day's weather report predicting a big hailstorm. They were planning to pull up what was left of their tent and move on. We'd be going on our way also. This was the way of campgrounds. We'd gather into a sweet little community for a while, get to know each other a bit, then say goodbye and disperse. We told each other, "Maybe we'll see you at another campground down the road."

It was time to say goodbye to our beloved Assateague. In my mind I said, "We cherish you dearly, we thank you for your pristine and sometimes harsh beauty. Thank you for resuscitating us when we were spent. When will we ever see you again? It's so hard to leave, but you'll always be alive somewhere in our hearts."

The wind had changed again, bringing the inevitable flies, and the sky had ominously clouded over. Assateague always let you know when it was time to move on. The weather would become unfriendly, making the goodbye a little easier. Like pulling off a Band-Aid quickly, we'd get going now.

HARLEY DRAWS ADMIRERS

Driving north on the Coastal Highway through Ocean City, Maryland, and on to Dewey Beach, Delaware, we pulled into our favorite dog-friendly motel, only a block off the beach. Tod and Steve, the managers, actually remembered us from a time some years before when we'd stayed there. We were welcomed and introduced to Chuck, the semi-feral cat, and to Marley, the old yellow lab who liked to lie down and relax in the parking lot. "Be careful of him when you're backing up!" They greeted Harley like a long-lost friend, and he returned their enthusiasm, wiggling and waggling and offering his head for pats.

We settled in to our room. Then carrying our instruments, we took Harley with us to a gazebo on the boardwalk where he became part of our act. People always loved to say hi to a friendly, good-natured golden retriever, so if our music didn't draw them in, our dog would. Tying him to the bench with his water bowl within reach, Peter took up the fiddle and I, the guitar. We played some tunes while partiers at the open-air bar next door looked on. Some people passing on the boardwalk stopped to pat Harley and listen to this unexpected Irish music at the beach, and sometimes an appreciative dollar would find its way into the open fiddle case.

One woman remarked, "Oh I play the fiddle!"

Peter handed her the fiddle and she played an old-time ditty and then asked, "Hey, where'd you get that fiddle?"

Peter answered, "My friend, Bob Morgan, makes them."

"Oh I thought I recognized the sound, I know Bob's fiddles through my teacher in Baltimore, Ken Kolodner." We asked ourselves, what are the chances?

"Renee Baldwin's the name," she called out as she was walking away. "Tell Bob I love his fiddles!"

Then an artsy looking woman approached, wearing an orange polkadot shirt and a big black straw hat. She obviously appreciated the music, and we got to talking. When she heard that we were traveling west, she exclaimed, "I'm going to have a show of my paintings in Santa Fe at the Kristen Johnson Gallery on July 12. Please come by if you're out that way. My name's Mary Ann Pollack." Peter was a devoted artist, himself, so they compared notes about oil painting and their individual styles. And then moving on, she called out, "See you guys in Santa Fe!"

We played for a couple of more hours, but wanted to give our buddy a good walk before we went out for dinner, then get him settled at the motel. In our room, Harley stationed himself on the kingsize bed, we pulled the curtains and turned on the fan for him, and as we were leaving, he heaved a great, delicious sigh of satisfaction.

At the Stoney Lonen, just the two of us at the table that night, the sky by our window at the booth darkened, growing grim and foreboding. One man started to leave the gang at the bar, took one look out the door, then turned on his heel and jumped back onto his barstool to order another drink. Our waitress was disappointed. We were the only diners so far and it looked to be a slow night, except for the rollicking scene at the bar.

As we payed for dinner with the bills from the fiddle case, I suggested, "Let's go park beside the Henlopen Hotel and just enjoy the ocean from there." And as we did, out from a dark cloud above the ocean emerged an astounding double rainbow, with the sun spreading its setting colors magically at the same time.

I told Peter, "Get your fiddle and play homage. Fiddle up a thank you to the rainbow sunset!" And while he played, we stood in awe as the grand spectacle gradually faded, melting away into the ocean.

A GOLDEN DREAM

The beach in Dewey was dog-friendly until 9:30 in the mornings. There were so many happy tail-waggers, play-ing off-leash in the sand together, and then we saw it was all golden retrievers. We asked someone, "What's going on with all these goldens here today?" He explained that it was Dewey's Golden Jubilee, held here every year to celebrate the state dog, the golden retriever. Goldie lovers from all around converged at Dewey once a year for this event, bringing their dogs to romp together on the beach.

In a little while, there would be a ceremony, with a speech given by the mayor, and then the blessing of the goldens by a local priest. It was an amazing sight, so many dogs, all different shades of gold, from light blond to the deepest red, all chasing balls and swimming in the surf, all speaking the same dog language. And we owners also spoke the same language: the love of these dogs! We saw a couple that looked like they could be Harley's siblings. They were dead-ringers for him. It all felt kind of surreal, like a beautiful golden dream.

After the morning's celebration, Harley ended up with another dog's tennis ball, proudly prancing back to our camper with his jubilee souvenir in mouth.

THE GREAT MACHIPONGO CLAM SHACK

There were streaks of lightening and booms of thunder, and poor Harley was shivering with fear in the back of the RV. We were driving south to the Outer Banks of North Carolina, so I checked the weather forecast for Cape Hatteras and it looked like strong winds, thunderstorms, and a tornado watch until 3 p.m. Maybe by the time we'd arrive, all that would have passed.

Meanwhile Harley had crawled under the bed and there was no consoling him. Thunderstorms were the hardest for him, his only solace to hide somewhere until it was over. Actually, even just riding in the camper caused him to pant with anxiety at times, so we tried to stop every couple of hours and give him some fun, swimming in a river or chasing balls on some grassy Baptist churchyard.

We found ourselves behind a stink bomb that morning, following a truck whose noxious fumes were wafting into our air vents. I lit a stick of incense to try to counteract the stench, but just then, the truck pulled into the Tyson Chicken factory. Ugh, rotten chicken parts. That's where the really bad smell was coming from. The poor people who had to work there, as well as those who lived nearby. The putrid odor was pervasive. Right next to the plant was an enclave of battered, broken-down old trailers and a terribly ironic sign reading, "Dreamland - A Touch of Class". Too painful. What did the people who lived there think every time they came back home from work and saw that sign? Or did they just become numb and immune to the smell and degradation? My heart went out to them, whoever they were. They probably felt so trapped.

Aware of our great privilege in being able to leave that tragic horror behind, we approached the Chesapeake Bay Bridge Tunnel. An engineering masterpiece, it goes for 17 miles, connecting the eastern shore of Delaware to Virginia Beach and Norfolk. It moves from a bridge, into a tunnel, and then into a bridge again, cutting almost 100 miles off the inland trip. It was so windy that Peter had to hold tight to the steering wheel just to keep us on the road. I didn't like to think about it too much, but couldn't help myself. I wondered how the bridge stayed in place so far out in the middle of the water and with tunnels on either side of it? And what kept the tunnels from shifting position and not being able to connect back up with the bridge? It was a relief to finally get to the other side and solid land. Still, the construction of that creation was miraculous, and I could really appreciate it all the more, having crossed over to terra firma.

The Great Machipongo Clam Shack. How could we not stop there for lunch? Great golden oldies were playing inside, and we couldn't keep from singing along. We ordered the fried catfish basket, with hush puppies and coleslaw. All local seafood and so delicious. The owner had a kind face and a strong fisherman's body, saying he, himself, had caught some of the items on the menu.

"Everything all right here?"

"You bet, it's the best!" we exclaimed.

A real family restaurant, it seemed like lots of locals were enjoying lunchtime there too. The owner's wife had painted murals of nautical scenes on the walls, decorated the chairs with seashell designs, even painted a colorful mandala on the floor. I searched the freezers in their store and found shrimp, lobster, all kinds of fish, and fresh clams for sale. Hard to decide between all that luscious seafood. I finally ended up getting some frozen rockfish and bay scallops, tucking them into our little RV freezer, like money in the bank for another day.

CAPE HATTERAS

Pulling in to Ocean Waves Campground on Cape Hatteras, we found a gorgeous beach where I took Harley out for a long walk on a stretch of impossibly white sand. The waves were muscular, and the wind was hefty! I buried his poop deep in the sand when no one was looking, rather than having to carry it around in a baggy where it would be deposited into a dumpster, where it'd eventually end up being buried anyway, only in a plastic bag that never biodegrades. This was my rationale anyway.

We met and greeted other campers, Will and Kathy from Northern California who had five kids, ten grandkids, and four great grandkids. "We like taking care of the little ones. It's our own kids that drive us crazy!" Kathy told us she had a florist shop, and that one of their grandkids who was a funeral director sent lots of work her way.

Then there was Mac, 87 years old and still sharp. "Now I'm not telling you no fish story here, I was in the army many years ago." He looked gray and grisly now, a stubble of white across his face. He said he'd been camped out there for a while, and bless him, he looked like it.

"Yeah, it's like they used to say in vaudeville. You should never follow a girlie show with a dog-and-pony act. I had me a nice Class C camper. Wilma could drive it. She's the only one I could ever travel with. Either her, or my best friend, Bill Harper. But see, then we got us a

Class A RV. Wilma got up there in the driver's seat. She just couldn't set her sights right. She drove just hangin' on tight to the steering wheel, but we had to put some pillows under her so's she could see the road. I've got her in a nursing home now. She's got the Alzheimer's, you know. Well anyway, I have high tea at 3pm. Y'all come on down to my site for that."

Peter and I went out exploring and came upon a quirky cafe that looked like a flying saucer. In fact, a pretty good replica of one. We were drawn to check it out. Inside, the owners told us how this idea had come to them and they'd been able to construct it with some help from friends who were big into extraterrestrial lore, just as they were. The coffee was good and we took our "to go" cups out to look at their bulletin board posted on one side of the saucer. One advertisement stated that there'd be a meeting of the Rainbow Gathering at a nearby campground and it was going on right then.

We decided to go see what it was all about, and found a raggle-taggle group of hippieish-looking folks of all ages, who were deep into a group project of making a big pot of vegetable chili for dinner that night. The Rainbow Gathering is an offshoot of The Grateful Dead, or "Deadheads", who have "the shared ideology of living in peace, harmony, freedom, and respect." So said Wikipedia. I'd had to look it up, never having heard of the group before then. They gather for a week or two at a time, usually in some remote area, to try as a group to embody their credo, while sharing the tasks of daily living. Like cooking dinner, for which we had come on board that day.

The first order of business was to find plenty of wood for that night's campfire. Peter joined the group going out to pick up some skids, or wooden pallets, and it seemed they'd found a free source for them. I joined the group chopping vegetables for the veggie chili. A big table had been set up, and we all stood around it, chopping and talking. It seemed like most of the people had traveled from places in the North Carolina area. Already I could see that there were some slackers, sitting and lying down on the grass nearby, offering no inkling that they meant to help out. But it looked like there was room for all types there. I fessed up that we'd only seen the flyer for the convention that morning, and had never really known about the Rainbow Gathering before this. But we were game for it. At least for a while, I thought to myself.

Finally, the guys came back with the wood, a fire was started, and the big pot of chili put on to cook. Meanwhile, some folks pulled out guitars, and we joined in with the music, mostly old folk tunes mixed in with an assortment of rock. The pot began to bubble away and there was a pretty good feeling among this mixed group that was trying to make it all come together.

But toward dark, it began to drizzle, and I wondered how it would go, as most everyone there was camped in tents and some just had sleeping bags on the ground. We were the only ones with a camper, and I began to have visions of a bunch wanting to share space and crowd in with us. Hmmm... Peter seemed to have had the same thought. So while they were busy dishing out dinner, we said our goodbyes, collected Harley, and made off back to our own campground, where we could plug in, turn on the heater if need be and climb under our cozy covers and even watch a DVD if we'd like to. Okay, we'd tried it out for an afternoon, but maybe Rainbow Gatherings weren't exactly for us. Or maybe we were spoiled! We snuggled in together while the sounds of rain drizzling on our roof continued off and on throughout the night. Feeling a little guilty, we really hoped our friends were managing to stay dry under those lean-to's.

WEST AT LAST

On our way out of the campground, we ran into Mac. He was bright and chipper, joking goofily, "Does a hobby horse have a wooden peter?" Then we fell into a discussion about the various routes out west. "Route 40," he said, "too many truckers. But 20 West or 10 West, now these are good routes. There's a lot of good camping out there in Arizona." We thanked him and hugged goodbye, Mac saying, "I sure am going to miss you."

We started off on 64 West, along the Alligator River National Wildlife Refuge, an alligator waterway running right alongside the road, with signs saying "Watch for Bears next ten miles" and "Red Fox Crossing". We would so loved to have seen them, and kept on the lookout for alligators as well, but none showed their faces that morning.

We were saying goodbye to the Atlantic Ocean, leaving behind the East Coast, the life we'd known. There was one last chance to hang on to the ocean at the juncture of 64 West and 17 South. We got off at the Dairy Queen with atlas in hand and sized up our options over lunch at the picnic table outside. Seventeen south would take us to the South Carolina beaches, or maybe down to Florida along the beach, and head west from there? What was called for? South to more beaches felt like enough already.

We'd been by the ocean for a few weeks. Not to mention, it was Easter weekend and bound to be really busy at the seashore campgrounds. But 40 West felt like such a push. That was the way we'd driven so many times before.

We were ready for something new, thinking outside the box, letting go of preconceptions. We were making it up as we went, paying attention to what felt right. Sometimes this journey took courage, some days more than others. There was no way to predict what would happen as we ventured onto unknown pathways.

Harley had his own challenges on the journey, with panting, shivering at times, especially during storms. He'd found a way to lie on the sofa so he could see us over the dog barrier that had been erected. Here's what it took to keep him from getting between our seats and up front with us, distracting the driver and driving us nuts with his anxiety: first, a suitcase, then a guitar case angled on top of that, my yoga mat, the laundry bag, and finally a single futon stuffed into the hole he'd learned to crawl through. I gave him the rest of my DQ cone, he wolfed it down, and we were on the road again.

We coasted along 64 West, to the spaced out, expansive music of Andreas Vollenweider on the CD player. A huge sky was skimmed over by high flying clouds. Crisp white linen dogwoods in bloom were scattered among groves of pine. A field of orange poppies was splashed unexpectedly along the shoulder of the road. We were heading west at last!

THE MYSTERIOUS LEAK

We settled in at the Super 8 in Claremont, North Carolina, run by our old friends, the Patels. We'd been there before. It was like home, the motel and the RV dealership in town, Carolina Coach. Some years ago, we'd traded in my old VW pop top camper and had to stay for a couple of days during the whole process. So we were familiar with some of the high spots in town. Now the dealership would service our camper, fix a mysterious leak, and get us road-worthy.

First thing, breakfast at Hannah's Bar-B-Que, best breakfast in town. James Hamilton, the owner, came to our table and told us of camping experiences with his group. "We pay 600 dollars a year for the membership. We've upped from the limited to the extended. We can go for unlimited camping all year at all their locations. We'll be going to Cape Hatteras in a few weeks!". I didn't tell him that we'd just come from there and had only payed 15 dollars a night for our beautiful oceanfront site. Simplicity was our modus operandi. No membership for us. We were freewheeling and feeling so open!

Everything was bright and happy that morning. We hung out in the town park after breakfast, and I brushed Harley, fluffing out his ears and tail with the dog brush we'd just found at the dollar store. I threw some sticks for him which he gnawed fiercely with great enthusiasm. As he chased stick after stick, his tail was held high like a flag, wagging with the sheer joy of life.

Peter was down in the pavilion playing his fiddle, while I sat on a bench practicing my harp. Two teachers brought a group of school kids to the park and set down the rules. "OK, no playing on the bridge, do not pick up sticks, no running near the parking lot, and don't wander off this playground. Now what are you supposed to do?" The kids dutifully repeated back the litany of no's (even though they probably could have used some yes's in their lives) and took off for the swings and sliding board. I imagined the one other admonishment that had gone unsaid, "And *do not* talk to those itinerants over there playing music."

We got the call. The camper was ready; they'd found the leak which was in the water pump. Next rainy day, we'd see if that was really it. We turned down a deal they offered, satellite TV for $1,650 plus a monthly contract. No thanks. We'd happily do without! We'd noticed so many people at campgrounds who stayed plugged in to their TV's all day when the beauty of nature was right there. We wondered why they went camping at all if they were just going to stay in front of the screen, just as they could do at home. But to each their own. There were all kinds of different approaches to camping. Some tent campers probably looked at us in our RV's and shook their heads.

After picking up the camper, we went by the Boxcar Restaurant, where the iced tea was super sweet, the rolls were fried, and the salad bar comprehensive. Not to mention those hush puppies that came in a basket with every meal. And part of the beauty of the place was that you could hear the trains, whistling their lonesome hearts out as they passed on by, reminding us that we also were just passing by and feeling a little lonesome ourselves.

54

PERVASIVE RAIN

We hit the road for Buck Creek Campground in Marion, North Carolina. It was a whole different mood that day, determined largely by the cloudy sky that threatened to dampen spirits and campsites. When you're living mostly outside, the weather has even more of an effect on your emotional outlook. Nature is more intimate and up close with no four walls to buffer and not so many distractions like when at home.

We found a beautiful site, right by the musical creek, with pine trees lining its banks. A circle of stones invited the possibility of a campfire, if the weather would just hold out. Right off, Harley pranced down to the creek, washing off the saltwater still in his fur from the beach. The water was clear and oh so cold, but he didn't mind that at all. He had his beloved tennis ball in his mouth and it was all good!

Down at the office where we went to register, the owner, Dan, told his story. "Seventeen years ago, I'd been an electrician at the local factory in town. I injured myself and found out that all the job security I'd thought I had was not there at all. So I put my butt way out on a limb and bought this place. Made it into a campground and a driving range. Luckily I had my three sons to help, it took a lot of work. But now, the campground and range stand on their own. People will drive 30 minutes to come here and hit golf balls. And later, you may see me out there if the weather holds up!"

55

But the weather did not hold up. It was rain, pervasive rain, throughout the rest of the day, the sound of rain steady on the RV roof. I was inclined to get going, but Peter said he didn't think it'd be safe to drive the foggy mountain road to Asheville in this kind of weather. Not my favorite cup of tea, being face to face with my own restless nature and having nowhere to go, I told myself "OK, breathe. Let's just see what this day can be." I opened the blinds in the bathroom and right there out the window were the pines and the creek. If we must be rained in, it was a beautiful place to be. After all, I coached myself, this was part of what our journey was about, practicing being able just to be with what was, knowing that we couldn't control everything, or maybe much of anything, except our own attitudes.

During a brief respite from the rain, we hastily built a campfire. I made a pot of seafood stew with the scallops we'd bought from the Great Machipongo, and we enjoyed it by the fire. But then, on came the thunderstorms again, so we raced back into the camper, bowls in hand. Bone-rattling thunder booms, streaks of lightening, the deluge throughout the night had poor Harleydog panting with anxiety and hiding in the shower, inconsolable.

PITEOUS CRIES

The skies were still dark the next morning, and so was our mood. We had our own personal thunderstorm and set out for the drive to Asheville in silence. Even though Peter and I usually flowed along easily with each other, we'd been too long inside that small RV with no respite from the rain. At least the camper hadn't leaked, and it had really been put to the test.

In Asheville, Malaprop's Bookstore/Cafe beckoned us for coffee and a quiche. On the shelf in the store was a book that caught my eye by Elizabeth Gilbert, *The Last American Man.* It was about a local guy, Eustace Conway, who lived off the land somewhere around there, and the clerk at the register actually knew him. "He used to come to our school and give talks about living in the wilderness. He'd take a group of us to his place on the weekend as part of a program at the time. He was a very intense guy, a man with a mission. Elizabeth Gilbert would meet with him here at this bookstore, interview him, and then sit at one of those tables over there with a cup of coffee and write on her laptop for a few hours." Intrigued, I bought the book to read later on, maybe on some rainy day in the camper.

A light mist falling, the weather was cold and damp and gray, and so were we. Where could you go when you felt like that? What would help to shift the gears? Moving out of that cloudy mountain vortex seemed to be the answer. "Let's just head to Tennessee and give the skies some time to clear," I suggested. But Route 40 passed through mountain tunnels and was pretty treacherous and steep in places, exhausting to drive with all the truckers bearing down on us.

So when a Day's Inn presented itself in Cookeville, it was a respite for the weary and for those desperately in need of a bath. Just as we were getting settled, the sun began to break through, its blessed rays streaming in through the motel window, kissing us awake again. We spread out a blanket and sat outside on the porch to play a little music. Like snakes, we were starting to wriggle free of our East Coast skins. Something new and fresh and free began to emerge. We were in Tennessee! Heading west!

After dark, a truck pulled in to the motel lot hauling some livestock. I guessed they were cattle, on their way to Texas to be slaughtered. During the night, we heard some piteous sounds coming from the truck parked outside our window. My heart broke for those poor cows and for their destiny. We'd passed by the slaughter houses in Texas on past trips, a horrific sight to see, like a putrid cattle concentration camp that you could smell for miles around. In my mind, I apologized to those poor cows in the truck who cried so mournfully that night. Made me so thankful I didn't eat meat.

Out in the parking lot the next morning, I asked the driver about those sounds we'd heard last night. He slid open the side door of the trailer and out popped a nuzzley little camel nose! The dear creature looked at me with these huge eyes and gave a cry, just like the ones I'd heard during the night. The driver explained, "They're baby dromedaries we got in Iowa. We're taking them home to our ranch in North Carolina." He entered the trailer and began to feed one from a big bottle with a camel-size nipple. Then, the dromedary looked up at me with his sweet heart-melting eyes and gave a contented milk-lipped smile. He was only three months old, and I was totally in love with him! OK, so much for the whole drama about cows, for thinking you know what's in the truck. And actually, so much for the stories we tell ourselves about anything. We just don't really know, and on this journey, I was coming to enjoy not knowing.

EASTER

A gorgeous, open, sunny Easter morning, and ah, life was reborn! And what better place to start the day than at the Starbucks outdoor porch in Nashville. We were greeted by a friendly chocolate lab, Hershey, whose boundless enthusiasm seemed right in sync with the optimistic day. Harley and Hershey sensed their common retriever spirit, their tails wagging fervently in unison. Then sniffing each other out, all was deemed to be well. We found a table, Harley keeping watch to see if a morsel of the croissant would come his way. And of course, it did. As he curled up on the ground beside the table, we toasted with our coffees to a brilliant Easter Day.

Nearby, a woman was doing something that looked akin to sewing or macrame. I asked, "What are you making?" She showed us her method of making coiled baskets, going into great detail.

"Okay, you just take some ordinary rope and wrap yarn around it three times, then stitch it down in a figure eight, tie in some beads, and voila. See? It's easy!" She bubbled forth all sorts of information about googling and websites, and ordering online from various sources.

Pretty sure I wouldn't be doing this myself, we bought one from her. We'd put it on our dashboard altar to hold all the treasures we'd collect along the way, like the obsidian pieces that Sandra and Anita had given us. As we drove away, we could see her on her cellphone, probably calling a friend and telling her the good news, an unexpected sale at Starbuck's on Easter morning. Life is so easy on a sunny day!

We got back on the "Music Highway" as Route 40 between Nashville and Memphis is called. Onward we went across Tennessee, where scores of signs for state parks beckoned to us as we drove on by. Our destination was Bledsoe Creek State Park, campsite 33, home until tomorrow.

There was an open, grassy expanse near the lake with little white wildflowers sprinkled everywhere like a blanket of delicate lace spread over the field. Harley ran joyously across it on his way down to the water, a good swim being his panacea for the rigors of being on the road. Now, all rubbed down with a towel and fluffy, he gave a big sigh of contentment. A wild turkey strolled by, allowing me to follow him briefly and take his picture. From somewhere nearby, a hoot owl was calling. The trees were alive with other bird songs which a real birder could probably recognize but which sounded sweetly melodious to me, without identifying.

I boiled some eggs and dyed them; those and some jellybeans made a perfect Easter basket to nibble for the rest of the day. Our campfire burned on in a little circle of stones all afternoon and into the night.

*** PART TWO ***

GULPHA GORGE

"This is momentous," I declared as we crossed the bridge over the Mississippi River. "We're in the West now! This is the dividing line; we're leaving the East behind." It felt exhilarating to finally be shaking loose of the East Coast and the scheduled and restrictive way of life it represented to us. We were breaking free of what we'd known, writing a new script moment to moment now.

We'd crossed the wide and lazy waterway with hardly a sign of its coming. Seemed to us as though it would have been a mark of respect for there to at least be a big sign announcing the river, so rich with its history and literary lore.

Finally arriving at Gulpha Gorge Campground in Hot Springs, Arkansas, we were road weary and ready to rest and take refuge. We lucked out and pulled into a great site, magically open, right by the melodious stream. Harley splashed in, washing off the miles, wagging his wet tail with sheer joy. Peter took his fiddle and went over to an open space to play, and I perched on top of the picnic table to practice my harp.

Soon enough, a couple came by and introduced themselves, Gene and Jerry. He played mountain dulcimer, she the hammered dulcimer. At 75, they were still tent camping. I played them a couple of tunes, and they were encouraging. "Hey", Gene offered, "you might really like the musical gathering at Mountain View next week! People gather in the square and just jam informally." I filed that idea away for later, knowing it would be Peter's idea of heaven. In the freedom of being on the road, we were able to spontaneously pick up on serendipity like this, so Mountain View might well be our next stop.

Another couple came by, Clara and Roger. "I play the rhythm guitar. He plays dobro. Would you like to jam together?" Musicians abounded at this campground and were drawn to each other by the sounds of music, just as the scent of food in the air draws the hungry.

So later on, Clara and Roger brought their chairs on down to our site, diet cokes in hand. We'd see how we could all harmonize together, which was really challenging since Roger's dobro was totally out of tune, and he might have been tone-deaf as well. But he had a good heart, and he was as enthusiastic as a big old dog. Clara, it turned out, had been playing since she was a kid. She was a wealth of old country songs, lots of Hank Williams and Willie Nelson, and she kept on cranking them out, along with stories all about her 5 children, and 10 grandchildren. "And I think there's about 10 great grandchildren by now," she added. Clara appeared to be a seasoned performer. She had her act together and it was good!

She and Roger were on their way from Yuma, Arizona to visit family in Michigan. They were proponents of the "no pay" system of camping. "We just travel the back roads, and pull off at any rest stop, church parking lot, or Walmart. We ask permission if we need to, and just stay the night. We end up meeting lots of people who are traveling the same way. Then, we save our money and go out to eat. Get a lobster or a steak sometimes."

With just a little encouragement from Peter, Roger went

and brought his car back, set up a big speaker, and his electric keyboard. Uh-oh. I had visions of a loud, blasting, out of tune session, which the others on the campground might not have appreciated so much. But divine providence interceded, and he couldn't get the electric to work, so no amplifier. We made do.

After a few more songs, a little hippie guy wandered up with his pan pipes slung over his shoulder. Peter invited him into the scene. He entered playing his pipes, and soon enough, Clara and Roger packed up and moved on, sensing a definite shift in tone. Nat introduced himself, admitting, "I smoked some medicine weed earlier and it was pretty potent. My friend from California sent it to me." We got a contact high just being around him. He picked up Peter's guitar and played in a way I'd never seen before, flat like a dobro, but plucking and tapping it so it sounded more like a sitar. I got my harp, Peter his fiddle, and we jammed together in a whole new way, inspired by Nat and his California medicine weed.

Nat weaved a story of his life so far, 27 years, raised in Hot Springs. "The vapors of this ancient site of Native American gatherings for peace just whirled me out of here. Out to Asheville NC, and traveling around, and finally back here to tune up the family thing." He explained that the Native Americans who first came to this area centuries ago called the hot springs "the vapors", and many around respected the tradition and still used that term.

Nat pulled his camera out and took some photos of us at stoned out angles. Then he got his cellphone and called a couple of friends who arrived soon after, Hayley and David. Hayley immediately fell into my arms for a hug. She was like a little fawn, all big eyes and innocent sweetness. "I've always loved a harp!" I put it in front of her and let her play. She was in her own little heaven: you could see that. She'd brought a small djimbe, so I took that up and we all got a groove going.

Then David told his story. "My mom and dad were never married. I didn't even meet my dad and two step brothers until a couple of years ago. It was weird at first, I didn't know what to say. But now I call him all the time, ask him for advice on building and stuff."

The afternoon got lost in a timeless sphere of flow we shared together. The sky began to turn dark and we talked about a campfire. I said we'd need kindling, and just like that, Hayley took off her shoes and socks and waded to the other side of the cold stream, gathering all sorts of sticks, and brought them to offer. Bobby from the next site over, who'd been hanging around on the periphery, came back with a beat up old plastic cup. "It's motor oil. Add it to the fire to git it goin'. Just don't let yer dog lick it." We thanked him. There was a moment of silence while we digested all that.

Nat invited us over. "I have a big fireplace. We could make some dinner, have some wine." But it became evident we'd be staying at the campsite that evening. So I made a big pot of miso soup with noodles and veggies. David asked, "What's miso soup?" and got a comprehensive answer from Nat, as well as lessons in how to use chopsticks. Not enough spoons to go around, so it was chopsticks instead.

David asked, "I like pepper in my soup. Do you have any pepper?" He seemed like a sweet young guy, who maybe hadn't gotten enough love or pepper as a kid. And I was so happy that we did have some of each we could give him.

It began to get cool, we gave out blankets to wrap up in, and everyone huddled closer to the fire, burning strong now thanks to Bobby's motor oil. We looked like an encampment of Native Americans, wrapped up in our buffalo skins. "How are you doing, ancient ones?" I asked. We all felt it. Magic was in the air.

Hayley ventured forth to tell us of the time she'd first seen a fairy. "We were sitting on my father's land. We had come down from ingesting some medicine. We'd had our realizations and understandings. And then I saw it, a light flashed by."

"What color was it?" asked Nat.

"It was orange, and I knew it was a fairy. And once more, it flashed by the other way. I couldn't see the details, but I knew what it was without a doubt."

"I understand", I said. "Peter and I used to have some land in West Virginia. We were walking in a place we hadn't been before. There was a little spring coming up out of the ground, with some moss and ferns. And then I saw it out of the corner of my eye, from a place that was not my rational mind. And I knew with conviction it was a fairy."

As the fire died down, a hush of shared understanding bonded us together for that one timeless evening at Gulpha Gorge. I really loved these young people. They felt like family, maybe my children, or maybe like I'd known them before in some other place or life. We exchanged phone numbers in case there'd be another time, and hugged each other goodnight. Then Hayley came back for one more hug. "That's so good", she said as she melted in my arms.

Sitting by the stream, while Harley splashes downstream

A GOOD SOAK

We awoke in the morning to the sounds of men's voices loudly calling out to each other. "Hey Sam, hold it there, I'll come over with the backhoe!" It was the Park Service construction crew, modernizing our old down-home campground. There would be water, electric, and sewer hook-ups at all the sites by that summer. The price would go up, too, from $10 a night to $30. We wondered what would happen to all the rubber tramps who depended on staying there as a cheap way to get by on the fringes of society. We used to really appreciate the variety of eccentrics this place attracted, people you'd never have had the chance to talk with or get to know in your everyday life.

We thought the town of Hot Springs might offer a respite from the noisy construction that day, but it so happened that the town park was the site of a commotion equally as loud. A large group was gathered, holding signs saying "Honk if You're for Lower Taxes" and "Don't Mortgage my Children's Future." Every time someone drove by and honked, the crowd by the road would go wild, hooting and hollering. Each honk fanned the fire of their righteousness higher and higher until they were in quite a frenzy. And it was right into the middle of this melee that the Irish Fiddler opened his case and began to play for those who could hear. Luckily, the sound of the fiddle carried well, and Peter had found a bench in a park a little distance from the crowd. As I walked away, a passerby had already stopped to listen.

I, however, sought the solace of a hot springs on Bathhouse Row. Actually a national park, celebrating the eight bathhouse buildings constructed around a century ago and maintained handsomely to this day. The bathhouses had been part of a culture at the time, and famous mobsters like Al Capone used to frequent them, along with people from all over the world.

Today I was at the historic Buckstaff, where I signed on for "the works". First, you soaked for 20 minutes in a big whirlpool of hot springs water. Then, a mountain lady with a thick backwoods accent came in and scrubbed you down, arms, legs, and back, with a loofah (four dollars extra). Next, you went to the sitz bath. Kind of weird, sitting down in this little square tub of hot springs water to soak your privates. After that, you lay down on a table while the mountain lady wrapped you in a hot wet towel, like a burrito. "And here's a cold towel fer yer face," she offered. Twenty minutes later was the steam cabinet, the old fashioned kind where your body was in the cabinet and your head outside it. And just when you thought you were about to faint, she brought a cup of cold spring water to drink. Then, you went into a cool shower, where the water sprayed from all directions, around, above and below. And last, a 20 minute massage, and you'd become a limp noodle in body and mind. All of this for $55 total plus the optional $4 loofah that you got to keep. Throughout the entire process, modesty was respected. There was an art to wrapping you in a sheet that would be reapplied at every station along the way. "Jes' you stand facin' away from me and I'll wrap you on up in this here sheet", the mountain woman intoned. From start to finish, only your bare back and butt were exposed. I gave her a nice tip and staggered out onto the street.

A big sunny sky greeted me and helped bring me back to this world. A young guy standing nearby asked, "Are you a visitor to this town? Well, I hope you're enjoying your stay!"

I answered from my bath-induced stupor, "It's wonderful here!"

I headed to the park to collect my Irish fiddler, but he was nowhere to be found. I checked a cafe at the local hotel, and found him there, having sought refuge from all the hubbub on the street. We learned that the group called themselves The Tea Party. It was the first time we'd heard of them, and they seemed to have a lot of supporters in this impoverished area. Although Bathhouse Row was looking proud, there were many broken-down and boarded up properties in town, art deco relics from a bygone era when this town had been in its heyday. Maybe The Tea Party gave them some hope of getting a better deal from the government?

THE CAJUN

We met our new neighbors from the next campsite over who told us they'd been living on the road for 7 years. They'd given up their home and sold everything, "We didn't want it anymore", they explained, and had been traveling ever since. On the back of their RV was a map of North America colored in for all the places they'd been, with only two white areas remaining, Mexico and Canada. They exuded great enthusiasm and vitality as they told us about some of the best places they'd been, like when they went to the Cowboy Poets' Gathering in Nevada for six days of poetry, music, dancing, and folk arts. Actually a whole segment of our population had become mobile, living only out of their RV's, campers, vans, or trucks, and otherwise having no stationary home. North in the sum-mer, south in the winter, moving on with a natural kind of rhythm when the mood struck, and making friends along the way who they'd meet up with later, like a new kind of family along the road. It was a sociological phenomenon that seemed to be on the rise. The freedom and variety of the gypsy life sure appealed to us, and our journey was open-ended so we'd just see how it felt as time went on.

I put Harley on a leash and walked him around the campground. An old, skinny guy, his camouflage pants hitched up with a belt, was rummaging around in the back of his makeshift camper. It looked like he had everything he owned there, small crates with various foodstuffs, bedding, toilet paper, and piles of clothing scattered everywhere. He had long white shoulder length hair, his face wrinkled with deep furrows. He wore some bear claws suspended from a rawhide string around his neck, and two beaded leather pouches hung from his belt. "They call me The Cajun around here." He told me he'd moved from Louisiana to Hot Springs "to take the waters", as he put it. He wanted me to see his pup who was in the front cab. "Best dog in the world," he attested, "part aikido." The Cajun seemed like a kind soul, with a sweet, gentle handshake. My heart went out to him, and I wondered how he got by on whatever little cash he probably had. Would he be able to afford to camp here after the prices went up? Who was looking out for him? I really felt for him, but figured at least he had a good dog companion to share life with.

As I returned to our campsite, I saw Peter talking to a guy who'd set up his tent near us. All I could hear was, "Yeah, listen to this, man. Listen to this," spoken in a loud and pressured voice. I decided to leave Peter to his own devices. I was too tired to try to rescue him. Crawling into bed and pulling the covers up, I heard Harley growling nearby in low tones, like a slow, steady complaint. Later, awakened by Peter coming to bed, I whispered, "Tell me about it tomorrow." Peter answered, "Yeah, the guy was amazingly exhausting." And then we both heard it, sounds coming from his tent, a loud voice calling, "Get away! Go on! Get outta my face!"

"Paranoid schizophrenic," I whispered as we drifted off to sleep.

ANGIE

We discovered I was right. Mike came over to our site in the morning, Peter offered him a cup of coffee, and we were off and running from there, getting a bigger dose of Mike's World than we might have wanted. He told us, "I've been living with my mother for a while now," complaining, " I don't like it there. She gives me a hard time". And we could just imagine why she did. He began to focus next on the campground host, saying she was plotting against him and might well try to poison him. He kept up a steady monologue in a voice way too loud for that time of morning at the campground, and we began to realize it might not be so easy to shake him. We got the idea to start packing up our camper, say our goodbyes, and go to town for a while.

When we returned later, we saw with relief that Mike had taken down his tent and left, and the campground felt noticeably a lot lighter and brighter. But having been a psychiatric nurse for so many years, I could really understand what Mike's life must be like. Eventually, he'd become a danger to himself or others, some neighbor would call the police, and he'd be committed to a psychiatric hospital where he'd be forced to take medication that would straighten him out for a while. Then he'd be discharged, stop taking his meds, and the whole process

74

would start all over again. Schizophrenia has no real known cause, though there may be hereditary or environmental factors. So it was through no fault of Mike's own that he had this illness. Still, we were thankful that he'd moved on to be someone else's problem.

We decided to change campsites, and since sites were not reserved, anyone might claim an open one. A primo site opened when the biker who'd been camped there pulled up stakes and drove off. We moved on it quickly, number 20, the last one down, with plenty of privacy, right by the stream. Harley immediately tried it out. I hooked him up to a long leash so he could splash away on his own all afternoon. The site was right next to the amphitheater, a perfect place for Peter to practice his tunes. Listening to Peter playing, I heard his fiddle, but then mingling with the sounds of a flute, so I went to check it out.

There was a young girl playing her flute, her dark hair in dreadlocks decorated with beads, ribbons, and colored strings, wearing a beat-up pair of jeans and a little pink embroidered peasant shirt. Angie told us she was 19, and had been on the road by herself since she and her boyfriend had split up. Since he'd taken the car and the tent, she'd been hitching rides with her backpack and sleeping bag. She said she was looking for a more deserted place to camp.

We immediately felt protective of her. She had a beautiful presence, but wasn't she living on the edge, living dangerously? I made a big salad and laid out some cheese, bread, fruit, and cookies on the picnic table. She particularly liked the date cookies. Angie told us she was from Romania, part Roma, and she definitely had the gypsy free spirit in her blood! She asked if I'd like a Tarot reading, and I said sure, mainly because I wanted to be able to give her some money. She fished the cards out of her backpack, explaining, "Someone gave them to me, but I had to get their energy out of them before I could use them." She unwrapped the deck from a red flowered scarf and laid out the cards in no particular order, seemingly led by intuition. She gave me a deep, sensitive reading, putting her finger on the situation that was up for me. My question, which I'd kept to myself, was about being on the road, how to stay open and yet have enough quiet time to myself. The Fool, representing new beginnings and spontaneity was balanced with other cards that indicated keeping my own counsel. She wisely advised me, saying, "It's not the dichotomy you think it is. Take time for yourself." Perfect. Peter and I felt so good to be able to give her some money for the reading.

Then Angie let us know she'd been sick, had a sore on her leg, and thought she'd gotten it from some guy. I asked her if she'd let me take a look at it and told her that I was a nurse. She agreed so we stepped into the camper for some privacy. She showed me about six sores on her upper thigh, all oozing and reddened. My guess was it was a staph infection, and I told her it was nothing to mess around with. If untreated, the infection could spread into her blood. We went out, and Peter and I insisted,

"This is serious. We can take you to a clinic where you could be seen and get on some antibiotics. Please let us do that. We'd really like to."

"Absolutely not. No way," she answered definitively. "I've been curing it by stuffing myself with fruit. No junk food. I'm planning to find an organic farm and work there, eat good, and take some healing herbs."

We advised her to keep it clean and rest. And please

consider changing your mind and let us help you get some medicine.

We were torn and didn't want to do her a disservice by underestimating her ability to survive by herself on the road. But there was a fine line between that and putting herself in harm's way. She could really have used some help, and we'd have so loved to help her, but she was adamant about doing it her own way. As we left later to go out, we saw her in her sleeping bag on the ground, looking so alone and vulnerable. She was someone else's daughter, but right then, I felt as protective of her as if she'd been my own.

TIM AND DYLAN

Peter had met a father and son who'd heard him playing on the campground and they invited us to their nearby home where they had a recording studio and wanted to record his fiddle music. So we were going to their apartment that evening, not knowing what to expect, but open to getting to know some local Hot Springs people. Tim and Dylan, father and son, both with long dark hair down their backs, both dressed all in black in the Goth style. They seemed to be good hearted people. It was a spartan home, with only two benches, two chairs and not much else. "We don't have much furniture, but we've got plenty of equipment." And they did, it looked like a professional recording studio in their living room. There were instruments everywhere, two keyboards, an upright Baldwin piano, and around six or seven guitars, among them a 12 string Gibson. "Best sound ever", Tim attested. A microphone was suspended from the ceiling and was hooked up to a computer with a special program for recording.

They got right down to it, Peter playing his repertoire of Irish fiddle pieces, Dylan working at control central. "When you see the green light, you're recording." Peter cranked out tune after tune, Tim and Dylan giving words of encouragement, "Sounds great. That's really good." The plan was, they'd travel to a studio in Las Vegas, where Peter's music would be mixed with other instruments, guitar, bass, keyboard, drum. They promised to send us a copy of the resulting CD.

As the evening continued, Peter, who'd been fueled by a couple of glasses of super sweet iced tea, remained focused and seemingly tireless. I had time to check out the room more closely, taking note of two big Bruce Lee posters, along with a collection of samurai swords, all hung on the walls. In the corner on the floor was a cardboard box with what looked like engine parts, and on a shelf above were lined up some Bruce Lee DVD's.

I began to get a sense of the strength of the bond between father and son. Tim admitted, "This is the only one of my kids I got to raise from the git-go. He's a really great musician, knows this computer so easily, and can also make jewelry, just like his old man." Tim showed us a book of photos of some of the jewelry he'd made over the past eight years. The pieces were beautiful; Tim was a talented artist. "But I gave up everything when my wife, Cindy Lou, died last year of cancer. She was only 40, the love of my life. I fell apart, everything stopped. I have a jewelry workshop set up here in the back room, but I don't have the inclination."

At one point, it sounded like the neighbors upstairs were making a lot of noise, but Dylan said, "No problem. We have a thing going on, our amplifier versus whatever they have to give us. We go back and forth. I can correct the recording for that." At the end of the evening, Tim and Dylan played us some music they'd composed on the keyboard and guitar.

Then when I reached my capacity, I said, "We're used to going to bed early on the campgrounds, and I'm starting to fade. It's been really amazing to be with you. Thank you so much!" We exchanged our info, then Tim and Dylan stood on their porch, waving goodbye as we drove off.

We felt really touched that they'd shared their lives and home so openly with us. And we'd see in time if that CD would ever materialize.

When we returned to the campground, we were all set to have a good night's sleep, but in our absence, a couple had set up a tent right on our site. Their dog started barking and Harley barked back, setting up a domino effect of barking dogs throughout the campground. Peter went out to speak to them, but it did no good. We could hear the couple arguing loudly in their tent. We finally gave up and moved over to Angie's site, but we barely got any sleep, hearing the sounds of police nearby in the night and not even wanting to find out what that was about.

Gulpha Gorge had left its mark on us, had taken us for an amazing ride, but we were so ready to move on. We were exhausted! It had been a powerful vortex of social and musical energy, with all the people we'd gotten to know, who'd touched our lives and our hearts, but who we might never see again.There was an openness on the road. We were all on a level playing field among people we never would have met in our everyday life back in Maryland. What a crazy, magnificent cast of characters in this extended family we were meeting along the road! I remembered my meditation teacher, who'd taught, "See God in each other." And it was just like that. We saw the beauty in all the people we met and loved them all. But now I felt I could really use some rest and quiet and I didn't think we'd be finding that there at Gulpha Gorge.

RETREAT

Peter woke up and popped his head out the RV window. "Good morning hon, what's up?" He could see me sitting at the picnic table, throwing the *I Ching,* an ancient text of Chinese wisdom and divination, and he knew this had a meaning. We had planned to go to Mountain View, Arkansas, to the big music festival that we'd been told about. We were to leave that morning. But I just couldn't seem to wrap myself around the thought of being around a crowd of people, no matter how nice, and hearing non-stop music for three days, no matter how good. There had been so much socializing and music at Gulpha Gorge during the past week, and it had all been wonderful. But now I felt desperate for some solitude, peace, and sounds of nature.

Amazingly, the *I Ching* reflected just that - hexagram number 33 Retreat. Know when to back off and disengage. After all, I was still adjusting after the death of my mother. I'd been so exhausted and worn down, I'd hardly even taken the time to grieve. And now, I was at my wit's end, just needing some rest and silence. But I knew Peter was so excited to play with other musicians at Mountain View. It had always been his longing to jam informally with a good banjo, guitar, hammered dulcimer, or actually any kind of player. How could I have denied him this? Still, something inside me couldn't go with it.
Well, he gave it all up in a snap, just like that!

He said "I know what it's like to not want to be around a lot of people. Let's go find someplace beautiful to be." And we did.

But first, we'd promised to give Angie a ride that morning on our way out of town. She wanted to hitchhike from Little Rock, but we were afraid she'd meet up with some rough character there. I told her about a guy I'd met who was camping with his dog in the hills just up from Gulpha Gorge, who'd said that the police never bothered him and just let him be. That sounded good to Angie. "And on the way to dropping you off, we could take you to a clinic and have someone take a look at your leg. Please let us do that for you." I gave it one last shot, but she was having no part of it.

So we all went to fill up our bottles with the clear spring water that poured for free from faucets in town, then drove Angie to the trailhead. We loaded her backpack with cheese, bread, fruit, and the rest of those date cookies she liked, slipping some money in a side pocket while she wasn't looking. She tied her flip flops onto the heavy pack and hefted it onto her back. It was a misty, foggy morning as we hugged her goodbye and wished her well. There was nothing more she would let us do for her, though she needed so much more. We watched as she climbed up the steep trail in her boots and disappeared into the fog, her flip flops swinging from the pack behind her as they finally faded from sight. And part of my broken heart went with her.

We headed south and west toward Daisy State Park in Kirby, Arkansas. Peter was able to release what he'd wanted and seemed to turn on a dime to embrace the new plan. Maybe it was all his years as a Zen monk that trained him how to let go, to not be attached. Before we met, he had lived for many years in Zen communities, had even been through three month-long meditation retreats by himself in remote areas. He had learned the art of surrender.

"We're in this together," he said, "and we're making it all up as we go!" I melted with gratitude.

On Route 70 West, all along those beautiful hills were beat up old shacks, testaments to the hard times in these parts. A roadside fresh produce stand drew us in with gorgeous fruits and veggies from Texas. Oranges "sweet as your mother's milk" as we were told, papayas, mangoes, green beans, spring onions, zucchini, green peppers (unwaxed!), avocados, big red tomatoes....We took it all! The guy behind the counter spoke in such a thick mountain dialect, I only caught the occasional word. But after so many excuse me's, I just ended up smiling as though I knew what he was saying. Inspired by the beauty of the produce, Peter grabbed his fiddle, and in a wave of expansiveness said, "I'll fiddle you up some business", and he went to play out by the roadside.

One of the other customers came up to me and started telling me how to grow avocados. "You just git yourself a glass like a votive candle sits in, just set that avocado seed right down in it and in six weeks, it'll grow a few inches high. I had me one when we lived back in Idaho, but I had to leave it behind. We left near everything when we came out this way. We prayed to Jesus to help us find the right place for us, and he surely did show us. We bought us some land right up the road from here. We're home now. You put yourself in Jesus's hands and he'll take care of you. He'll show you yourself. If you haven't got Jesus, if you haven't got yourself, you don't have anything."

I thought to myself how fortunate Peter and I were to have each other and Harley too, of course. How fortunate we were to find a true home inside ourselves in the silence of meditation. And how we'd find our home that night at a campsite where we'd feel blessed by the bounty of nature.

And it happened just like that, right beside the sparkling Lake Greely, sunny campsite 26, Daisy State Park. The breezes rippled across a big expanse of lake. An eagle soared above. The feeling of peace, penetrating and healing, was just what the doctor ordered. A campfire, a pot of soup on the stove, a few fiddle/guitar tunes, a leftover Bud Light from when Derek visited us by the beach, the sun going down all red on the distant shore, everything combined to make the perfect medicine. And Harley had been treated to a dose of his panacea for the road: swimming repeatedly after sticks in the clear water.

We watched as two elderly couples hobbled along with their lawn chairs, down to the lake to witness the glorious display at end of day. And at night, the peepers serenaded us to sleep.

There was a lot of tossing and turning that night as I entertained a parade of doubts and fears, my mind running like a wild pony. Maybe it had been the wrong path not to go to the Mountain View Festival? I apologized to Peter, saying, "I'm so sorry you didn't get to have that experience this time."

He said emphatically, "No, you were following your intuition, and I trust your intuition. You know, it sounded great, but maybe something not so great would've happened there. So we really need to trust our sense of things, especially on the road."

What Peter said rang true, so I put all doubt out of my mind. We were on this trip together, and I couldn't think of anyone I'd rather be doing it with than him. And Harley, too, of course!

THE LEAK

We tore the RV apart looking for the source of the pesky leak that had left a water spot on the carpet. It was a persistent problem, a mystery that remained unsolved. Numerous theories had been proposed. Maybe there was rain coming in the window by the emergency exit. Maybe the side of the RV needed recaulking. Could it be that rainwater was splashing up through the rear wheel guard? At the RV dealership in North Carolina, they thought it was the water pump and they supposedly fixed that, but it was still leaking, so what gives? Peter was finally able to track down the culprit. A puddle under the camper, a big clue, pointing the way to…yes, it was the water pump. We could see it in action when we turned it on. They hadn't really fixed it back in NC.

Woodall's Camping Guide showed an RV service station at the far end of Texarkana. We would go there; a phone call confirmed it. The service guy sounded like he had a can-do attitude, and an appointment was set for 1:30 that day.

Route 70 West took us across the border into Texas, the towns looking decidedly western now. Wide streets with flat-fronted buildings were lined up side by side close to the road, and we could imagine a horse or two tied up outside a saloon, with some gunslingers bursting out the swinging doors. Many of the people on the street were wearing cowboy hats and boots, looking like stock characters that had been cast in a western movie.

That afternoon at the Shady Pines RV Park and Service Center, all kinds of business could be taken care of. Peter showed the service manager the crux of the matter with the leak, and the guy seemed relieved. "Leaks can be tricky business to track down, and you've done that work for me." We could see we'd be in good hands here.

While the leak was being taken care of, we gathered our laundry and headed for the pavilion at the RV Park next door, where we loaded two washing machines with efficient dispatch. We set up our office at the picnic table and before we knew it, emails were being answered, bills paid, money transferred, phone calls made and received. All the while, storm clouds were gathering across the expanse of sky. Then they finally all let loose. Jagged streaks of lightening and huge kabooms of thunder cracked closer and closer until the whole pavilion was shuddering. This was poor Harleydog's last straw. He hid under the picnic table, shivering, shaking, panting feverishly. It was a full-on doggy anxiety attack, and no amount of stroking his head or reassurance offered helped to calm him. It was only when the thunderstorm let up that he was finally able to relax.

Then a guy wandered up to our table and introduced himself as Charley. He was an elderly, rotund man, sporting shorts and a T-shirt that barely covered his sizable belly. A scar on his head was visible through his short gray hair. "Yeah," he started in, "me and the wife have been at this RV park for over a year now. Back then, I kept falling and we didn't know why. So the wife takes me over one day to the ER, and it turns out I've got this brain tumor, see, right on my pineal gland. Right there, on the spot, they put in a shunt to take the pressure off my brain. The doc said I was darn lucky nothin' worse happened. They sent me up to Little Rock to have the doctor, second best brain surgeon in all the country, take care of me. He said I should have the tumor taken out. The surgery lasted 12 hours, but here I am now, all healed up and hair growed over the scar. They're going to do an MRI next week to make sure, then we're on our way to Missouri. We met a couple who told us about an RV park there where you can stay for four dollars a night, longterm. You can get a job working at the local cinema taking tickets or selling popcorn and they give you free tickets to the movies. Yes ma'am, I am one lucky man. I was never religious before, but after this, I feel the man upstairs is looking out for me. Me and my wife have started going to church every Sunday now. Well, looks like the rain's let up now, I'd best be gettin back or my wife'll wonder if I've been washed away."

Charley had poured out his story without pause, with me offering him oh, I'm sorry's and yes, you were lucky and good to meet you and best of luck, and then he was on his way, never to be met up with again. Peter and I found that so often, people just wanted and needed someone to listen. And so often, listening seemed to be our job. A slice of Charley's life remained with us as one in the ever-growing family we were part of on the road. I really loved him, and wished I'd hugged him goodbye.

Then it all came together, the laundry was done, the water pump repaired, the window and side of the RV had been recaulked, our office work completed. Harley had recovered his composure, and we were all ready to hit the road again. If the water pump had not been the problem, it would be put to the test that day. The weather system seemed to be pervasive and the rains were torrential, coming in waves throughout the night.

88

GYPSY BAD LUCK

We decided on sheltering at a cozy motel for the night. The bed was so high that Harley was discouraged from jumping up there to join us. He found a spot on the sofa, thoroughly spent from his difficult day of being a dog on the road. But he was with his people and that was all that really mattered. His good natured acceptance of whatever came about, without complaining, was a true inspiration.

Next morning, Peter rolled over in bed to greet me as I returned from walking Harley. But Peter was at the edge of the bed, and just as he was mid-sentence, he slipped over the edge and landed on the floor quite surprised. It was a long fall from that high bed, but luckily somehow a soft fall, and he narrowly avoided hitting his head on the bedside table. Once we established that he was unhurt and all was well, then it was safe to laugh. Quite comical, though sometimes comedy is terribly close to peril. This time, it was a light touch, a reminder to start our day with a thankful heart. Being on the road, we were more aware than ever how vulnerable we were, and how good luck can sometimes turn sour. Peter had said we needed some "gypsy bad luck" at times along our way to balance things out. That point of view always seemed to make the rough edges feel a little softer, the bumps a little smoother. And we trusted that even if the worst did happen, we would still somehow be OK.

SUSAN

We pulled up to the home of Peter's sister, Susan, on La-Fayette Road in Fort Worth. Our road-worn and dusty camper parked in front of her house was a definite eyesore in her upscale neighborhood. Alas, Harley was relegated to waiting in the RV and just going on leashed walks now and then, as Susan's dog Lintz was a bit wild and Susan feared we wouldn't have had a moment's peace to talk together if Harley were to come into the mix. As it was, there actually wasn't a moment of peace as Lintz in the house and Harley in the camper barked back and forth together, each quite audible to the other, each quite aware of the other's presence. It seemed they were both curious to see what this new arrangement was all about. We finally decided to put them on leashes so they could meet in person on neutral territory. Once they sniffed each other out, all was quiet on the doggy front.

One of Susan's students at Texas Catholic University where she taught painting was giving a concert that afternoon. He had composed all the music and TCU students would be playing the pieces. A piano and violin sonata, a classical guitar piece, piano and flute, and finally the whole orchestra. Discordant, amorphous, somewhat melodious, at times quite tedious. After the concert, there was a tour of the gallery where the composer's paintings were hung. What an interesting life Peter's sister had there in Fort Worth, and we were happy to have shared a taste of it.

Later, saying goodbye to Susan, we took 20 West toward Abilene, where a whole colony of wind turbines were spread across a distant hill, silently whirling in submission to the winds that blew steadily across this land. We passed flat pastures where horses, sleek and strong, grazed under an open sky as though they had forever. Purple wildflowers carpeted the shoulders of the road, and along the median strip, groups of prickly pear cactus flowering red clustered in the sandy soil.

Susan's friend, Joachim, had been surprised to hear our trip was open-ended. "I know what it's like to go on vacation for a month," he had mused. "But I can't imagine having no deadline."

It was beyond our comprehension too, but we were simply taking it a day at a time. And the truth was, a moment at a time. On this journey we were being trained in the art of being present. There was no list of things to do, no goal oriented mind, no schedule or pushing ahead, no striving to get somewhere. Just being, enjoying, appreciating whatever appeared as it all unfolded. What a luxury, though it seemed like just a natural way to live. This was a gift we'd given ourselves, a gift we'd been granted.

ONWARD

We passed Sweetwater, Texas, the self-proclaimed "Home of the Largest Rattlesnake Roundup." Once a year, hunters would bring all the rattlesnakes they'd caught during the past 12 months to Sweetwater. A jamboree was held, some of the snakes were roasted, cooked in various recipes, and sold at food booths outside. Others were killed for their skins, also offered for sale, and would end up in boots and purses.

At last, toward the end of day, we arrived at Lake Colorado State Park on a branch of the Colorado River, but didn't find the campground at all to our liking as it was right in the city, too busy and loud. It was late in the day to be looking for another campground, so we made our way to a Days Inn in Snyder, Texas. I cooked dinner for us in the camper and we ate out on the porch of our motel as the sun set slowly along the flat horizon.

Well-rested, we started out the next morning on Route 180 through west Texas, in the middle of nowhere. It was a good road, and I took the wheel all morning. The dirt was red, with an occasional rocky outcropping. Scrubby growth abounded over this desert flat land, where cattle were somehow able to graze, and so many miles from any observable ranch. When was the last time these cows checked in at home base?

And then crossing over the line into New Mexico by the town of Hobbs, Peter exclaimed, "We're home!" He'd always felt a special kinship with the land in New Mexico and I loved it there, too. We bypassed Carlsbad Caverns. The day was too beautiful to be underground, so we proceeded north on 285 to Brantley State Park. Here, the Pecos River was dammed, forming a huge green lake that beckoned our road-weary Harleydog. Sticks were thrown, and he plunged in, swimming with a big smile on his face, as if to say thank you, thank you.

In contrast, we heard that the desert land all around here had had only one tenth of an inch of rain during the past six months. Several varieties of cactus were able to eke out a living on this parched landscape, but all around the campsites, it was like an oasis, with junipers and cedars thriving. As we learned, an underground sprinkler system irrigated them at 11 each morning. Every campsite had a shelter painted as blue as the cloudless sky, and all the campers, us included, were thankful to take refuge under them from the intensity of the afternoon sun. A refreshing breeze blew through and helped give the illusion of coolness. Still just the end of April then, July and August must have been brutal there. I found myself drinking huge quantities of water, the air was so dry. The wet spot on our carpet where the pump had been leaking had finally dried within a few hours of being here. No matter that my hair dryer had broken, after I washed my hair, it was dry in a few short minutes. Repeated applications of lotion were required to combat lizard skin and lips.

The pace of life had slowed down; nothing seemed that urgent in this heat. Walking Harley down to the lake, I threw some more sticks for him. I'd have liked to go in too, but the shore was too rocky and it was hard to get down to the water. That didn't bother Harley's bare doggy paws though, as he ran sure-footedly over the rocks with never a slip or twisted ankle. Remaining focused, intent on the stick, and swimming back with the prize in his mouth, he looked at me with an expression of deep satisfaction. He was doing what he was born to do, fulfilling his mission as a golden retriever.

Afternoon drifted away gradually, imperceptibly, into dusk. The sunset lingered forever. It was almost 10 p.m. before being officially dark. A new moon and a world away from any lights of city or town, the conditions were perfect for gazing up at the numberless points of light in the sky. We three slept sweetly that night in our little camper in the middle of a staggeringly vast starry universe. The desert air had become deliciously cool and fragrant.

DARE TO NOT HAVE A CARE

Awake before dawn, Peter had had a numinous dream that he was flying. He was feeling full of energy, and now I was awake too, so we packed up and headed out just as the huge red sun made its appearance on the horizon. A refreshing and welcome coolness was in the air early that morning. The plan was to drive north on 285 to Artesia, then west on 82 to Alamagordo, but then we learned that there was a heat wave and it would be in the 90's in the south.

This sparked a question, whether to go north or south out of Alamagordo. I had really wanted to go south to the sweet old town of Mesilla where there was a campground nearby. But it promised to be another scorcher. I was disappointed to miss visiting Mesilla, but began to realize it wasn't the actual agenda of what we saw or where we went, so much as the state of mind we were in. My intention was to experience a restfulness and sense of ease, just being able to go with whatever came up, like adjusting our route for this heat wave. What was the point of this journey, anyway? It was to open our minds, to experience joy and appreciation for all the beautiful landscapes and people we met. I aimed to let go of tensions, to see what was underneath all the resistance, grasping, and trying to make things go my own way. Let's slow down and lighten up! I remembered a van we'd seen before we left on this odyssey, and painted on the side was the message, "Dare to Not Have a Care". Perfect words to live by!

A magical road unfurled before us, the landscape gradually changing from harsh, sparse vegetation to cedars and junipers with huge bunches of prickly pear cactus growing along rocky outcroppings. Slowly we climbed, up in elevation, gradually so we hardly noticed it until our ears started popping. And soon, ponderosa pines and aspen were carpeting the mountainsides all around.

Just as we were getting really hungry, we came upon a little cafe where people were friendly and you could get a breakfast burrito, which Peter did, while I got the veggie omelet with green chile. Those with two mugs of black coffee, so satisfying. We stopped at the trading post next door, where Kim, an upbeat woman with eyes alive and conscious, in jeans, blazer and buzz cut, was ready to tell her story.

"Yeah, I came here nine years ago. I was just passing through on my way to Austin, Texas, and I ended up buying some land here and building a cabin, all solar. I haven't paid utilities in nine years. But now my kids want me to move out to Tennessee to be closer to them. I don't have any grandkids, but I do have a couple grand dogs. First I've got to sell my cabin, though. I've been advertising it for a year now, but maybe no one wants the solar thing. Heck, I'm 66 years old. If I can do it, anyone can!"

She pulled out some photos of the cabin to show us.

"It's beautiful. The solar ought to be a selling point," I offered.

"Well, when it sells it'll be right. And then I'll move to Tennessee."

As we headed out, she bid us goodbye, saying, "Blessings to you on the road."

97

I really liked her and somehow felt a real kinship with her, as if I'd known her sometime, somewhere before.

Little RV parks abounded up in the New Mexico mountains, some, quite inviting, beside a creek. It seemed all the ranchers figured they'd make some extra money. Just throw up some electric and water hookups down in the pasture and there you go. You're in business. We pulled into one campground, and while we were considering it, the woman who ran the place was watching us. But no, we didn't feel like stopping, though she probably could've used our business. On down the mountain we went, the road dotted all the way with truck runaway brake ramps. It was a relief no truck was bearing down on us picking up speed on the downhill as they sometimes had done in the past. And into Alamagordo, where we stopped at a health food cafe to discuss our options. Chai for me; black coffee with organic sugar for Peter. It looked like the best route would be north to Ruidoso, a ski area and home of Smokey Bear Historical Park, where the original Smokey was buried.

Various campgrounds presented themselves. We were shopping for real estate just for the night. We finally came upon an appealing one at the juncture of 48 and 220, Elk Ridge. But it was deserted and no one answered the phone. We pulled into number 10 but didn't hook up. We felt tentative, undecided. We spread out our new rug on the ground, but Harley didn't even lie down, since he wasn't sure about it either. Just then, Peter spotted a "sun-dog" in the sky. Purple, red, blue, green, it was like a rainbow all reflected in a cloud floating past the sun. Maybe this was a sign to relax already and breathe deep! There we were, nestled in the ponderosas, a vista of snow capped mountains right before us, birds calling out their songs in the breezes through the valley. What was not to like?

"OK," Peter declared, "want me to hook us up?"

"We might as well! If the owners return and want to charge us an exorbitant rate, we'll just be outta here. But for now, we're here!"

I started planning what to make for dinner...sautéed green pepper, onion, mushroom, and zucchini, with couscous and tahini. Sounded good! We ate at the picnic table as the sun's rays stretched low across the sky, illuminating our meal. And Harley, with his bowl of dog food right by our feet, was ready for any morsel from our bowls that might fall his way. And he knew that they would!

A parade of mule deer grazed by our RV in the deepening dusk. What could they possibly find to sustain life with here in this dry brown grass? It looked like they were thriving, though. Gentle beasts with long ears and white behinds, they moved sensitively and quietly along, swishing their tails, aware of our presence and alert to any sudden move. At the click of my camera, the mule deers gave a twitch, but went right on nibbling away at whatever it was that was keeping them going. One little rogue deer separated off from the others, coming right up to the RV window and agreed to pose for a photo. Luckily, our watchdog, Harley, was asleep on the sofa, so no barking to scare the little one off.

Peter unplugged the RV in case we needed to make a quick getaway, and that kind of set the tone. We were way out there, all alone on a campground where the owners seemed to be away. Was there a chance they could return and shine a flashlight in the window at one in the morning? That night I dreamed we decided to cloak ourselves in invisibility. I was looking for Mom and found a man who knew where she was, but he couldn't take me to her for some reason. I awakened briefly in the night. The mountain air coming in through the window smelled so fresh and pure. Oh, life was good.

MANZANO WINDS

Awake at dawn, we made ready and in 10 minutes were on the road. Route 48 North to Angus, and on to Route 380 West. Breakfast was at the only act in town at Carrizozo, huevos rancheros with green chile, the hot kind. A woman sat next to us at the counter. "I just got off night shift at the Allsup's gas station across the street. I can't eat anything right now. I'm too tired." However, she proceeded to watch us eat and advise us on exactly how that should be done. "If that chile's too hot for you, just sprinkle some salt on the lettuce and that'll take the heat right out. Go ahead. Just sprinkle on some salt and take a bite. There, see? Next time, you should ask for more lettuce and never mind the tomatoes. And that'll help you right there." I began to realize the drawback of sitting at the counter as opposed to a table. She was sitting awfully close, and watching every bite I took. And I had the distinct feeling she believed she could do a better job of eating it than me!

Singing, our hearts and souls were singing with the huge expanse of this land and cloudless blue sky. We felt free and open to any possibility that might present itself. Along 54 North to Corona, past buff colored dry grasses with red soil peeking through, the fields were dotted with junipers and cedars as far as our eyes could see. Cattle were grazing on old dry grass, their headquarters nowhere in sight. On to Route 60 West, the mountains were beginning to take shape, looking as if they were moulded out of clay. Up we went, past 7000 feet elevation to Mountainair, "The Gateway to Ancient Cities", so the sign said. Petroglyphs, or rock drawings, were prevalent there, dating back to the 1400's when the ancient Pueblo culture had thrived around the area.

And in Manzano, a sweet little unexpected store yielded the perfect congratulations on your new baby card to send to my nephew Rob and his wife Jen and their new baby, Madison. Also some fresh tomatoes, lettuce, eggs, and cherry cider made their way into our little fridge. At Manzano State Park, we pulled into campsite 8. The lofty sound of the wind moving through the ponderosa pines spoke to me deeply and called forth something primal, timeless. I listened. This was the perfect medicine I'd been longing for without even knowing it. I breathed the sound in and let go into a forever afternoon. The huge trees were thick and they swayed in the wind like a troupe of dancers.

Kay from a couple of campsites down came over and said how much she loved our tablecloth and we took off from there. She let me know she had a MSN in nursing, but had been doing other things. "For three years, Bruce and I lived on our sailboat, a beautiful 38-foot boat made of teak, off the coast of Mexico. It was a great adventure. We'd swim and fish off the boat, and we met so many fantastic people. Like you! You know how it is when you travel. But then, I'd had enough, I wanted a home base again. We came to Ruidoso NM and ended up buying an inn. It was a house with ten little cottages we'd rent to vacationers. Lots of people would come up from Texas for the summer to get out of the extreme heat. It sounds like fun, and it was, but it was a lot of work and it was really hard to take time off. So when Bruce had to have a valve replacement of his heart, we sold it. Now I'm going to Tunisia with a friend in the fall. Bruce said I should just go ahead and go. So I'm reading up on the art and architecture of Tunisia. I've got a book if you'd like to take a look at it."

Kay exuded enthusiasm. She spoke with her whole body, particularly her arms and hands. And you got the feeling that she might have had no idea how to stop talking. Finally, picking up an old dented soda can, she found an exit strategy. "I found it on the ground while I was walking. Better go put it in recycling", and she pushed off with a "See you later!"

Wow, that was a lot to digest. I liked her a lot and she felt somehow familiar to me, as if I already knew her. I took a deep breath and came back to the sound of the wind. But just then I got a text message on my phone from my son Derek, saying "the only cloud in the sky" with a picture of one white puff of a cloud floating in a sea of blue. Amazed that my phone worked way up in the mountains since there were so many open spaces in the-West with no internet or phone reception, I realized how important it was to me to be able to stay in touch with family and friends. Not ready at this point to fall completely out of the known world and get lost in oblivion, there was only so much letting go I felt comfortable with! Thus began a torrent of emailing throughout the afternoon.

The day felt timeless, but I did want to sink my teeth into something before it all slipped away. Hearing there was a lake a couple of miles down the road, I got the idea to walk Harley down there and let him swim. The road was steep going downhill and seemed like it went on forever. I was sure we'd walked more than two miles already. Then a spectacular vista opened up, clear and in focus, but no lake in sight. Ponderosa and aspens covered the mountainsides as far as I could see.

Hiking back up the steep hill was another matter, and I was huffing and puffing, the atmosphere thin at this elevation. Harley was free, off-leash for now, ears pricked, tail held high and wagging. Carrying a big stick in his mouth, he didn't seem to feel the lack of oxygen at all. I hadn't told him about the possibility of going swimming (he did know that word) so he was perfectly happy and satisfied with just this. I could learn a lesson from our dog, being totally content with just this, whatever it was.

Peter asked if I'd like to play some music together. I noticed I felt some resistance, the old story about how he's so talented and it's taking me so long to learn the harp. But now on this trip, I wanted to try something different. Let's just see what it's like to forget about that story and have an open mind. And we actually sounded good. It was fun. The old mental pathways that had worn ruts in my brain had been rerouted a little. I was growing younger!

THE FRONTIER

"What are we doing on this Earth anyway?" I mused. It was five a.m. and it looked like I wouldn't be going back to sleep. It was a question I didn't need an answer to, but after it was quiet for a while, Peter said, "To live in bliss. That's what we're doing here."

It's just that living in bliss is not exactly something you can put on your to-do list. Maybe it's more something that gets revealed as you continue to weed the garden, as you cut away the dead wood. So for starters, I lit the incense, rang the bell, and we sat together in the silence, as my mother used to say.

Well, we agreed that after a few days here, it was time to push off and leave Manzano State Park. This was a bold move, to leave on a Saturday when campground real estate was at a premium. But we were all in the spirit to go to the Frontier Restaurant in Albuquerque for some breakfast, where the huevos rancheros were absolutely the best, and the restaurant was alive with interesting people having intriguing conversations. People who you'd like to pull up your chair and join, who you'd like to get to know. It's a happening place, right across from the University of New Mexico, in a culturally diverse neighborhood.

That day, however, I have to say we were the most interesting people I saw, and I was so happy to be sitting at the table with us. And the huevos were not actually the best, just pretty good. But the fresh squeezed orange juice *was* the very best. The truth was, we'd always come here just as we were ready to start out on our return trip back home to the East Coast and feeling a little sad about leaving. Maybe our judgement had been clouded by sentimentality. Maybe it's a good place to come when you're saying goodbye, but not as great when you're saying hello? Or maybe it was just an off day at the Frontier.

REDEEMED

I was sitting at a picnic table facing the Sandia Mountains. The nearby American flag was snapping around like crazy in the strong wind. The sun was setting, its light glowing pink on the mountains. Hence, the name Sandias, which means watermelon, about the color they looked right then at sunset, the angles of their rocky faces dramatic in the changing light. Cottonwood trees lining the banks of the Rio Grande River below were dressed in a new green, just beginning to leaf out in the spring.

We were at Coronado Campground on ancient Native American soil. Back in the 1200's, there was a drought, and the encampment moved to the shores of the Rio Grande to plant where the soil was moist. Ruins of their community were right next to the campground, and there was also a kiva, or circular sacred meeting place, that had been preserved there. The kiva had a white tent around it to protect it from the elements.

What an afternoon it had been! That morning, we'd felt as if we had all the time in the world. We had left our beautiful campsite in Manzano on a Saturday, no less, and had thrown our fates to the wind.

We did laundry, grocery shopping, banking, and had made our way to the holy land of the Jemez River valley

107

where the rocks were brick red, the Sangre de Cristo's were in the distance, the blood of Christ, given for us that magnificent afternoon. We'd stopped at the fry bread stand, where the Pueblo women had a fire going, so fragrant, of cedar wood, with a deep pan of hot oil on top. When we ordered the frybread, they had patted out the dough with their hands and plopped it into the hot oil, turning it with a stick and then onto a paper plate when it was done. You could get beans and onions and tomatoes on top; that was called an Indian taco. Or you could choose to put honey or cinnamon sugar on it, and that was the route I'd taken. We'd eaten at a picnic table in the sun by the brick red rocks; their deep color seemed to open our hearts. The day had felt like it would last forever.

At Vista Linda Campground, though, we'd discovered that it was full, not a single empty site for us. It was a Saturday night, and people were off for the weekend and ready to have fun camping. I'd thrown sticks for Harley in the Jemez River which was gushing from spring snowmelt down from the mountains. Harley was drenched and happy, shaking off the excess water all over me. A certain kind of blessing. Still, I'd had the optimistic feeling that all was well. But driving on up the mountain, every single campground had been full, and we'd begun to wonder where we'd be sleeping that night. The local inn had a sign posted that said "no dogs excepted" and we'd hoped that meant they'd not leave any dog out from their motel. But no, it had just meant they didn't know the difference between except and accept.

We were feeling tired and getting a little tense, and headed back to Bernalillo to try to find a dog-friendly motel there. But along the way, we saw a sign for Coronado Campground at the national monument. Everything was difficult: parking the RV in the last available space, getting water, agreeing that this was the best place to be. It was all a rough and rocky road. And then, we discovered we were right there beside the ancient Pueblo holy lands. Our RV window looked out on the kiva where the Ancient Ones had meditated. Peter and I walked the paths with Harley, even though the site was closed for the day. The wind was blowing all the while, blowing away the tensions, the harsh words and fiery emotions. We were redeemed.

Peter said it was just like in the Paul Bowles novel, *The Sheltering Sky,* where the couple was in a troubled state with no place to stop for refuge, until finally they came upon the last place open, and discovered they were resting on sacred land. The temple was right there, they entered and were blessed.

That night we had been healed, provided for once again, reminded that even when all seems lost and ruined, when we're tired and irritable, we could just *be* and that would be enough. What if "the worst" had happened and we'd found no place to stay the night? We could have done what Clara and Roger did. Pull into a Walmart parking lot and call it a night. Fear of the worst is worse than the actual worst, which is somehow still doable.

As we headed to bed for the night, I caught sight of a coyote pausing up on the ridge near our campsite. We looked in each other's eyes for a long moment, then he turned and disappeared over the ridge.

PARADISE

Up at 4 a.m., Peter found a tick under his arm and pulled it off. It seemed like it'd been there a few days. He'd thought it was a skin tag. We looked it up online, and it was questionable, but best to take preventative action in case of Lyme Disease. Within a short period of time, we'd located an urgent care center, Peter had been seen by a nurse practitioner, ("she was an angel and so thorough"), the prescription for doxycycline had been filled, and he had swallowed the first dose with a slurp of the Star-buck's coffee I'd gotten while waiting for him.

And now once again, the towering Jemez mountains beckoned us and invited our hearts to open. A huge blue sky bestowed its optimism; it was a new day! Campsite 7 at Vista Linda Campground, the primo spot right by the river, was open. We'd been blessed and pulled into our new locale in Jemez Springs. We were home for a while.

The sound of the water gushing over rocks was music to my ears and fed my soul. I could get lost in that music. Sometimes it sounded like tabla drums playing, some-times like voices singing. A bird so blue I couldn't believe it was flitting around our campsite, and I wondered if he was a character straight out of Disney. The afternoon was ours, each moment stretching out to forever. I took Harley to the river for a swim. He chased sticks into the water with endless enthusiasm, his tail going round and round in circles as he pounced on each stick, bringing them to the shore where he fiercely gnawed his prize to bits. The water was deeper by the rocks and he got tossed around a bit, but that did nothing to dampen his spirits. He was energized! When the supply of nearby sticks was exhausted, he even retrieved twigs as long as I threw them.

After Harley was finally exhausted, or more accurately after I was finally tired of throwing, I came to rest on the picnic table and played my harp for the river and the red rocky hillside. Practicing the harp used to be something I'd do; it'd be on my list to learn the new pieces before the next lesson. But this was another way to play, it flowed organically from within. The mental commentary that often ran on - "it's taking so long to learn this song, I'd learn faster if I were more talented" - that voice of the critic was somewhere else today, taking the day off. It had been working too hard. And what was left was just the playing, which was the right word for it. It was fun, like play! It didn't have to be perfect or good or anything. Later, Peter woke up from his nap and said, "I had the most delicious nap. I fell asleep to the sound of your harp. Are we in paradise?"

A gorgeous campfire crackling, a vast sky full of stars, an exhausted and happy dog curled up on the blanket beside us... Yes, this was paradise.

ANIMAL CONTROL

Chai, the best since the ashram days, made by Pema at the Highway Four Cafe. She told us her parents had a restaurant in Darjeeling, India, and she'd brought their recipe all the way here to Jemez Springs, New Mexico. I got a refill in my to-go cup, taking the breakfast panini, which didn't really do it for me, to maybe repair later with more veggies from our fridge. I wasn't starving, so why eat something that didn't taste right and wouldn't satisfy? But the chai, ah, the chai! It conjured up early mornings at the Siddha Yoga ashram, where after meditation, my mother and I would sip from our steaming cups of the milky sweet brew while awaiting the morning chant. I would always go back for a second cup and then maybe have a third during breakfast. I never was able to recreate the chai of India myself, but that might have helped to keep it special.

Peter and I went to soak in side-by-side tubs at the Jemez Springs Bath House. The tubs were long enough you could really stretch out, and made of rough cement so you could rub the soles of your feet on it like a pumice stone. Filled with hot spring water straight from the ground, the tubs' hot and cold water faucets could be adjusted to make them just the right temperature. My sweetheart needed some encouragement in the personal hygiene department. He'd been on the three-day method, a shower once every three days, and by that third day, things were getting a little ripe. Thirty minutes was what we signed up for. The attendant came by our curtained room to tell us when the time was up. A lot of deep down grime can soak off in 30 minutes!

At Los Ojos, the popular cowboy bar and saloon across the road, a mural on the wall outside pictured a few old time cowboys. Inside, rustic wood stools lined the bar, and every seat was filled. Tables and booths were still available, so we sat right by the huge stone hearth where a roaring fire could warm you on a chilly day. On the walls hung various animal skins: bear, mountain lion, rattlesnake, as well as some Native American rattles and drums. During the weekends, local musicians would play up on the stage, and people could dance when the tables were pushed aside. Bikers stopped off here in big groups on the weekends, their shiny motorcycles lined up outside the bar. Los Ojos was a happening place in the small village of Jemez Springs, where there were only two other restaurants available.

Some emailing at the local library stirred up a hornet's nest of emotion about my son Derek. He was all excited about going on a trip to Ireland with his father. Ugh, hate to admit it, but I was jealous and wanted to go along with them. Back at our campsite, I sobbed straight from my broken heart and Peter held me with compassion. I was Derek's mother, we were close while he was growing up, and that was our time. I'd made a lot of sacrifices to be a good single mother after the divorce, but I didn't get any glory or recognition for it. And now, he wanted to be with his father who really knew how to show him a good time. They would leave for Ireland that Thursday. My highest reframing of it was that it'd be great for them to share this special time together, and I was happy for them both. Just let it go and say bless it all. I couldn't hold on to any of it and didn't want to cause suffering. Let this heartache dig a deep hole and compost the soil. Plant a seed of hopefulness that something good would grow out of this feeling. Straight and true, like the field of sunflowers we once saw in South Dakota, with all their happy faces pointed toward the sun.

As I was making my internal peace with the Ireland thing, Harley had started barking nonstop at the guys in the animal control truck parked at the next campsite down. We ended up having to put him in the RV, since no amount of admonishing him made him stop. Finally, we went talk to the guy and asked him, "Have you had any unusual animal sightings around here lately?"

"No, actually someone reported a golden retriever at your campsite off leash in the river."

We admitted that, yes, for a brief time we did let him off leash to chase sticks in the river.

"Of course, you know that it's the park's rule to keep your pet controlled on a leash at all times. But man, I'd do the same thing."

We gave a sigh of relief. It looked like no citation would be issued. Then we wondered to ourselves, who could possibly have seen Harley in the river yesterday or would have even cared? Our best theory was that it might have been the guy a few sites up from us who had been fishing. Maybe Harley had disturbed the waters for him, in which case, we were sorry for not paying closer attention to that. At any rate, it was strange that Harley hadn't liked that animal control truck and had continued barking from inside the RV until the truck finally pulled away. Our Harley was one smart dog.

SANTA FE

I awakened early, around sunrise. Peter later called it a vision. It was definitely more real than a dream. I saw Derek, standing beside me, looking intently at me. The unspoken communication was "I love you. I will always love you." I was surprised to see him, so real, and said, "You're here". Again, the communication was wordless. We were in the Burnbrae house, the place we had last lived together. He hugged me, I could feel the bulk of his body. He was absolutely present, his attention totally focused on me. I knew that he had come to reassure me and to say, "It's okay." This was more than a dream, it was a soul communication, and I got it on a deep level.

And yet...ugh, I hated to admit it, but I still felt an aching nostalgia, a sense of separation. After feeling our closeness in the dream, the fact was, we were so many miles apart. Maybe it's just the human condition, believing we are separate when in fact we are all one? Maybe it's a choice, whether to entertain that thought of estrangement, or not. I resolved to focus on the feeling of love, which transcends all division.

That morning, we were to go hear the Roshi, or enlightened master, give a talk at the Bodhi Manda Zen Center up the road. But Hosen, the friendly abbess at the center, appeared to tell us, "Sasaki Roshi is not feeling well, so there won't be a talk. But maybe this afternoon, if you'd like to give a call."

We thanked her and said goodbye; this was our cue to head for Santa Fe and adventures as yet unknown. Our first stop in Santa Fe was seven miles up on Artist Road to Hyde State Park. We scouted around, sizing up the campsites, and finally paid our money for number 41, leaving a blanket behind on the picnic table to alert others that this one was taken. We were way up there in elevation, among the tall ponderosa pines and aspens. Dedicated bicyclists, lean, mean, and young, somehow biked up this steep seven mile road then turning around, zoomed back down at breakneck speeds. I hated to limit myself, but I didn't think this would be me in what remained of my lifetime.

Back down in Santa Fe, there was a fantastic parking lot on the alameda where RV's were allowed to park, a mere few blocks from the plaza. There was a little line of them into which we fell in place. All day cost only $7, a real deal! In fact, you were allowed to stay the night for that price, and the idea occurred, why not? If we didn't feel like driving all the way back up the mountain, we could just stay here. Peter didn't seem to see the attractiveness of that possibility, but I tucked it away on the back burner of my mind. You never knew.

Peter renewed his Santa Fe buskers license and set up on a bench in the Plaza. Part of his act was having Harley tied up next to him looking adorable and, Peter hoped, appealing to people to come give a listen and drop some money into the open fiddle case. There was plenty of competition that day, two guitarists and a one man band. According to the city legislation, buskers were to maintain a 150 foot distance from each other. Not so easy to do if one was right in the middle of the plaza with an amplifier. The one man band approached Peter, irate.

"Thanks a lot man, you ruined my gig here."

Peter apologized, but in fact, he'd been as far away from the other musician as he could possibly get. And besides, the other edict was that after two hours of playing, it was time to move on and give someone else a chance. And that guy's time was up.

I walked around Santa Fe, window shopping at all the trendy stores, and people watching. Before long, I'd had enough of the mobs of tourists. This was definitely a tourist town, and merchants depended on them for their livelihood. But I wondered if it might be a love/hate relationship. The rampant consumerism, the desire to acquire, the kind of skimming the surface, and checking it off your list of sights to see. Peter told me he'd once overheard a couple of old Hispanic men sitting on a bench in the plaza, talking about the tourists and shaking their heads in bewilderment at the stylish, well-outfitted yuppies who'd been shopping at all the New Age stores. Quite a change from the old days, Santa Fe had become a kind of mecca for the wealthy, beautiful people.

We were both ready to make the drive back up the mountain and seek respite in the clear, pure atmosphere at 7000 feet elevation, with the music of the wind moving through the tall pines. Peter pulled out his saw and cut up some dead branches we found lying on the ground. They burned so efficiently in the fire ring, even though small, and glowed on into the night. The wind had quieted, a quarter moon shone through above the treetops, a deep silence pervaded. This was the right panacea, the prescription we needed. It was fun to visit the city, but the stillness of this mountain top was our refuge that night.

Stars gave us their blessing for a peaceful night's sleep as we three nestled in together, the bustle of the city left far below us.

A SPECIAL DAY

Peter was sitting on a stone bench, playing his fiddle in a park with a fountain, off the beaten track. I stationed myself on a bench in the plaza, right in the middle of town. Some school children filed in, kept in an orderly line by their teachers. Carrying their paper bag lunches, they found seats on the ground all around the center monument where they ate. The monument honored the soldiers who had fought in New Mexico during the Civil War, but it had become very controversial due to some wording about the "heroes" who died fighting the Native Americans.

As I was sitting, a guy came by with his two dogs, asking "OK if I sit here?"

"Sure," I said. "Nice dogs." I thought of Harley who was with the Irish Fiddler right now and would have loved to play with these two.

"You from around here?"

"No," I answered. "Actually, we're on the road right now, traveling for an indeterminate time."

"I've been thinking of doing that myself. Been looking for a little RV on Craigs List. Last year, I went tent camping just to see if I could do it. Really never been camping before. It was great, me and these two. My father had just passed away. In fact, today is the one-year anniversary of his passing. I took care of him myself. He had Alzheimer's. The hospice people got involved, and eventually they helped ease him out of this life. Just giving him two cc's of morphine, then two more. By the way, my name's Greg."

I told him how sorry I was, thinking of my mother who had also been taken care of by hospice at the end, only three months ago. So I could really empathize with him. The hospice staff was a strong support, compassionate and caring.

Greg's cellphone rang and he told someone, "Just doing as much of nothing as I can. Pretty easy going here."

Then returning to our conversation, he said, "Yeah, it was my girlfriend who'd gotten me in shape for taking care of Dad. She became a quadriplegic, and I took care of her till her family said they wanted her with them right at the end. She went just before Dad. It's her I miss the most."

As his eyes began to fill with tears, I offered, "I'm so sorry. It's really hard to lose someone you love, particularly when they're young."

We fell silent for a few moments, then, "Well I'm going to move on here. I really liked talking with you, Susan." Greg collected his dogs who'd been lying under the bench in the shade. "C'mon guys! You have a great trip now!"

I sat for a few moments more, feeling so much love and compassion for all of us who have cared for family and loved ones near the end of life. That experience can be hard and sad, yet it's part of life, and I supposed that some people never had an opportunity to understand the richness that caring in this way can really add to your life.

As I looked around, I phoned Peter and told him, "Come on over to the plaza. There's no one else playing right now. The place is yours!" Before long, I saw him sitting on a bench at the other end of the park, Harley at his feet.

Peter was fiddling away while people stopped left and right to put money into his case.

In fact, there was enough in that case by the end of the afternoon to pay for dinner at the outdoor Cafe de Paris, on Burro Alley. Fashioned into a little world of its own, the alley was shady, with breezes moving gently through. Big planters of ferns and flowers lined one side, tables and chairs set for dinner on the other side.

I asked the waiter, "We'd just like some appetizers. Is that OK?"

"Sure. I recommend the Pinot Noir and the pate de maison." Our waiter's accent was decidedly not French. More like the Bronx. We overheard him commiserating with a friend about how slow business had been. "But maybe tonight, with the show at the Lensic going on..."

The Pinot Noir was great, a healthy-size glass full, with crusty French bread to mop up the garlic butter in the escargots, which we'd ordered instead of pate.

"Where's Dadou tonight?" I asked. He was an accordion player we'd heard when we visited this cafe a few years ago. Dadou had played little French songs on his accordion all during dinner, creating a magical French atmosphere right there in this Santa Fe alley.

"Not here tonight. Maybe tomorrow," the waiter answered.

There was just enough time for a coffee from Starbuck's, and a quick walk for Harley. Then he'd go back into the RV where he'd fall asleep on his (our) king-size bed. Then we headed to the Lensic Theater, where the gifted Nadja Salerno Sonnenberg played her violin in her own unique and astounding style, vibrant, energetic, dramatic.

She was accompanied by the Assad Brothers, Sergio and Adair, on their guitars. Together, they made the music come alive, playing everything from Gypsy to Debussy, from Bach to Romanian folk dances. Wow, played impeccably, the music was spirited and animated. Sergio had arranged all the pieces; apparently there hadn't been much music composed for violin and two guitars. And the Lensic was such a grand environment for it, with its Moorish architecture and magnificent hall and acoustics. Just being in this unique theater would make any show that much more special.

Awed, we made our way back up the mountain and thankfully found one last campsite open. Straight to bed we went, drenched in the afterglow of the night's superbly rich concert.

DAY OF REST

The sounds of a playful squirrel chattering right outside our RV window was our alarm clock in the mornings at Black Canyon Campground. The air really chilly, I closed the window and turned on a warming blast from the furnace. It felt like there'd be rain this day; the sky was completely gray. Peter wasn't feeling well, he thought from the antibiotics he was still taking for his tick bite. We'd take a day off and just rest here. We did two sittings of meditation, both fiery, as if some kind of dross was being burned off. It felt like a new phase of our journey was beginning, we were really slowing down, listening, our awareness more finely tuned to the moment. It had taken a while for the East Coast pace to drain out of us. This day seemed to be some kind of turning point. As we sat, we began to hear the tap tap of raindrops on the RV roof. I swept the kitchen and unrolled my yoga mat. There was just about enough room to stretch out and unkink my body.

At a break in the rain, Harley and I went for a hike along the trail. The campground had just been built and had been opened up for campers by the U.S. Forest Service the day before. I looked around and saw everything appeared to be so well crafted. Heavy wooden picnic tables and fire rings graced every site, each one spacious and far enough from the others to provide some privacy. New pine outhouses with green tin roofs, masterful stonework along the walkways, it was all a work of art. Ponderosa pines stretched up toward the sky, while fluttering aspen leaves played their music in the breezes. Patches of snow still remained in the shaded nooks and crannies along the path.

Walking with Harley, I was aware that bears could have been around watching us. The campground hosts, Pat and Caroline, had told us that a hiker had seen a mother bear with her cubs up here just a week earlier. Mothers with cubs are the most dangerous kind; they're fiercely protective of their young. Somehow I felt if I just stayed on the trail, we wouldn't have any problem, but Harley didn't seem to share this feeling. Off the leash, which had been left behind in the camper, he was trotting all around, following some intriguing scents. In an effort to reroute him, I threw sticks for him, making sure they landed right on the trail. Tail held high, ears perked, he loved this! But the thought of a possible bear nearby brought us back toward our campsite. We returned just in time. The rain started up again and we climbed back in the RV to wait it out.

Pat and Caroline invited us to their trailer to look at the jewelry she'd made out of glass. She had Pat fetch the boxes and boxes - looked like we'd be there a while! - of necklaces, bracelets, earrings, bookmarks, Bible-markers, watches, barrettes…yikes. She fed us some cake she'd made to keep us fortified for the long haul. Their place was spacious, with two slide-outs, cozy and warm with a space heater going. They had electric and water hook-ups since they were the hosts for the summer. The rest of the sites had to do what's called dry camping, using our generator if we wanted to bake something in the oven, using the water in our own tank and turning on the pump to access it.

124

We emerged some time later. Let's just say we did our part to help support Caroline in her business. Pat had been looking at us the whole time from his La-Z-Boy recliner, just shaking his head. We wondered, was this a phenomenon among hosts, having a business on the side and inviting campers to "come see what I've been working on"? Caroline's work was beautiful and I was happy with what I'd bought. And she was absolutely glowing with satisfaction at having been appreciated.

Another lull in the rain allowed for a campfire, and incredibly we got one burning well. Peter had wrapped the wood and stashed it under the RV. He was such a good camper! He was experienced from all the months of tent camping he'd done when younger during his solo meditation retreats. So even though there was a scarcity of dry kindling, huge wads of an old New Yorker magazine, the program from Nadia's show, and some Trader Joe's shopping bags did the job and helped ignite the firewood. We played a few games of hearts by the fire, as Harley curled up nearby. And then, plop plop plop, the rain started up again and that was it for the night. No need to douse the fire before bed; the rain took care of it.

It had been good to take the day off and rest here. So often we'd been moving on, wanting to experience the joy of being on the open road, seeing new environments, novel campgrounds, meeting new people. But the restlessness of our early days on the road was beginning to wear off and we wanted to settle a bit. We were learning to trust that what was ours to experience would happen at the right time and place. Just take a deep breath, relax with the flow, and take our time.

A DREAMY DAY

I dreamed of Mom and running uphill in the sand after her. She was pushing a cart loaded with oranges, and I took off after her. But the elevation had me winded, gasping for breath, and she slipped out of view. Where was she? Where did my mom slip off to? Sometimes I felt her so close, but maybe it was my imagination. Mostly I simply missed her, and would have loved to be able to contact her. It's all a mystery, life and death. But again, I knew I could focus on the sense of separation, or focus on the love I felt for my mother, and that approach made me feel better.

We bid adieu to Caroline and Pat, returning back down the mountain into Santa Fe. Breakfast at the La Fonda cafe, where at the next table, a Japanese couple was sitting. When their breakfasts were served, but before either one of them could touch it, a photo had to be taken. Actually, several photos. He zoomed in with a state-of-the-art Nikon lens to photograph. First, the untouched plate with the fruit crepe, and next, the ham sandwich with béchamel sauce. Close up, without utensils, then from a little distance with her in the frame. A few more from various angles, then finally they were able to begin eating. Presumably, their friends back home would be most interested to see what they'd eaten while here in the USA.

Wandering around the streets, we felt pretty low-key

and slow moving that morning. We found some fetishes carved by Zuni Indians, purchasing a few for friends and family. Fetishes are small Native American carvings, from stone or other materials, that are used in their ceremonies. We found a turquoise frog with coral eyes for Peter's mother, Inge. A hyalite bear, symbol of healing and power of the inner life, with coral eyes and a power pack on his back for our friend, Jay. And a little hyalite beaver with turquoise eyes for Lucy, who used to care for Harley when we were away.

Drifting out of town, we found ourselves camped again at Coronado Campground, overlooking the Sandia Mountains and the Rio Grande River lined with cottonwood trees, their leaves fluttering and flashing in the sun and the steady breeze. Banks of clouds rolled in across the huge sky. So expansive! The laundry that hadn't fully dried at the laundromat flapped away outside on hangers to finish it off. Sitting at the picnic table, facing the deepening shadows on the Sandias, Peter and I played music together into the dusk. Clouds stretched out all along the mountains as they gradually turned pink, then gray. A half moon rose. Joyful sounds of laughter and camaraderie washed over us from a gathering at the next campsite. They sounded like really nice people.

Moonlight poured in through the open skylight of the camper as we three - yes, Harleydog was definitely part of our pack - nestled into bed, covered only by a flannel sheet that night. We fell asleep to the sounds of geese honking as they flew down the Rio Grande in the night, Harley too sleepy to even bother barking.

BEARS

Sun salutation on top of the picnic table. When the ground was too stony or uneven for my purple yoga mat, I'd spread it out up on the table. You had to have a good sense of balance up there and not look down too much or you'd lose it.

On our way out of Coronado Campground we were greeted by the group next door, three couples, self-proclaimed "full timers", overflowing with enthusiasm and information. One couple had been living in their RV for 12 years, the others, for 9 years. They congratulated us as if we were newlyweds when they discovered we'd been at it for only a few months. Business cards with email addresses were exchanged, various recommendations made. "Aspen Lite makes the best fifth wheel around. On a windy day, I can hold a match inside by a closed window and it doesn't even flicker. This baby is airtight!" They advised us to check out the website escapees.com. "We're 'The Boon-Dockers'. That's the group that has no rules, no leaders. We dry camp mostly, never the RV parks for us. We get the most out of the solar panels on our roofs. This way of life is not about deprivation. The full-time RV life is about comfort, having all the comforts of home. We'd never last otherwise."

We bid each other happy trails, maybe we'll see you again down the road, and as we drove off we told ourselves we had a plan for comfort that day too!

Sitting in a hot spring pool later that morning near Las Vegas, New Mexico, we gazed dreamily at the abundant ponderosa pines on the adjacent hillside. Harley was tied up on a nearby coyote fence, preventing our little coyote-dog from trying to get into the hot pool. The coyote fence is made from rustic cedar sticks or small branches of all different heights and strung together with wire, thus reminding me somehow of notes on a musical score. There were three pools there: one too cool, one too hot, but one was just right! We relaxed in that pool until we became limp like well-done pasta. Up from the pools on a distant hill was what looked like a castle, and we found out that it was the United World College, founded in 1982 by philanthropist Armand Hammer. It was a boarding school for high school students from around the world, but the castle originally had been built by the Santa Fe Railroad as a hotel where one of the main attractions had been these hot springs.

We dried off and went for breakfast at Pancho's Cafe where the huevos were great. The very same waiter we'd had all three times we'd been at the restaurant, over the past nine years, was still there and took our order that day. He had the air of one who had grown to be able to take whatever life dishes out with great forbearance. Peter thought maybe he was Catholic and just kept repeating his rosary over and over while waiting on tables, taking orders, bringing food, clearing tables, day after day, year after year. Throughout all the years we'd been living out our drama in Maryland, this man had been at this cafe, persevering the whole time.

The campground at El Porvenir was calling us, and driving on, the mountain began to come into view. From a distance, the granite rock formation looked like a giant gorilla, maybe King Kong, lying on his back looking up at the sky. As he must have been doing for millennia now. He seemed to command the whole area with his massive presence.

All along the road to the campground was a raggle-taggle collection of adobe huts, beat-up old trailers with rusted out pickup trucks in the yard, and finally giving way to some quality log homes and haciendas. As we wound our way up the mountain, there were ponderosa pines everywhere with their beautiful butterscotch brown trunks, stretching up toward the sky. Peter pulled over and invited me to smell one of the trunks. Circling my arms around the huge tree and pressing my nose against a fissure in the bark, I inhaled. Butterscotch, aah, the scent was delicious!

Rounding one curve, a vast vista opened up and the whole valley lay spread out before us. Some ranches were visible, tucked away in the hillsides, and we wondered what hardy souls made their homes isolated out here. We finally came to the campground where no other campers seemed to be around except for one old truck parked nearby. On bear-proof trashcans were posted signs stating "Beware, This is Bear Country". We were really out in the wilderness, and it felt pretty exciting and maybe a little scary, to tell the truth.

As we were reading the signs by the trailhead, a burly guy emerged from the trail and introduced himself, John Anderson. He turned out to be a good story teller, telling us how he'd been living in western New Mexico and eastern Arizona all his life. "My stepfather bought up land all around here. He wasn't an educated man, but he worked hard and would buy up land at three cents an acre whenever he made a little money. He had huge hands, and earned his money by making feed bags. So every time he made a little more money, he'd go and buy a little more land. We owned all the water coming from the springs in the area. But eventually I got burned out on ranching and maintaining fences on all that land, so I went to college, and later worked for a large construction firm. I'd come up here after work to hike and fish."

John told us about places in the area where we could set up a tent if we hiked a few hundred yards into the forest. I was quite sure that wouldn't be something I'd want to be doing, particularly with all the signs warning of bears. "On the weekends," John continued, "people from town come up here to drink and fish, but no one will bother you on a weeknight."

I'd actually have felt better if there had been some other people to bother us that night. It wouldn't have felt so lonely and isolated. But we said goodbye to John, and as he drove away, I realized again, it would be just us that night on the adventure, us and the bears. I wasn't planning on taking any long hikes deep into the woods with Harley.

First order of business was to build a good campfire and keep it going. And then to figure out what was for dinner. Opening a cabinet, I discovered that the lid from the can of tahini had come off, and there was tahini everywhere. Yikes! Wouldn't bears be drawn to the scent of this nice, oily, yummy sesame butter? They'd have been able to smell it from miles around. We began mopping up the mess with paper towels, using the entire roll to do the job. I stuffed the gunky paper towels in a bag and carried it over to deposit in the bear-proof trash bin. At least I hoped it was bear proof. I remembered a time when we'd camped at Long's Peak in Colorado and we'd seen a camper that had been totally bashed in by a bear trying to get at the food inside. With the fragrance of tahini still permeating our camper, it was going to be a long night keeping watch.

But the next morning came, we were all safe and Harley had not alerted us to any night prowlers. Let's make some coffee, meditate, and hit the road!

COYOTE CREEK

The campground at Storrie Lake State Park proved to be kind of a strange place, the vibes a little creepy, so paying attention to our intuition, we weren't given to staying that night. Just long enough to throw the ball for Harley into the lake over and over until he finally just lay down in the shallow water near the edge. He ignored all calls and requests to come, simply lying there and looking at us placidly, as if to say "Why bother? I'm totally happy here."

What did he care that it was time to push off…until some dog food was rattled in his bowl. That did it. He couldn't resist. Even though it was the same dry food every day of his life, he always gave a leap into the air in absolute joy when the full bowl was about to be placed in front of him. He came trotting up out of the water and allowed himself to be leashed, and giving a good shake all over me, and proceeded to crunch away on the morsels in his bowl.

The road unfurled across mountains and canyons. We ended up at Coyote Creek State Park, campsite number 10. The healthy looking creek was a haven for fishing. One woman proudly proclaimed, "We caught our limit. Five trout yesterday and today!" The bounty of the creek provided dinner for many on the campground that night, but not for us. We had no fishing license, or bait, but we did have miso noodle soup and broccoli, and that was so satisfying to us.

We built a healthy campfire, the wood dry, burning big and bright. Harley curled up on his rug after an afternoon of splashing in the creek, no campground host or ranger around to enforce the leash law. He'd sleep well this night. Maybe coyotes, elk, or bear would roam this valley while we slept. This was their land, their territory. For sure there would be gophers, their holes were everywhere.

We gathered at dusk with the other campers for a brief time. They'd been playing horseshoes all afternoon, drinking rum and coke. One couple was there from Albuquerque for the night with their father. She specified, "Just for one night only, I'm not a camper." The father, Jose, looked in great shape for 82. He said, "I used to always RV camp with my girlfriend, but since she had a heart attack last year, she doesn't like to go to remote places anymore." Both Jose and his son had been in the Air Force, and the guy from the other couple in the Navy, so they bonded.

I felt oddly removed that evening, holding myself in reserve, though they all seemed nice, particularly Jose and his son. Peter brought over a cup of wine that tasted a little of dish soap not rinsed off enough. We drank it anyway, and when it was done we said goodnight. A restless night's sleep for me, tangled up in blue. My energy and enthusiasm felt like they were running low. Too much thinking. The only panacea was the mantra I had been given, so many years ago in Siddha Yoga. Om Namah Shivaya, repeated again and again until finally I drifted off.

TAOS HIPPIE

At 8am, two big busloads of school kids pulled up on the campsite right next to us. They were all looking happy; a day of freedom and fishing awaited. One of the teachers said, "Yeah, but I have to cook for all of them!" We wished them all a wonderful time as the kids took their backpacks and fishing rods and headed on down to the creek, boisterously chattering away with excitement. Their energy generated a wave throughout the campground, probably rousing even the late sleepers.

Up the winding road to Angel Fire, we stopped at the post office to mail the presents we'd bought in Santa Fe for friends. Everyone was friendly, as if they already knew us. A huge bank of PO boxes indicated there must have been a lot of people living on the outskirts around here who came to pick up their mail rather than being able to have it delivered. And on to the Enchanted Circle, a gorgeous drive around Taos with grand views of snow-covered mountain tops, the Sangre de Cristos, in the distance. This was the route that Dennis Hopper and Peter Fonda took in the epochal movie, *Easy Rider*, in which two hippies are traveling free, in search of spiritual truth. Not unlike us!

The road wound along beside a creek, water splashing over rocks, tall ponderosa pines and spruce everywhere, crystal blue skies above. Along the way, we stopped at the Lama Foundation, a spiritual retreat center, where decades ago, Ram Dass had written his iconic book, *Be Here Now*. The blue school bus in which he'd written the book had been turned into a shrine, where his presence still seemed to linger. We were told that there would be a Native American peyote ceremony that evening, which sounded interesting, but our four-legged buddy Harley wouldn't have been invited. No dogs were allowed on the grounds.

Breakfast was at Michael's Cafe in Taos that day. Now in our search for the best huevos rancheros, this was definitely the best anywhere! Perfect: beans, veggie green chili, eggs, tortilla, and a pancake for Harley which Peter packaged up neatly in a little napkin. His great Aunt Moofy had taught him the Japanese art of "furoshiki" or wrapping a gift in an artistic bundle. We shortened the word to froshki, and it was a word that Harley came to know meant something good was headed his way!

It was going to be a summer of festivities in Taos, celebrating the fortieth anniversary of Easy Rider and Hippie Taos. Signs were everywhere, announcing the occasion, and it promised to be a real tourist attraction. We treated ourselves to a stay at the El Pueblo dog-friendly motel. Our room was very New Mexican in flavor, with a kiva fireplace, vigas or rough-hewn logs that lined the ceiling of the adobe walls, Mexican tiled sink in the bathroom, rustic furniture, wooden pegs on the wall for hanging clothes, and a breezy porch overlooking the mountains. So restful. That was the state of mind we were aiming for!

We stopped to visit Tony, an old friend, in his gallery. He seemed to be caught in his lifestyle, complaining, "I haven't had any time to play music. Had to sell my third guitar. Business is down, but who needs three guitars anyway?" We did our part and bought a beautiful wool rug with natural dyes, three by five feet. "Hey, come by around 5:30. We'll go for drink!" Tony suddenly had a new air of optimism. Maybe this sale portended for him a more hopeful change in business.

Peter played his fiddle on a bench near the stores while I walked around town and found a great birthday present for him, some wool to make a basket like the one we'd bought on Easter morning, and last, a stop for coffee from One World Cafe. Their kick-butt brew kept you going all day, and it was a great scene, sitting on a bench outside the cafe with all the hippies and various vagrants. You always met someone unusual. That morning, a guy with a beat up old guitar, stickers plastered all over it, played an amazing version of Leonard Cohen's "Hallelujah". He was a diamond in the rough, his voice pure and clear, so heartfelt and moving. I gave him some money and he lit up, saying, "OK, now I can buy my morning cup of coffee and some breakfast!" He looked pretty shaggy and grubby, and I wondered if he'd been living on the street with his guitar.

I went over to pick up my Irish Fiddler who'd had a good morning too. Harley, tied up to the bench beside him in the shade, his bowl of water on the ground, was an integral part of Peter's act.

Later on, we went to meet Tony, but the shop had closed early and he wasn't around. The only act in town seemed to be at the Taos Inn, where the open courtyard was popping, and celebration was in the air. It was Cinco de Mayo and the summer was getting kicked off. Dinner at Doc Watsons Restaurant in the hotel was quiet, at least for a while. Peter recognized the men sitting at the next table. "Famous artists", he said. "I saw their picture in the magazine in our room." There was going to be live music that night at the Adobe Bar, but Harley awaited us back at the motel.

It felt so good to walk through town after dinner in the cool evening air, back to our comfy motel. We took Harley out to the courtyard where Peter played a few songs on his guitar. A man who'd been sitting nearby came up and told us how he also loved playing a guitar, so Peter asked him if he'd play a couple of tunes. He seemed like a friendly, easygoing kind of person. We enjoyed his music and his company for a while, then he went on his way. Peter said, "Do you know who that was? That was John Nichols, the local New Mexican author who wrote *The Milagro Beanfield Wars*. Nice guy!".

Later, we stretched out on our bed, while Harley curled up on his own little sleeper sofa, where so many dogs before him had probably slept. Our campfire that night was in our own little kiva fireplace, right in our own cozy room, campsite number 127. The firelight flickered and danced on the wall as we surrendered ourselves to the mystery of sleep.

LAMA BLESSINGS

"Whatever a person possesses through the strength of their own nature cannot be lost". So said the *I Ching*. Oh dear. I realized that somehow I'd lost the skein of beautiful wool I'd bought yesterday, and the store wouldn't be open before we left. Alas. Peter offered the possibility that maybe someone had found it, and they just loved it and felt so lucky. OK, let it go! If you lost it, it wasn't yours to begin with.

We took the road north out of town, then west on 64 past all the "earth ships", a sprawling community of eco-friendly homes built partly into the earth on three sides with the front side facing the sun. Some looked like sand castles, others like sci-fi spaceships. Who were these people living way out here, and what kind of life was it? What did it feel like to be living partly underground? Not for everyone, it sounded claustrophobic to me!

We pulled off at the Rio Grande River Gorge, which was like a mini Grand Canyon with huge high rocky cliffs and the river far down below. Lisa from Pueblo Hot Blood Tours, as her T-shirt read, called out. "I have a rule - I must meet every golden retriever I see!" She ran over, glass of champagne in hand, to greet Harley who was to-tally willing to offer his golden head to her for pats.

"What are you celebrating?" I asked. "Because my rule is that I'd like to share in every champagne occasion that I meet up with!"

Lisa explained in her professional voice, as she must have done many times before, all about the history of hot air balloon travel, and how in France when they'd land, people on the ground would break out the champagne, and there'd be toasts all around, even for the peasants (like us!).

"So now," she continued, "we just left the Taos area this morning, went for about an hour flight down the Rio Grand Gorge, and landed here where our trucks will meet us and drive us back to Taos. There are two balloon companies in the area, but we're the best. If you'd ever like to go, I'll take care of Harley for you during your flight!"

At Ojo Caliente, literally "hot waters", it was our first time to camp there. We found a perfect spot, and took Harley for a controlled dip in the raging river. The current was so strong, we feared he could be washed away downstream. So he chased sticks tossed close to shore, and was hauled back in on the long leash attached to his collar. We mastered the art of setting up our RV awning, so with some shade and the breeze, our four-legged buddy would be nice and cool while awaiting our return from the hot pools.

There was a special feeling of peace at this ancient abode of natural springs, a healing atmosphere. But unfortunately, there was an awful lot of chatter going on at the pools that afternoon. Some guy was talking too loudly about all the urgent things he had to do when he got back home, people he had to call, what he'd make for dinner, and on and on. Enough of your self-importance, we thought, and moved to another pool where it was quiet and we could really enjoy the soak. Every once in a while, one of the staff would walk by carrying a sign that read "Silence, Please Whisper", though not everyone heeded that request.

In a while, someone came by and made an announcement that there would be a monk giving blessings by the entrance to the steam room. So I wrapped up in my towel and joined the line, all of us in our bathing suits dripping wet, awaiting our blessings. When it was my turn, I looked up into the Lama's eyes where a beautiful sweetness exuded. A moment of silence, and my mind stopped as I fell into the depth of his eyes.

Later, Peter and I introduced ourselves and talked with Lama Losang and his friend, Soo Kyong. The lama told us how he and his family had escaped Tibet in 1959, making the treacherous journey across the Himalayas and into Dharamsala, where he later became the Dalai Lama's personal assistant. Speaking with a peaceful voice that induced a sense of calm, he said, "I learned the art of making sand mandalas, and in time, traveled around the world, making sand mandalas for peace." He related to us how he'd met his friend, Soo Kyong, a professional viola player, here in the US and together they had moved to Philadelphia, where he set up a meditation center. "We have some friends here in New Mexico who invite us to come stay once every year." We bid them safe journey, saying earnestly, it was so good to meet you, we hope to see you again sometime. We walked back to our campsite, feeling very blessed indeed to have met them both.

Harley got a long walk on the leash, then it was time for our dinner reservation at the only restaurant on the grounds. Our table by an open window allowed the gentle breeze to refresh us while we ate. I got the barbecued

144

salmon with fried spinach, Peter, a rich pasta with cream sauce which he couldn't finish. The waiter asked, "Would you like to take it to go with you?" Simultaneously, Peter said "no" and I said "yes", so he wrapped it up and handed it to me. I stuck it in our little RV fridge for another time.

After the cool of evening arose and Harley was curled up contentedly on the bed, we returned to the springs for another soak. This time, things were much quieter, and we overheard a couple of men whispering "Mescalito", and "Did you get off yet?" A starry night, the moon was almost full, while big rocks up on the hillside were illuminated dramatically by spotlights. The fragrance of the piñon wood campfire in the plaza drifted out to the pool; there was a magical feeling in the air. The ancient Native Americans used to soak here, the ruins of their pueblos right up the hillside from these pools. I had a sense of their presence looking down on us peacefully that evening.

Everything slowed down as we lingered in the hot water, until finally the security guard came around and let us know, "The pools are closing for the night." We emerged dripping, languid, half asleep already when we returned to the RV, pushing Harley over so we could all fit in bed. I dreamt of the Ancient Ones, and a kiva, where something mysterious happened, though I didn't remember exactly what.

ITS OKAY TO BE HAPPY

We threw the coins and the *I Ching* gave us the hexagram 15: Modesty, Qian. Mountain or Keeping Still is below, Earth the Receptive, is above. "Moderation will return you to your authenticity and hone you for the next level of growth." OK, that sounded about right. We could go with that. But first, we wanted to indulge a little at the gift shop! I tried on two pairs of Crocs, but the guy working at the shop, Rich, said, "I used to work at a shoe store, and I can tell you these are just too small for you." I took this as a message that I didn't really need them. And anyway, what about moderation? Peter, however, had picked out a whole bunch of things and laid them on the counter: two packages of incense, two Cokes, two cans of Arizona green tea, two dark chocolate bars, a package of cookies, and a new pair of swim trunks. Hmmm...

Rich said to Peter, "Oh your eyes are so beautiful, I'm not coming on to you, man, they're beautiful!" Peter extended his arms and openheartedly hugged Rich. I loved that he did that. Rich told us, "You know, living here is a dream come true for me, I got here by the law of attraction."

I smiled and nodded. My mother's group had been into that for a while. Peter's face, however, registered blank, too New Age-y for his tastes. But all during the years when I'd been growing up, for as long as I could remember, my mother would hold her weekly "Miracles" group. They'd begun by reading *A Course in Miracles* together, discussing, sharing their experiences, then meditating together as a group. Subsequent to that, they'd focused on books about manifesting what you want in life and the law of attraction. My mother had ended up writing her own book, *Journey to Awareness: Healing through Spiritual Growth*, about her awakening experience and describing how she'd become a healer. The group had used her book as a guide, always starting and ending with a period of meditation. I was still in touch with many of these women, all of whom had been younger than my mother, who had really been a woman ahead of her time. One of them had even led my mother's memorial service, after which a lunch had been held in her honor, complete with colored balloons, as Mom had wanted. How could it be, that had been only a few months ago?

Traveling toward Jemez Springs, for once we didn't get lost in Espanola, the Bermuda Triangle of New Mexico. The town apparently didn't believe in signs indicating which road led to our destination. We drove on, past Bandelier National Monument with its rocky cliff dwellings, past the velvety looking grasses of the Caldera, site of the volcano a million years ago that formed these red rock mesas, past Spence hot springs, only one old hippie in the parking lot today. Down, down, down to the Jemez valley, past the land we'd once thought of buying, past the Zen Center where the Zendo, the meditation room, contained a whole world. Past the Highway 4 Cafe where I'd definitely be coming the next day for a cup of chai. And finally down to our home for the weekend at Vista Linda campsite 7. Strong breezes welcomed us, and as always, the sound of the river washing by. Our awning was up already by the time Harley and I had walked back from registering, half-price here, five dollars with my senior golden access pass.

Peter tackled the river, crossing over on hands and feet to retrieve some blanched old branches that had gotten caught in the middle of the river, tangled up on top of a logjam, and therefore dry and fire worthy. Peter gave it a valiant effort, liberating some large branches and sawing them down to size, and then giving them a heave onto the shore, where Harley greeted them gleefully, ready to gnaw them and sure that they were all for him.

After the sun went down behind the mesa, we went over to meet the guy at the next campsite, Jayson, who in the spirit of John Denver, was irrepressibly upbeat, interested in everything and everyone. It all received equal emphasis and enthusiasm. He exuded good health, and spoke with a defined and definite cadence, giving every syllable of every word an underlined importance, as if he was confidently creating and bringing into being every subject to which he turned his attention. He gave it all his affirmation. He was adorable!

Gathered at his campsite were Carol and Jack, and her granddaughter, little Athena, who sat under her own little cloud and was told repeatedly to hush and not break anything. Peter compassionately handed her his squeeze box to play and showed her how to work it. But she was afraid; it came with too many warnings from the grandparents. As we played music, she wandered around, lost in her own world of make believe, making swishing sounds, as if she were flying. So dear, this blond Athena. I'd have liked to rescue her and preserve her untouched innocence. So very precious.

Jayson took a turn playing, classical guitar. He had his music written out on a board. "It's about an approaching storm", he explained. "I have six guitars, two electric, two classical, two steel string. I'd like to have a wall and hang them all up, with paintings in between. You might ask why I have six guitars and can't play any of them well, but I love them all." He actually did play pretty well, though he said he'd only taken lessons for two months. "I have to read the music. I don't know it by heart."

We bid them goodnight, returning to our site 7 to build a campfire, when we discovered the unfortunate truth. Although the wood Peter retrieved burned well, it had a terribly unpleasant odor, acrid. Alas, we backed off a bit from the fire, which was still going strong and not about to go out.

And then we both saw it. A few of the leaves of the cottonwoods above us were twinkling as if lit up with lights. What was this apparent piece of magic about? Something outlandish, like fairies or angels or extraterrestrials? And then, there it was, the full moon, coming up over the mesa and illuminating everything, catching just a few glimmering cottonwood leaves with its divine rays.

"Is it really okay to be so happy?" I asked.
And Peter responded, "I always feel God is very pleased when I'm happy."

BIRTHDAY BLUES

It was Peter's 55th birthday, and I wanted to make it a special celebration for him. But what he really wanted was just a quiet, relaxed day. He made a pot of coffee in the French press; we began the day sipping a cup of the strong, dark brew. Then ringing the bell, we sat together, with Harley curled up beside us. That right there was the most special gift, that we could share meditation, the expansive feeling of melding with this place of power in the Jemez Valley, at our favorite Vista Linda campsite 7 by the river.

I handed him his present, a Case knife that I'd bought on the sly from a shop in Taos. He loved it, and got the idea to use it for fishing that day, so we headed out to San Ysidro for a license. But when we discovered that it cost $32 for an out-of-state license to fish for one day, I said, "Yikes, that's so expensive! I don't think that's for us." It happened that the forest ranger was in the store at that moment, and we were glad he heard our response, thinking maybe he'd decide to change the fee, but no. So an alternate plan evolved.

At the Walatowa convenience store, I purchased a roll of fishing line and a couple of trout flies. We figured as long as I wasn't using an actual fishing rod, it wasn't really official. That, and I probably wouldn't catch one anyway. Stopping for breakfast, a piece of fry bread at the Pueblo stand, we partook of a kind of communion at a picnic table surrounded by the brick red rocks under a limitless blue sky. We were invited to share a table with a Pueblo family, where a grandfather was teaching a young boy a song in Towa, their language. We felt honored to be included in the sweet powerful tradition, dating back from ages past.

A feeling of deep longing began to come over me, from where did it arise? Maybe sparked from witnessing the tender, ageless scene between grandfather and child. I thought about how we're all here on Earth, longing for an understanding of the mystery of this life, only given partial glimpses of the whole, aching to return to what we already are. I was a philosopher at heart, and there was no real cure for it that day.

Maybe it could help to go do something, I reasoned. Engaging in activity might help bring me out of the existential funk. A book signing was scheduled at the library, so I entered, but it looked like a sad event. The co-authors of the book *Jemez Springs - a History* were sitting alone in the empty room with a stack of books on the table in front of them. A big pitcher of lemonade and a plate of cookies remained untouched on a nearby table. Kathleen Wiegner and Robert Borden seemed to be experiencing a dearth of paying customers. She looked withdrawn and despondent. He brightened briefly, remembering my name from a year ago when I had subscribed to the local paper, *The Jemez Thunder.* After buying my own autographed copy of the book, I told them, "I'm going out to that parking lot and tell those bikers to come on in here and buy a copy." And I did just that, but the crowd seemed to have their own agenda. They were about to gather at the cowboy bar, Los Ojos, across the road for something to eat and drink. Not a one of them was interested in learning more about the place that they'd come to today. But I'd given it my best shot.

Later around the campfire, the guy at the next site, Josh, came over to talk a while. He told us he'd grown up here in the Jemez, but now lived and worked in Utah. We showed him the book and let him borrow it. He returned it later, all aglow and enthusiastic about the book. Part of the glow might have had something to do with the number of brewskis he'd had to drink, but there was also a genuine interest. "My wife and I loved seeing all those old photos! We're going to go get a book tomorrow. I want the people where I live now to see where I came from, to see how beautiful it is here. All those Mormons in Utah think I'm a heretic. They know that I drink and smoke, and that I'm not going to convert. I'd love for them to know there's a tradition of value here to appreciate, even if it's different from theirs." I decided to give him our copy. It meant something personal to him, and I felt he should have it. As I handed the book back to Josh, he was so thankful that I wished the authors could have witnessed it. Maybe that would've helped cheer them up.

We never did rig up the fishing line that day. It had been a low-key day, just what the birthday boy had requested. Peter wanted to eat around the campfire, so we'd go out for a special birthday dinner another night. And truly, the ambiance there at campsite 7 was the best around. It'd been a kind of lonely, achey-breakey heart day. Missing something, feeling an existential sense of aloneness, a fundamental awareness of my own insecurity and impermanence. Feeling that none of us really had anything to hold on to, we were all on a one-way trip through this life. Peter and I curled up and took a nap, while Harley slept on the floor. And when we awoke, the wave of emotion had crested and passed on.

We lit a fragrant fire that night with lots of juniper and cedar that Peter had found on the ground. No more of that stinky cottonwood; we'd learned our lesson on that one. We played our tunes, harp and guitar, into the dusk. Jayson and his girlfriend Christine came by and listened for a while. They gave us a container of watermelon, delicious, and we spit seeds into the fire as the moon slowly rose above the mesa. It was a magical birthday night. We felt one with the land. And the river washed on by, like a lullaby throughout the night.

NATE

I awakened in the night, dreaming about putting on some clothes, breathing life into them and they actually did become alive. "There's consciousness in everything!" I exclaimed. I remembered my teacher, Sally Kempton, with whom I'd taken many courses on the ancient Hindu texts. And one principle that was repeated in so many of those writings was that everything is made of consciousness, of divine energy or intelligence that's called Shakti. The *Shiva Sutras,* the *Bhagavad Gita,* the *Yoga Sutras,* all those texts spoke of the all-pervasive awareness in everything. And the modern science of quantum physics bordered on substantiating this truth that the ancients knew.

Up and out of Vista Linda, without meditating or coffee or anything, and on to Starbuck's for coffee and its clean bathroom, and then to Grants to do laundry. There, an old Native American guy, Nate, greeted us outside while the washing machines did their work. He was probably not that much older than we were, but it looked like life had been hard on him. His breath smelled of last night's whiskey as he told us of the time when he'd been in the Marines in Vietnam back in 1968-1972. "I told my men, watch me, follow what I do, and then we all ran for it and jumped in a ditch. I got hit in the leg here. My left eye is gone." He lifted his sunglasses up to show us his missing eye. Once he found out we had both been nurses, he lifted his T-shirt up and showed us a long scar extending from his chest, down to his stomach and abdomen, and disappearing somewhere beneath his shorts. "I served my country and protected the people." We thanked him for his service, then wondered to ourselves but didn't say, "And what did your country do for you?"

Nate then pulled out two silver bracelets studded with turquoise. "Now I make these. My people support themselves by making arts and crafts. "I'll give you one for $20." But truly, all we had between us was a $100 bill and two ones and some change for the dryer. We told him we had no cash. "Then I'll give you both of them for $25."

"No cash" we again told him.

"Then one for $10?"

We pulled out our wallet and showed him the two ones (not the hundred) and he smiled and hugged me. "Happy Mothers Day, I know you must be a mother." We gave him the two ones as a gift, and wished we'd had change for the hundred. "My great grandfather was Geronimo. This is our holy land here."

Peter answered, "We love your holy land. It's very beautiful here."

We all went back inside the laundromat. He had a load going too. Nate introduced us to his nephew who looked a little uncomfortable and standoffish, as though maybe he had an attitude about Anglos, but we didn't know if that was actually the case. There was a good feeling with Nate, though. He was open-hearted, a good person. Gathering up the laundry from the dryer, we bid Nate and his nephew goodbye. Outside, we told Nate how very thankful we were to have met him, and we meant that. Any time we could have an interaction with someone from another culture or way of life, we welcomed the opportunity to expand our understanding and love of this one human family of which we were a part.

Later, there was a Happy Mothers Day call from Derek as he was on his way to work. He told me about his trip to Ireland. "It was totally fantastic. The people were so friendly and they all loved Obama. They wanted to know all about life in the US. And everything there was so green. I love you so much, Mama! You're the best mom I could ever have had!"

I was so happy he could take this journey abroad that helped to expand his perspective and experience of life. It had been a great opportunity, a special one to share with his father. And a great opportunity for me to expand my heart generously.

Bluewater State Park. It was like a mirage to see that big blue lake in the middle of all the dusty desert land. There was so much poverty around the area, but heart warming to see all the families at the day use picnic tables enjoying a simple Sunday afternoon together, laughing and eating. We found there were no good campsites within view of the lake and that was an absolute deal breaker for us and Harley, so after a good swim for him, we retraced our steps back to Grants, then south on 53 to El Morro National Monument.

El Morro, land of peace. The land exuded a feeling of stillness, despite the wind that was blowing steadily that day. We settled in to number 4, and soon, Chris from the next site came over to join us with his glass of wine in hand. We really connected. He was one of those people who was just easy to be with, a good-hearted person. We fed him some hummus I'd concocted on bread with a slice of tomato on top. We talked of music, told our life stories, and asked where he'd be headed next. Chris was on a two week trip, had to get back and take care of his

82 year-old mother whose health was failing. Oh yes, how well we knew what that was like. Our hearts went out to him. He'd be going on tomorrow to visit friends in Albuquerque and get a long overdue shower. "It's been five days, and I can't wait!"

At dusk, we all went to his site where he was tent-camping with his two dogs. "The wind has died down enough, but I think I'll put on a paper fire-log just to be safe." And eventually he added a couple of small pieces of wood. We all gathered around, sipping on mugs of tea, when Chris spat his out on the ground. "Ugh, must have been a moth that got into my tea and it was too dark to see him." He got a bag of gingersnaps, saying "This'll take the taste out of my mouth. They're my favorite. Really good!" And they were, spicy and crunchy, and we all crunched away together around the fire.

Every star we could ever imagine, and more, was out. The moon hadn't risen yet, so we could really see them clearly. The vastness of the night sky opened us to a great sense of awe, a reverence for the unknown that we all shared together that night. We hugged Chris and wished him happy trails until we meet again and trundled back to our RV where our Harleydog awaited, warming up the bed for us. "Good night and sweet dreams," we called out to the night sky, feeling a sense of oneness with the mystery of it all.

THE ANCIENT WAY

We were headed to the Ancient Way Cafe for breakfast, but on our way out of the campground, we met a couple from British Columbia who were traveling the old Route 66 from L.A. to Chicago. "We found a book on this route at a yard sale for three dollars and we took it as our personal message to go. It's a wonderful, slow path and you see all the small towns and sights along the way. It's been so much fun!" They were in their VW pop-top camper which he had outfitted himself. "I made the screens and the curtains, I used to make sails for our boat, so I have a little sewing machine that does the job. And I used to be a pilot. Let me show you my cockpit." There, beside the driver's seat was a laptop computer on a special pullout swivel table. "Everything's organized and downsized. We're used to that since we moved from a big house to a small condo. It's a good feeling to downsize, to learn to live with less. So now we do just fine in this little camper together." Peter and I used to have a VW poptop camper in the old days, and we knew just how small that bed was. Not a single, but definitely not as big as a queen. And sleeping in the bunk above could be a claustrophobic affair. Plus, there was no bathroom on board. So this couple had our respect and admiration, though they seemed to be happy as clams in their little shell together!

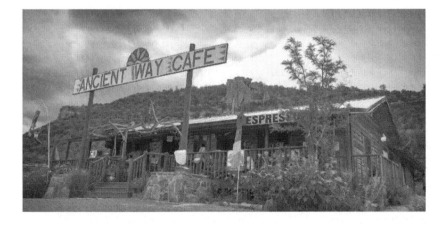

The Ancient Way Cafe was a small, rustic place, with pine benches and tables, enough seating for maybe around 25 people. There was a shelf and small refrigerator where

some of their baked goods were offered for sale, everything looking delicious. As we went to find a seat, we
were greeted by a large, friendly man who said, "You
should have been here last night. There was lots of music
and people. It was so great!" We learned that he and his
wife had made the journey out here from Florida to attend
their son's memorial celebration last night. They asked us
to join them at their table, where their daughter and
granddaughter were sitting as well. They told us how their
son had gotten involved in drugs and became very sick
with a terminal illness, how he'd come here and had been
nursed and taken care of by this community of healers.
"He loved it here. There were so many people, all different
kinds in this community, that knew and loved him. Last
night, there were thirty-some people here to celebrate his
life with drums and Native American ceremonies. It was
really great. We were so moved. These people opened
their hearts to us like they'd known us all our lives. Today,
we're going to go clean out our son's trailer where he
lived until he passed on."

We offered to help. "Our hearts go out to you, is there
anything we can do?"

But no, it was their labor of love to perform, and they
went on. We were taken with how conservative they appeared to be, and how this community seemed quite un-
conventional, with their crystals and alternative healing
methods. And yet, love was the common language between these two cultures. And it sounded like their son
had been dearly loved.

Our waiter, Standing Feather was his name. When he
first came to the table, it took our minds a moment to get
it. He was an unusual person, tall and slender, wearing
short shorts, a T-shirt fully stacked, long fingernails

painted red, a long curly ponytail hanging out the back of a baseball cap. His eyes were clear and beautiful, with mascara and eyeliner. Long beaded earrings completed his outfit. His whole presence declared "This is who I am, now just relate to me as a person" and we did, including it all. We immediately really liked him and respected his unique beauty. Though to be respectful, I should have been calling him her.

After breakfast, Peter, Harley, and I went to hike around the El Morro National Monument, past the 20 foot-deep pool where rainwater had collected for centuries. A semicircle of huge limestone cliffs stood watch above the pool, a silent witness to all the years. This apparently had been a much-used watering hole on the way through this desert territory to the West. Many had carved their names, like hieroglyphs, on the rock known as Inscription Rock, names and dates from the conquering Spaniards, and later from the Americans who pushed their way west during the time of expansion some called "manifest destiny". But originally this land had belonged to the Native Americans, as the ruins of their pueblo culture up on the clifftops attested.

Peter and Harley headed back to the campground. No swimming was allowed in the pool here for dogs or people. I continued on to hike the two mile trail up to the sandstone cliffs to see the ruins of the ancients and the incredible views of the surrounding caldera. All this territory had been formed by volcanic activity more than a million years ago. I watched the precarious path and followed it very carefully. Some years ago, when we'd been here, I'd gotten lost on this same trail and had found myself out on a steep promontory with no idea how to get back on the path. No one had been in sight, and I'd freaked out, with a racing heart and huge anxiety. Dark would be coming soon and Peter would be worrying about where I was. I'd tried every possible way to retrace my steps, but had become even more lost. Finally, I'd heard some voices and had been able to follow them until I got back on the path. No way I was going to repeat that episode! I was vigilant and keeping alert. The trail did get pretty sketchy in places.

There was something special about this land here in the Zuni Mountains which drew us inward to a place of stillness. As our waiter this morning at the cafe had told us, "It's all the Ancient Ones who lived here, and it's the water which sustains life that gives this place such a healing vibration." I didn't know what it was, but the feeling of peace was palpable.

There was no campfire that evening, though Peter had found some gorgeous cedar and juniper and had sawed it up into fire-friendly sizes. But the winds kept up and were too strong. With all the dry trees and shrubs nearby, it was better to be safe and prevent an errant spark from being carried off by the wind. It was a different campground that night, not so friendly, just isolated groupings interspersed around the sites. I walked Harley around the loop and saw a guy camped by himself, sitting in his chair. No tent, just his car to sleep in. He nodded silently in my direction as we passed. And that was perfectly OK with me, I felt happy to simply enjoy the tranquil feeling, so Harley and I returned to our quiet home for the night, campsite four. Peter and I lay down on top of the picnic table and looking up, surrendered ourselves to the stars, vast and unfathomable.

A PLAN

Peter dreamed of going over an impossibly high waterfall, and when he finally landed in the water below and resurfaced, he was in a heightened state of consciousness. The journey we were on was like that long descent down the waterfall. Where and when we would land was not something we could figure out with our rational minds. And we were aiming for that heightened state of consciousness every day by being present in each moment with a quiet mind to the best of our ability.

Sitting at a table at the Ancient Way Cafe, we threw the *I Ching*. It gave us the hexagram "The Wanderer", and cautioned us to remain humble and flexible while in a foreign land. "The land that is nowhere, that is your true home. Remain open to what the unknown can teach you." Bingo, those words really hit home. This was what we'd been practicing on the road - finding our true home within, opening ourselves to the unknown, the mystery unfolding each new day. Trusting whatever came up. We were being trained in how to live a good, simple life, free from expectations.

We could feel it was time to move on. Although it was wild and gorgeous at this campground, we were definitely off the map and needed to be able to be in touch with family and friends. Peter broke camp while Harley and I walked a mile to the one spot where I was able to get cell phone reception as long as I faced east and the wind wasn't blowing. We were out in the middle of a vast wilderness, and incredibly it worked, and I was speaking to our old friends from Maryland, Bob and Jenny! They were out in Arizona on vacation, taking a brief 10-day respite from caring for Jenny's mom whose health was declining. We made loose plans to meet up at the Painted Desert or maybe at the North Rim of the Grand Canyon, where they would have a campsite reserved that they'd share with us. True to our *I Ching* guidance, we'd remain flexible, as this plan might happen or not. We'd see in time.

Traveling on 53 west, past the town of Ramah, we stopped at its well-stocked feed store, staffed by two Native Americans who were looking sad and life-weary. We bought two yellow kitchen sponges and an Arizona lemon iced tea. I looked in the cashier's eyes and we met there for just a moment. And somehow all differences in culture and life experience, all sense of separation dissolved for that one wordless moment of our shared humanity. At least, that's how I'd experienced it.

Then on through Zuni, where numerous trading post signs declared "Buy direct from the artists - Buses and dealers welcome." We didn't stop, but drove onward, past the "Welcome to Arizona" sign, goodbye to New Mexico for now. Lyman Lake State Park was a wide open, sun-baked outpost where the lake was a reservoir formed by damming the Little Colorado River. Harley loved it, though he never met a body of water he didn't love. Chasing sticks thrown way out into the lake, he swam and swam in total joy. He was born for this! But he'd gotten covered in burrs, which we had to painstakingly remove from his tail, armpits, ears, even the pads of his feet. He submitted to this, gentle soul that he was, and as long as he could sniff every burr as it was removed, he was satisfied to let us do the job.

Peter was out of commission that afternoon from the heat. We were plugged in to electric, so he cranked up the A/C and holed up.

I asked, "Are you okay?"

He answered only, "I'm fine", but I could see that he was not. I found other ways to ask what was going on; he found other ways to fend off my questions. Finally I decided he just needed some space. So Harley and I went to walk and walk. Scrubby junipers and cedars, dried grasses and some prickly pear cactus were the only plants that could survive in this desert land, and after an unfortunate run-in with a cactus, Harley knew by now to avoid it. There were petroglyphs very similar to the ones at El Morro, drawings in the rock, traced ages ago by the ancient Pueblo Ones and lasting to this day. Pictographs representing rain, corn, and birds were drawn in a rustic and simple style. The winds were blowing so strong that I didn't feel the heat, but I wouldn't have wanted to be here any later into the summer. You could fry!

Finally, later the sun began to sink low in the sky, and Peter emerged from his cocoon. He told me he'd had chest pain, though it had eased up. What was to be done with him? I made a mental note to buy some aspirin the next day, for starters. And please tell me, I said, please let me know when you don't feel well so we can do something at the time. He explained that he hadn't wanted me to worry, but I wondered how could I not be concerned and want to help? We needed to look out for each other, particularly at this time of vulnerability while on the road.

At dusk we all walked, Harley on his leash per campground rules. Coming toward us was a man in a motorized wheelchair with his dog on a leash in his hand. He introduced himself as John, from Virginia originally, on the road for 8 years now, in a camper he'd inherited from his father. He was a wealth of information about Quartzite, Arizona. "From May through October, there's nothing there. It's a ghost town", he told us. "Then come the end of October, it begins to fill up, and by the winter, there's 100,000 RV's and a whole town springs into being. We stay at RV parks, do some boon docking, where you're not plugged in. There's music, arts and crafts, groups for everything you can think of. Like a giant retirement community, it's mostly people around our age who've taken early retirement, but also some older folks who've been retired a while. It's a whole segment of society, a sociological phenomenon, if you will. You should go there and see for yourself. I may not be there this year. My hips are bad and I need to get them taken care of. I was rode hard and put away wet".

We thanked him and wished him well, returning back to our camper for the night. Feeling thankful that we didn't have to go to Quartzite, we could tell it probably wasn't our style. We were happy to be at our peaceful little state park enclave where all was quiet that night and no groups were being organized.

VICTOR

Over beans and eggs in some cafe in Holbrook, Arizona,
we hatched a plan. We'd stay with Bob and Jenny on the
North Rim come the next weekend. Meanwhile, it was on
to Sedona, taking 89A South to Oak Canyon Drive, winding past incomprehensible beauty, rocky cliffs, pines, red-
rock formations, descending into the spiritual New Age
vibrations of Sedona. We were very happy to find a
campsite at Rancho Sedona RV Park, right beside the
creek, and a short walk to town. Harley gave his OK on it,
dripping wet as he emerged from the cold creek with stick
in mouth. We were fully plugged in here, electric, water,
cable TV, all the comforts of home! We thought back on
the boondockers we'd met at Coronado Campground
who were all about comfort.

While Harley took refuge in the RV, we walked up the
road to the Javelina Restaurant, where we had a long-
awaited birthday dinner for Peter. We sat inside in the AC
with mostly older people, while some younger folks were
seated outside on the porch in the breezes and shade.
But, the birthday boy had chosen, and it was his party
tonight. Plus, that heart problem was part of the equation
as well, though at least he had some aspirin on board
now. This birthday dinner was brought to us by Mom's
Tuesday group, the American Express gift card they'd
given me as a good-bye present when we'd left Maryland.
Such dear women, faithful to Mom always, were carrying
on the group in her tradition now.

167

On our way back, we stopped in at the New Age Center and took a look around. I remembered how Mom and I had come here to have our auras photographed and read only a few years earlier. She was always game for any spiritual adventure. An intense looking man approached Peter and me, asking would we like a reading? There was a moment of hesitation, and then, yes we would. We went with Victor up to his office which was filled with a variety of crystals, wind chimes, whimsical toys, bumper stickers, and assorted New Age memorabilia.

He began by talking to Peter. "You need to take better care of yourself, stop doing whatever you've been doing." I could have told him about all the excesses of butter, mayonnaise, Cokes, coffee and sugar. But why go into detail? He had the gist of it, and I was thrilled he was the one who was saying it this time. "Drink four quarts of dis-tilled water a day and take some herbs. It's simple, not complex." He definitely had gotten Peter's attention. Pe-ter's eyes were filling with tears. Victor talked on and on, no scarcity of things he had to say, in a steady flow, like poetry. "Do I need to be right? No, it's coming from all that is. It's coming from the Source, and that is the One, the Nameless in all."

And to me, "Play, experience joy, remember the lilies in the field, they toil not. Your only purpose is to just be, and through the love that you are, your presence will affect everyone around you."

I liked this prescription. It sounded sweet, pretty low maintenance, nothing too fancy! Then Victor asked Peter and me to repeat after him, while holding hands, a long vow to be happy, to create joy, to be simple not complex. It was like a marriage vow, and we both felt this ceremony had somehow deepened our bond. We'd actually been

168

engaged and living together for 17 years, but had never felt the need to get formally married. Our relationship was easy, sweet. We were in sync together.

As we staggered from Victor's office and payed our $90 with a Visa card, we headed back to our RV. We watched a show on PBS about Michelangelo and his works of art toward the end of his life. It was proposed in the show that he basically was with the Revisionists who felt that God could be known directly in the individual's heart. However, the Catholic Church, which had hired Michelangelo and paid him as their patron artist, held that God could only be known by the clergy who would then interpret the experience for the masses.

Ah, when the TV went off, we could hear the music of the creek out back, the sound of the eternal speaking directly to our hearts; no clergy needed to interpret for us. And the sounds of Harley, who we loved so much, sleeping at the foot of the bed. Goodnight Sedona. Your wisdom spoke directly to us through Victor this day.

VORTEX

Awake at 4am to the sound of a lone bird chirping out
back, and then the sounds of water spraying. I thought
the hose to someone's RV must have burst, but Peter
whispered "sprinkler system" and we fell back to sleep.
Being a light sleeper was sure to make you vulnerable to
any sounds unique to that campground.

Later on, up and on our way into town, we found the atmosphere in Sedona was elevated, expansive, despite the
whole tourist thing going on. We sat together under shade
umbrellas, overlooking a vista of red rocks. A big thing
here was the vortexes, certain focal points on the Earth
where healing and meditation energy was thought to be
heightened. Several such vortexes in Sedona were listed
on a map available free around town, one within view of
where we were sitting. I recalled a time when Derek was
11 and we took a train trip out here from Maryland. He'd
been very interested in going to a vortex, but as he stood
in the middle of the circle of stones marking the power
spot, he said "I don't feel anything, Mom." Just then I saw
a coyote right nearby and silently pointed him out to
Derek. The coyote stood still, gazing directly at my son for
a long few moments before running off. "Awesome!",
Derek had proclaimed. "This vortex is really cool!"

But this day, we didn't even have to stand in a vortex to
feel the special energy in the air. We took care of some
mundane tasks, getting my bicycle tire fixed, buying

170

supplies and groceries, but with all of it happening in a kind of slow motion sense of peace. I took Harley for a walk along a trail of red dirt, past flowering cactus, and otherworldly views of strange rock formations. The day heat was staggeringly intense, and we returned to rouse Peter to go to the creek for a swim. The only one who got in all the way was, of course, Harley. All I could manage to submerge was my feet which became numb pretty quickly. The rocky creek with its ice-cold water was idyllic on this hot day where everything was moving languidly. It must have been a blessing, a kind of paradise for the Native Americans to have discovered a clear, cold stream in this valley of red rocks.

I insisted we go out to dinner again that night, this time to the Mandarin Palace, where the food was quite honestly the best Chinese I'd ever tasted. Moo Shu shrimp - I ate the whole thing - minus the pancakes. Peter took a pancake and folded it like a handkerchief, froshki-style, placing it in his pocket to take for Harley. The waitress, someone's sweet, well-loved daughter, laughed and brought us a little to-go carton filled with fortune cookies for our well-loved doggy.

I wanted to go looking for the road that all the tourists took to watch the sunset. We drove up Sunset Road, and ended up in a little park, throwing balls for Harley. I was pretty certain that this was not the view that'd been marketed as the spectacular sunset attraction, but now the sun had gone down and it was a done deal. And I was satisfied with it, and everything, just as it was. The whole time we'd been there playing with Harley, we'd also been watching a guy at the far side of the field practicing his Tai Chi. With his knees bent and hands poised as if holding an invisible ball in front of his belly, he finished up and waved to us.

"How ya doing?", called out Peter.

"Spectacular!" he answered, giving Harley a pat on the head as he passed by.

TV seemed to be part of this plugged-in life. We watched a PBS show about a nature preserve in South Africa where endangered species were shipped in and allowed to live in a natural balance of predators and prey. The preserve was a success, the animals thriving: lions, zebras, giraffes, elephants, hyenas, leopards. Gorgeous, wild creatures eating and being eaten, the way of nature. But our darling Harleydog was safe there with us, feasting on good fortune cookies, which he had been trained to patiently wait for, drool dripping down from his mouth, until I'd read his fortune. Our dog was advised "Now is the time to make that investment".

PSYCHEDELIC MOONSCAPE

Four a.m. The sprinkler system was our new alarm clock.
But that morning, there was no falling back to sleep, and
the raucous birdsongs sealed the deal. Finally I surrendered, getting up at five a.m. to go online, pay some bills,
and take care of some business. I never knew when we'd
have good reception again. Later, our neighbors at the
next campsite said there'd been a javelina, a wild boar, in
the campground last night. They'd heard him snorting and
rummaging around in the middle of the night. He got into
a container of their dog's food and left the container empty and battered somewhere up the hill. Sort of like the
PBS show on the African preserve, it was survival of the
fittest. Luckily, their dog had been in the camper.

We packed it up, heading back up Oak Canyon Drive to
89A past Flagstaff toward Page, Arizona. The day was
wide open, taking us past the Painted Desert, with its
mounds of rippled sand in astounding shades of aqua,
blue, green, red, pink, and yellow. It was a psychedelic
moonscape, staggering, as if we'd been drugged and
found ourselves in a different reality. I gave my sister a call
while there was still cell reception, and attempted to de-
scribe the amazing surroundings, unable to capture anything but a hint of the reality of it all.

The landscape changed, and massive rock cliffs began
to emerge for miles and miles. We crossed the Colorado

River Gorge, and the little rickety bridge that I'd been so fearful to drive across 16 years ago when I'd been here with Derek, that bridge was now a footbridge for tourists to walk across and take pictures. The new, wider bridge, looking a lot more reliable, took our RV safely across. And if I could stand to look, way down there ran the powerful, emerald green Colorado River, looking dreamlike, with rafters floating silently down river far, far below. Driving on, the Vermillion Cliffs to our right were lined with a phantasmic aqua blue. The grandeur, the massive scale so incomprehensible, it stopped the mind.

Slowly ascending into ponderosa pine forests, we came to Jacob Lake Camper Village. Everything was a big production here. They'd just opened for the season, and total chaos and anxiety reined in the office. They tried to fit us into the next open slot, number 37, but the site was small and we felt cramped and hemmed in there. So back in the office, I asked the seemingly impossible. "We'd like to change campsites to number 89 please." After the initial shock and resistance, they did finally manage to make this happen, and 30 minutes later, I had the receipt in hand to substantiate it.

We were all exhausted. Peter from driving all day, and I hadn't felt well from a headache which had now become front and center. And Harley had puked up his dinner and was lying down under the RV, a behavior we'd not seen before. We needed some sleep badly. This would be a Tylenol PM night for sure.

BOB AND JENNY

Though we'd reserved our campsite for two nights, we
packed up as if we wouldn't be coming back that night,
and we hoped that this would be so. The campground felt
too busy. Driving on, we passed the site of the forest fire
of 2006, which had started out as a "prescribed burn" by
the Forest Service, but ended up raging out of control.
What was supposed to be a "managed" 300-acre fire, had
spread across 100,000 acres. It was heartbreaking to see
the vast devastation. Those Forest Service workers who'd
been on duty that day when the winds had picked up unexpectedly were probably still haunted by it. The theory
behind managed burns is that by burning off low brush in
a controlled way, when a forest fire does get started, it
doesn't have as much fuel to increase its spread.

Finally, the forest changed from blackened chars to
green again, and there, by a fresh meadow ringed with
pines, was DeMotte Campground, a little oasis. We pulled
into gorgeous number 2 and claimed it as our own for that
night. The campground hosts came over and introduced
themselves, Tom and Gwen; they'd be there until October.

Gwen and I talked as if we'd known each other always,
and I felt right away she was like a sister. She was a
mother of nine children and untold grandchildren. She
told me her story. "Back in March, I had an accident. Fell
down the steps and landed on my head. It was six days

175

before I knew who I was, or who Tom was. They told me I'd had a subdural hematoma, and gave me big-time steroids to reduce the swelling in my brain. I had to learn to walk all over again; my balance was off. It wasn't until just four days ago that I started feeling like myself again. Before that, people would look me in the eyes, but it was like I was removed, no one home. They won't let me ride the motorcycle again for one year. I can't even ride on the back of Tom's. I have to go back for CAT scans of my head every so often for the next year. How vulnerable we all are. Our fate can change, turn on a dime." Peter and I were quite aware of this while on the road, doing our best to stay alert and aware as much as possible.

We talked about our mothers, how hers had passed away five years ago. Gwen teared up when she told me how she and her sister had sent a Mother's Day card to the niece in whose care their mom's ashes were. The niece had placed all the cards around the urn. I told her about my mother, how she'd passed away just four months ago. How she'd driven until she was 94 and how that last year after her stroke had been so hard, that I'd been happy for her when she passed on. "It takes so long to get used to it. I still catch myself thinking I'll call her and tell her about something that's happened that day. But then I think, oh yeah, she's not at that number any-more." Gwen understood.

Peter and I decided to go over to the North Rim Camp-ground to check it out, and there, sitting at a picnic table with her back to us, was Jenny! It was unbelievable, dreamlike really, to meet up with them in this wondrous place. We picked up as if we'd never left off. Peter had originally met Bob and Jenny when they all worked to-gether as nurses on an oncology unit at Johns Hopkins

176

Hospital in Baltimore. They loved playing music, Bob was on the fiddle, guitar, and mandolin, Jenny played hammered dulcimer and concertina. We'd get together, share some dinner, and jam informally. Once, Bob even set us all up with a "gig" at some women's luncheon group he knew of. Our friendship with them meant so much to us, and it seemed like a stroke of serendipity that we could meet up here together.

But unfortunately, Bob had been suffering from cluster migraines on their trip and was in pain. He'd had them off and on for many years, but it seemed the altitude here had kicked them off again. He didn't have his Imitrex with him, and that was the med that usually helped. He was barely getting by on Tylenol and Motrin, but had some of Jenny's oxycodone that she took for fibromyalgia. He was ready for that heavy artillery now. We all shared some lunch around the picnic table, then Bob went into their rented RV for some down time, while Peter played his guitar outside.

Jenny and I took Harley for a hike along the wooded forest trails where the ground felt like it was padded with the build-up of centuries' worth of pine needles. We shared stories of how protective our mates had become. Jenny told me, "When I go off for a hike, Bob says 'Don't go far. Don't be gone long. Be careful'." I agreed. Peter had been saying the same kinds of things to me. We decided that it must be our age. We were not as invincible as we'd thought we were when young. And especially while on the road, things could happen when least expected. And we decided to leave it at that. I thought of Gwen's fall and didn't want to tempt fate.

Later on, we all shared dinner and music by the

campfire. Bob emerged from the camper, looking a little loopy but still able to eat and play music. "No alcohol for me", he said. "That'd be suicidal." And thus we knew the extent of the pain he was experiencing, abstinence being a true measure of that for him. They both looked pooped, so we made it an early evening. Peter and I retreated to our peaceful DeMotte campground. "Good night. See you guys tomorrow!"

The next morning, it was back to the North Rim where we checked in and got settled at number 59, just a few sites away from Bob and Jenny. They wandered over, and we all had some lunch. They'd been pretty much living on PB&J, so I made some shrimp salad sandwiches, and we all lived it up. Jenny and I went for a hike with Harley along a trail with awesome views of the silent geological giant by which we were camping. The vast canyon had been carved eons ago by the Colorado River and by rain, wind, and erosion. The massive cliffs changed color with the time of day, and right then, they looked vermillion, but that evening, they'd turn a rich hue reflecting the sunset colors. People came from around the world to witness this vast chasm, to hike or ride a mule way down to the floor of the canyon where the Colorado River had carved its path ages ago.

When we returned from our hike, Peter and Bob were jamming, guitars and fiddles, and we pronounced ourselves the campground's best band. There was "Ashokan Farewell", followed by "Whiskey Before Breakfast", and Bob fiddled "Nail that Catfish to the Wall". We were loud, and getting louder as the evening progressed. I was sure all our neighbors were totally sick of us and our music and voices, but we were having a great time. It didn't help that

Jenny kept nipping away at her little bottle of Crown Royal. Her voice, which was normally loud, kept ramping up the volume with each swig.

I figured some food might help, and baked a luscious piece of salmon saturated in barbeque sauce and wrapped in foil over the campfire grill. Some broccoli, last night's rice and beans sautéed with some onions and green peppers completed the meal. It was delicious! Later, around the campfire, we put aside our instruments and told ghost stories and talked about weird dreams we'd had. Jenny was at full volume, still nipping away at her bottle. By campground quiet hour at 10 p.m., we all trundled off to bed, in just under the wire with the noise factor. Our neighbors must have given a huge sigh of relief. It seemed as if it took a while for all the sound waves we'd created to settle down, but Peter and I could actually now hear the wind through the trees, which sounded so peaceful. It would be a good night's sleep right by the vast deep silence of the canyon.

THE PARTY WAS OVER

Bob showed up at our RV door holding the sleeping bag we'd lent him last night. He told us he'd had a rough night, and we believed it. He looked absolutely ravaged. His headache had returned with a vengeance, and he'd taken the last of Jenny's oxycodone. "We've decided to go to the nearest hospital or clinic. I need some meds that work, and that's Imitrex."

As they packed up in a hurry, I went to the ranger's station and learned that Kanab would be the closest place with medical help, some eighty miles away. We looked it up on the map and got the route for them, hugged goodbye, then off they drove.

There was a major mood deflation. We were sad to say goodbye to our friends, especially so unexpectedly. Things felt empty; our balloon of fun together had suddenly popped. I was already missing them badly.

Peter and I looked at each other, "OK, this is a turning point. Let's rein ourselves in and begin a new way of eating after breakfast today, like our Sedona psychic recommended." That decision seemed to kind of sober us up, but it felt like more than that. The sky was clouding over, the pace slowing down, a kind of somberness descended. I was missing the fun we'd shared with our friends.

We went to do our laundry and then to have our breakfast at the lodge. Huge picture windows looked out over the vast North Rim of the Grand Canyon, and we took an empty table right by the window. The waitress chided us, irritated that we'd sat at a table that hadn't been cleared yet. We told her to take her time, we weren't in a hurry, and besides, this table had the best view of the canyon. She was coming from a whole different vantage point, though. We felt like we had all the time in the world, whereas she was harried, hurried, and probably just wanted to be done with her shift. We could remember what that kind of stress felt like; we'd lived lives like that back on the east coast, not that long ago.

The breakfast was not so great, but we were really there for the ambiance. This huge lodge with its massive log beams and rough rock walls was first built back in 1928, and then rebuilt in 1938 after a fire. I remembered being here with my mother only a few years ago. She was 92 at the time and had wanted to go for one last visit to the Grand Canyon. So I'd brought her here and we'd stayed at the Yavapai Lodge. I'd made dinner reservations at this dining room. But Mom hadn't felt very good, the altitude was affecting her. I'd told her, "You don't have to eat dinner. Maybe just some soup, but the view there will be worth it." As she was scanning the menu, she looked up, her eyes following a waiter who was walking by to another table carrying a hot fudge sundae in a tall glass with whipped cream and a cherry on top, the works. It was a no-brainer for her. She ordered that instead of dinner, eating the whole thing, and exclaiming, "That went down so easy, I feel much better now!" What a character she was!

Peter was playing some lonesome songs on the guitar. The sky had completely clouded over. I heaved a big sigh, and decided a hike might cheer me up. I leashed up my four-legged buddy and together we took off up the fire road to walk the blues away. Through a thick growth of pines in a wild forest, we went up, up to the top of the ridge where there was an expanse of pines as far as I could see. The tapping of a woodpecker resounded in the distance. Two horned toads sat completely still on the side of the path. Harley looked at me as if to say what now. We turned around, going back to the campsite, but there they were, the blues, still waiting for me. Then the rain started up, and I remembered that this was all part of the mix. Fullness and emptiness, togetherness and aloneness, gaiety and sadness, hello and goodbye, it was all part of the fabric. Harley took shelter under the RV and we hid out under the awning. Big dark clouds took over the sky. A heavy curtain of steady rain descended. I'd have liked to move on, but there we were for the night, so we'd just be with it, however it was.

"OK, what's for dinner?" We started our new program, Peter with his simple rice, I with my raw salad. The rain let up and we got a modest campfire burning, played some music, and it was all just fine. We agreed to an early bedtime. We both needed a major reset and our doses of Tylenol PM before bed that night would ensure a solid sleep. I awoke in the middle of the night, thinking, yes we'll stay another day. That'll be good.

*** PART THREE ***

AN ADVENTURE

"Let's hit the road!", I heard Peter say as I awoke in the morning. And with those words, my heart thrilled. I was so happy at the thought of getting back on the road again! I made some tea, lit some incense, we sat to meditate on the bed, as always, Harley curled up beside us. And the tone for the day was set. A spacious sense of freedom. Open to whatever evolved that day!

Making a bold suggestion, I asked, "What about California, the Pacific, beaches, ocean? What do you think?"

Peter lit up at the idea. We consulted our Rand-McNally Road Atlas, and planned a route. We'd head south, then west. Our buddy Harley, along for the ride, would have totally agreed if he'd known he'd be on his way to the ocean again.

I made a pot of super-strong coffee for the road. We got going early, south to Roper Lake State Park. Harley went for a good swim in the lake, chasing sticks, erasing the miles. It was peaceful and quiet, until a bunch of magpies came around, busily chattering away to each other, hopping about. Peter and I took a look at a map and realized we were somewhere near the Peyote Way

Church of God. We'd found this church online before we'd left Maryland and believing in their cause, had become members by donating a little money. But now that we were nearby, we felt drawn and considered visiting.

"What do you think?" Peter asked.

"Maybe we should go check it out. We don't have to actually do the peyote, right?"

Well, for that night, we didn't have to do anything but rest. I sat on the picnic table playing the harp while in the distance Mount Graham's snowy peaks became bathed in the delicate pink of sunset hues. We watched, while gradually, an astonishing sky full of sparkling stars emerged, vast and miraculous.

The peyote church was situated down an 18 mile bumpy dirt road on 160 acres of wilderness. The road was so rough and rutted, we had to slow way down to 15 miles per hour to maneuver it. We figured maybe they didn't want this place to be too accessible to riffraff or curiosity seekers. A house, surrounded by a low adobe wall decorated with mosaics and tiles finally became visible at the end of the road.

Inside, we met Annie and Mathew, and despite whatever else they may have had planned to do this day, they made themselves available to us. They took us on a tour of their pottery studio, and then, on to the peyote greenhouses. What a powerful environment. We could almost feel the peyote just by being in their nursery where hundreds of the blue-green buttons were silently growing.

Hovering on the fence, we asked about making a donation, and bought some pottery. Then finally we asked about the possibility of getting some peyote "to go", but no, legal concerns prevented this. They told us about the history of the church, and all the legal battles they'd been through for so many years in order to establish this church within the law. We thanked them, and there was silence in the camper as we considered the possibility all the way back down the bumpy dirt road.

Then I suggested, "Well, we could stay in the area another day and go back tomorrow..."

We called Annie to see if returning the next day for a peyote "spirit walk", as they called it, would be possible, and it was. Hmmm... We put our heads together. This was not a recreational drug but a medicine, nothing we took lightly. We viewed it with respect, envisioning a spiritual retreat under the influence of the peyote.

Peter asked, "Well, do you want to?"

"Yes", I responded, taking yet another leap into the unknown.

So we called back and we'd be on for tomorrow. We were to fast for 24 hours and we'd take the peyote the next afternoon. Of course, the first thing we wanted to do was go eat lunch! And we really savored it, tofu salad, tortilla chips, and avocado slices at the picnic table. Now we'd start the fast. A swim for Harley, out to get some cash, and we were on our peyote way...

Arriving at the church around 5 p.m., we set up camp. The grounds had some campsites already plotted out, and we found one on the west side where there was good sunlight with a view of the mountains. Expectation mounted. What would it be like? Did we really need to do this? Could my body and mind take it? It was all part of the process of entering into a retreat and dying a certain kind of death, letting go and taking a plunge into we knew not exactly what. But we hoped that we would experience new and enlightening states of consciousness. Harley, always trusting, was unaware of what his people were about to enter into. It was a clear, starry night out there in the wilderness, not a single trace of civilization in view. We'd start our peyote walk around noon the next day.

SPIRIT WALK

Patience. We were already getting the picture about this peyote experience; it was all going to take some time to get started. Mathew kindly came down to build a fire for us. "All you have to do is light the match." He hung some tarps to help shade the sun, and brought down some chaises for us to relax on later if we'd like. Mathew regaled us with story after story, about his time in India in the old days, hanging out with the sadhus, getting sick from lack of B vitamins, traveling on to Scotland, enrolling in divinity school but finding it too cerebral. And on and on, weaving these tales, until finally Annie came down and putting a sharp end to it all, said, "Oh that's all so old. Tell something new, about what's going on now."

She let us know it was time to go up to the kitchen to sign some paperwork making us official members of the church. Then she got out two pint jars filled with a thick green liquid, a kind of peyote puree. We were told to sip slowly over the course of four hours, and to think about things other than nausea. "It's best to be humble," she suggested. "That way you don't have too far to fall."

Back at the campsite, lighting some sage and bowing to each other, we took our first sip. Yikes, it was really bitter, like medicine. Annie had also given us some peyote chips to hold inside our cheek. "It helps keep things going between sips."

I was feeling really on target, in focus. I wanted to be taken over by the peyote, to surrender to the experience. So I kept reminding us to take another sip, probably more often than the recommended 20-minute intervals.

At first, it was hard to tell. We had both already sensed the peyote in the air here, in the environment. We were watching and waiting to see. What would it be? Soon enough, one thing was clear. It was very quieting and calming, meditative. We sat silently, with eyes closed, or open and gazing out in stillness. All was quiet in this protected location, with only the occasional sound of a bird, or bee flying nearby. The groves of mesquite trees, the Saint Theresa Mountains along the horizon, the warmth of the sun, a gentle soft breeze. Annie and Matthew had created a perfect abode in nature for what they called a "spirit walk", one in which we might not actually be doing much walking.

After about two hours of sipping, Peter said that was enough for him, but I wanted to go further and take some more sips. Aside from the peaceful, contemplative state, there was also a prevalent discomfort, an ever-present nausea. From time to time, I vomited a bit, then felt better, and took another sip. After about four hours, time kind of slowed down to the eternal moment. "Maybe we've peaked," I suggested.

But not so. The experience became thicker, with a more trippy kind of energy. Seeing some lights with visions taking shape. Peter became active, and walked down to the house to look at a painting done by the founder of this church. I couldn't imagine how he was able to do all that, but figured he probably wasn't feeling it the same way I was and hadn't sipped as much as I had. I sat in the lengthening rays of the sun, so happy for quiet and sinking deliciously into an experience, an understanding given to me by the intelligence of the Peyote Spirit. It was a very small, humble feeling, of being completely one with the earth and all livestock and gentle beings. A sense of awe came over me, the beauty of this earth, how alive and conscious she is, to walk softly on her and gently with love. I knew I did not need to accomplish any big thing in this life. Just to be was enough, to love this earth. To surrender.

As the sun began to go down, Peter returned, lit the fire, and the velvety depth of the night slowly revealed itself. When he began to play music on his guitar, it sounded familiar, yet new and enchanting, and I found it incredible that he was able to manage the physical act of playing. I walked off toward the last patch of setting sun, spread out my shawl on the ground, and became filled with gratitude for this simple life. In a little while, I noticed Harley beside me, coming to check on me, to see what was going on.

Harley. What a beautiful friend. He'd been off leash all afternoon, staying faithfully by, looking out for his people, entering into the spirit of things. Just lying there with us all afternoon, peaceful, settled in, respectful, as if he understood that this was a special time. We walked back to the fire, but I was unable to get comfortable. I was getting cold and didn't seem to have enough clothes on. The sky gradually darkened. And out of the turquoise depths, stars slowly and magically arose. So grand and lovely.

But eventually, the air became really cold, despite the fire. Peter wanted to head into the camper for the night. I didn't see how I'd possibly be able to confine my energy inside there, but I'd give it a try. I had a hard time settling.

Just too much energy. Finally, I made some Sleepy Time tea, and that seemed to level me out a bit. It was clear that Peter was ready to sleep, but I felt nowhere near that. The trip just seemed to go on and on, unfolding layer after layer, so soft and deep and silent. I finally was able to lie down on the bed, looking out the window at the stars, waiting for the peyote energy to subside. Listening to the sleep sounds of Peter's and Harley's breathing, I felt comforted by the beauty of their music.

Peter was still snoring on in the morning, Harley and I were awake and waiting. Finally, I got up to begin the morning proceedings. Let Harley out, feed him breakfast, heat the water for tea, wash the face, brush the teeth. Still pretty trippy.

Peter made the bed, then we shared the grapefruit that Annie had given us. "It'll take the taste of peyote out of your mouth", she'd advised. And to some extent it did. We cleaned up, meditated as best we could. Annie came down and handed us our car keys. "I keep keys as a safeguard against people taking off in an altered state, and driving down the road seeing purple snakes."

We said thank you. This is a special gift you give here, a safe place to explore the depth of our peyote experience. I really connected with Annie. She was so spacious. Goodbye and thank you to Mathew, too. Yesterday, he'd generously set the stage for our comfort.

Then back down the bumpy road to find some hot springs, where clear water dumped down onto our heads from a waterfall in our own private stone tub, helping to bring us back to some semblance of reality. And then back where we'd started, to Roper State Park for the night. We treated Harley to another swim, regrouped, aired out the bedding and our heads. The next day, we'd hit the road again!

YOGANANDA

Oh life was so good! We were California-bound and expected to arrive that day. Barreling across Route 8 West,
past border patrol checkpoints, where a dog had been
trained to be some man's best enemy. "Do you have any
fruit with you? No stems or leaves where bugs can hide
out?" We showed them our orange and were allowed to
pass go. It felt kind of creepy, like the border patrol was
suspicious of everyone who passed through, guilty until
proven innocent. The border was visible as we drove on, a
great, unfriendly wall of fence extending as far as we
could see. On we went, past sand dunes, then acres of
green farm growth, artichokes and what else I wasn't
sure. Mountain ranges lined the distant horizon. And up
from sea level to 4,000 feet elevation, where mountains
with upsurging rocks were unlike anything we'd seen. The
In-Ko-Pah Mountains, where bedrock had weathered into
dramatic piles of rocks and boulders, shifting upward at
strange angles, resembling some weird moonscape.

   We pulled into a little coffee shop in Pine Valley, California. It was an oasis, with cheerful red and orange peonies
everywhere. I struck up a conversation with a woman who
had moved there from Philadelphia. When she heard that
we'd be camping up the coast of California, she exclaimed, "Oh, you've got an amazingly beautiful journey
ahead of you! It's the very most gorgeous drive ever!" She
told us how she'd driven south along the coast from

Washington state and had landed here in Pine Valley and never left. "And go check out Oregon Dunes. It's the best beach campground ever!" Well maybe, but our hearts belonged to Assateague National Seashore.

We proceeded onward toward the Pacific, got lost, then found, and finally arrived at Encinitas. Peter was astounded at how it had grown since he'd been here last, 25 years ago. It was a beautiful, warm, sunny southern California day and everyone was out enjoying it, biking, jogging, walking, eating at outside restaurants.

Then we came upon a splendorous golden lotus dome standing tall atop an archway, marking the exquisite haven of Yogananda's ashram. The sun glinted and played along the dome, catching my eye and inspiring my heart. So glorious! But first, we needed to find a place to stay.

The campground by the ocean was completely full, and after some back and forth and here and there, we located a dog-friendly Econo-Lodge nearby. The motel was manned by a gentle, welcoming soul from India, Mr. Patel. "We are making your room very nice for you. We are winning award for the very nice rooms here. You will be liking this. And here, very nice books for you. You may take a book if you wish."

Oh yes, I loved all things India. This place was for us! Harley immediately settled into the room, lapping up an ice-bucket full of water, stretching out on our bed, and settling peacefully with a big sigh, probably relieved to be out of the camper and stationary for a change.

Peter and I took off for the ashram, making note of all the eateries along the way and filing our findings away for later. But first on our agenda, Yogananda's Meditation Gardens. It was a place of delight, intoxicating. Walking up the steps, we entered the magical mature garden paradise that had been lovingly maintained since it had been planted in Yogananda's day in 1936. Huge elephant ear plants, flowering cactus, exotic bird of paradise flowers - it was a lush tropical wonderland. Large koi swam lazily in a pond, shaded by the low hanging, compassionate arms of an old pine tree, the sounds of a waterfall nearby. A path led through the grounds and alongside a sweeping view of the Pacific way below. And there by the cliff's edge was a square tile with a blue star, marking the original location of Yogananda's Golden Lotus Temple which eventually had slid right down into the ocean due to erosion.

On our way back to the motel, we enjoyed an early dinner at a Thai restaurant we'd eyed on our walk to the garden, then a stop at a fresh air market for some strawberries, and back to our Harley-boy with some fortune cookies for him, one of his favorites! He sat and patiently waited for his treat while I read him his fortune. "You will be taking a long journey". Wow! We set two alarms that night, so we'd be there in time for morning meditation at the temple.

DARSHAN CAFE

Just as we were about to take off for the temple the next morning, our Indian innkeeper ran out to the parking lot in his jammies.

"Are you now checking out?"

"Yes, thank you very much, it was a wonderful stay!"

Peter asked him how he'd slept last night, and he responded, "There was a ring on my phone around 3 a.m. and again later. It is being very difficult to sleep with all this calling going on."

We wished him well and found our way to the temple, securing a primo parking spot. It wasn't open yet, but the Darshan Cafe was! Entering, there before us lay an array of gorgeous pastries in a glass case. A man in line exclaimed, "They're all made with love, and that's why they're so good!"

Another person advised, "Ask for a free sample of chai." It came in a little expresso cup, and it was the real thing, straight from the chai-wallah in India!

When we were done, the temple was now open, and we entered the sublime atmosphere. Pictures of saints lined the front wall, Lahiri Mahasaya, Babaji, Shi Krishna, Jesus, Yogananda, and Sri Yukteshwar. An ethereal white-haired woman conducted the prayers and chant, playing along on a harmonium. And then, a deep meditation.

Peter said later, "Oh, that's what it is to really meditate." We were drunk on the celestial energy in the temple.

Finally we went on to our campsite which we'd been lucky to find available for just this one night at San Elijo Beach Campground, site 150 right on a cliff overlooking the Pacific. We backed in so all we could see out the back window of the camper was an endless expanse of ocean. It was an overcast, cool day, so we built a fire and played a little music together around the fire ring. I made some shrimp gumbo, spinach salad, and opened a bottle of wine. We couldn't have asked for a better ambiance than at this restaurant. I appreciated and imbibed every little thing so deeply: the sound of the waves, sitting out at our picnic table overlooking the ocean, our furry friend asleep by the campfire. I loved this campsite by the eternal tides, ebbing and flowing like the pulse of the universe. Later, the sound of the surf sang us to sleep so sweetly, just like a lullaby.

SAN ELIJO

The winds that buffeted our camper all during the night had stirred up the ocean into choppy whitecaps with lacy waves coursing in to shore. I took our Harleydog down the 108, maybe 125 steps - I lost count - down to the

beach. Letting him off leash for an illicit morning romp, he ran wild and free, at least until the lifeguards would arrive to patrol. All along the cliff, a vast wall of cement tried its best to hold back the forces of erosion, which eventually would surely win out. Huge houses with swimming pools hovered on the edge, awaiting their fate in time.

Tromping together back up all those steps, Harley secured on a leash, I put out some egg sandwiches on the picnic table, and we ate breakfast overlooking the vast gray ocean and skies. So deeply satisfying, all of it, the ocean, being together, just being alive. The van got swept and de-sanded, at least somewhat. Peter played some songs on the guitar; I felt so homesick for I knew not what. A brief window of blue opened in the skies and the sun spilled through for a while.

Then we had to bid goodbye to number 150. We'd only been able to have it for one night, and so it was back to our Econo-Lodge. At the front desk our Indian friend, Mr. Patel, told us his first name was Gunart.

"Isn't that the name of a character in the Mahabharata?" I asked.

"No character, it is quality. Quality my mother and father gave to me."

There was something so pure and simple about this man. We just loved his qualities. We were to return in about one hour after Consetta had cleaned the room.

I took Harley walking and we discovered a route down to the beach that didn't involve quite so many steps. Called Swami's Beach by the locals, it was a haven for surfers. The waves far below were dotted with their surfboards. We walked around the park overlooking the ocean but signs were posted "No Pets Allowed on the Beach", so we took a path along the cliff parallel to the beach. Walkers, joggers, parents pushing strollers, lots of us were out enjoying this beautiful walkway today. Beside the path grew flowering bushes, bird of paradise plants, and palm trees. I paused to take pictures from time to time, identifying myself as a visitor to this exotic landscape. In the evening after getting Harley settled in at the motel, Peter and I went to a special ceremony at the temple for Yogananda's Mahasamadhi, the anniversary of his death. Devotees were lined up to honor him, bow, leave a flower or a donation, and receive a blessing. It was amazing to see the numbers of people, one after another going up to bow. Row after row, a wave of devotees came, the perfume of their devotion wafting by us while sweet chanting filled the temple.

Back at the motel, a car alarm outside went wild for a while, in sharp contrast to our peaceful evening. Harley, too tired to even perk his ears at the sound, remained happily nestled beside his people in his (our) king size bed.

THE GORGEOUS PACIFIC

Route 101 took us north through foggy mountain lands
where vineyards spread along the hillsides for miles and
miles. We were very picky, saying no to Pismo Beach
Campground, no to the campgrounds at Oceana, Grover,
Morro Bay and Morro Strand. But we said yes to the dog-
friendly beach that Peter spotted beside the road! Harley
and lots of other dogs played freely with abandon along
the water's edge. There's nothing so happy as a good dog
beach. It did our hearts good to see their joy.

We stopped for lunch outside in the glorious sunlight by Cambria, with the Pacific below, crashing against rocks, its spray erupting high into the air. Magnificent! And then, innocently we set our sights on Limekiln State Park, 35 miles up the coast. But what a road. Hairpin turns along a precarious Route 1, hovering above a 1,000-foot drop, no guardrail at times on the southbound lane. The road was hanging on by its fingernails, hugging every rocky cove and inlet along the shore. On the northbound lane, there were numerous warnings of rockslide from the steep cliffs jutting up to our right, practically scraping our camper at times. We were treated to unbelievable views of the Pacific, sparkling and vast way down below, deep blue-green in color. Mile after mile, with six miles left to our destination, when on the right emerged Plasket Creek Campground near Big Sur. We took it! Peter pulled in to the first available campsite. No searching for the best real estate this evening. By 4 p.m., we weren't so picky anymore.

Through the pine trees at number 10, we could see the great ocean below and hear its ceaseless crashing. Harley chewed on his bone which yesterday he didn't care about but now was just great. I gave a sigh to be here. Sometimes the evenings could feel a little sad, kind of insecure and unrooted, like missing a home that we didn't even have. The camper was our home, this threesome, our family. And life doesn't offer security, not really, just the mirage of safety and security. I was never so aware of this truth as when we were on the road.

A PERFECT HALF MOON

Early the next morning, the ranger came by our campsite to alert us to the news. Japan had experienced an earthquake earlier that morning, a 9.0 magnitude undersea megathrust earthquake, and it was expected to cause a tsunami to come roaring to the California coast sometime that day. Our hearts went out to the Japanese who would be caught in this disaster and its ensuing devastation. But then, Peter and I began to wonder about the most prudent route to take. Should we head inland for safety? Would there be widespread flooding along the coast? We heard from the ranger that all seaside campgrounds would be closed that day as they waited to see what would happen. We tried to decide whether to head inland or to take our chances and continue north along the gorgeous Pacific Coast Highway. We consulted the *I Ching* and it recommended keeping on our original path, and we agreed.

So on we went, as the highway wound along impossibly steep cliffs and narrow curves. All looked calm so far down on the coastline. Campgrounds up by the towering redwoods looked as though they'd be safe from any flooding, but they were kind of dark, and I'm a sunshine girl. Onward, past Big Sur, with its staggeringly gorgeous views, past the occasional awesomely-placed multi-million dollar home on the cliff. We pulled over to look through binoculars at the sea lions below; I loved those innocent little darlings! There was a whole community of them raucously barking and playing along the rocks, unaware of us humans watching them on the cliffs far above.

We stopped for a while at Riverside Campground & Cabins, just north of upscale Carmel. Harley took a refreshing swim in the Big Sur River, where the water was so clear, we could see the rocks on the bottom glimmering in the sun. But after some ado, we found the available sites were dark and shaded. I was trying to be open-minded about the campground for Peter's sake, and he was trying to be the same for mine. Yet in the end, neither of us wanted to stay there in this dark and gloomy place.

It was a wonderful, free feeling to be back on the Pacific Coast Highway under a big sunny sky. Like the van we once saw painted, we "dared to not have a care" about where we'd be staying that night.

Pulling in to Half Moon Bay State Beach, we found it had bravely reopened. There were no really good sites available, but a few were left, so we reserved one and went out to get some supplies. On our return, we saw a great site right by the ocean that had opened up, so we claimed it as our own. Someone must have cancelled their reservation because of the tsunami, but the coast looked perfectly clear right then. How lucky! We learned later that people had to reserve six months in advance at this coveted campground. We settled in, so thankful for our good fortune, especially on a Saturday night!

We built a campfire, Peter started playing the guitar, and I was on the harp. Soon enough, our neighbor from the next site came over and wanted to jam, and so the Saturday night scene began.

James introduced himself. He was expansive, calling

out to us, "I've got margueritas, beer, tequila, whatever you want!" But we came to find out, he was hurting. He told us of his good friend who had just died a couple of days ago. There would be a memorial the next day, "a celebration of this incredible musician who inspired me so much. He was such a big-hearted man." Our hearts went out to James and we figured he was seeking refuge in drink in order to deal with the grief. James's wife, Angie, and his brother, Geo, and Geo's wife, Jeannie, this was the cast of characters we'd call our neighbors and friends/family for the night.

All of them were wearing sunglasses. Geo explained, "Yeah, I have a cottage industry selling sunglasses on eBay. Thought it'd be my retirement plan." Geo had long dark hair. He came across as an old, spaced out hippie, and we immediately liked him.

And so, the party continued with music and singing, Geo sort of howling along with the songs, making up his own words. He was a wild man! I gave him a tambourine to play, but what he really needed was a drum which somehow would have suited him better. Another guitarist, really talented, Parker, joined us, and the party took off. The music was great!

After a while, I went in the camper to make dinner, enough veggies and rice, fish and chopsticks for everyone. There was a wonderful familial feeling that evening among our little group.

We feasted by the campfire, the wine flowed, laughter abounded. Geo threw more and more logs onto the fire, and more and more words into the conversation. He talked on, saying, "Jeannie and I had to do intensive psychedelics the first two years of our marriage to get it all out there and work it all out. I'm the fire; she's the ice, cutting through everything to get to the truth." As the stars continued to fill the night sky, we all shared some of our life stories in the spirit of gathering close together around the universal fire circle.

And finally the last notes were played, the last stories told, and the fire died down. We said goodnight, with hugs all around. This had been our wonderful family for the night. We'd drawn close and poured our hearts out to each other. But we might never see any of them again, and in the morning, Peter and I would break camp and move on.

As we headed to bed feeling so thankful for this very special evening, we looked up to see a perfect half moon shining brightly that night, sparkling across the water on Half Moon Bay.

OUR SERVICE DOG

Sipping our cups of hot black tea, we meditated, then ventured forth to greet the morning. Geo and James, no sunglasses on as it was cloudy, were heading out to fish. Harley made a getaway toward the beach, running right past the sign stating "No Dogs Allowed on Beach". I took off after him before anyone could raise a fuss. We rounded up our errant doggy, saying goodbye to the guys and wishing James well at his friend's memorial that day.

Angie let us know how lucky we were on two fronts. "First, getting a beachside campsite when you usually have to reserve six months in advance. But thanks to the tsunami scare, you lucked out. Second, the sunny weather yesterday was lucky, as usually it's gray and rainy here this time of year."

We said farewell to Angie and Jeannie, exchanging phone numbers. We ended up giving our Yogananda video to Jeannie once she told us she used to go to the ashram in Encinitas with her mother when she was young.

"Here, it's yours," I said as I handed her the DVD, and she hugged me like a sister, heart to heart.

Following Geo's directions, we made our way out to Maverick's, the place he'd told us about, where the highest paddle-out waves were 50 feet plus, though it was low tide right then. Harley was in heaven! Despite all signs saying "Dogs on Leash Only", local dog owners had commandeered it as dog-friendly beach territory. Tails were wagging, four-leggeds running, chasing balls, playing together, free! Harley joined in the fun, and we took a multitude of photos of this joyous romp-fest where everyone was happy, dogs and owners alike.

Then on to Fish Trap Restaurant, their porch overlooking the bay where the sun, which had broken through, sparkled on the water. And where our eyes were bigger than our stomachs, so we had fried oysters, clams, fish, coleslaw, with plenty left over and packaged to go.

All around the porch were pots of flowering plants, a riot of pinks, purples, and yellows. The air was a perfect temperature, so comfortable and soft, with a gentle breeze. If we had lived there, we'd have been frequent flyers at this restaurant. As it was, we were so thankful to have discovered this little gem.

Back onto 101 North, all the way to San Francisco, where we snuck Harley into a Travelodge, and where the sign read "Service Dogs Only". Truthfully, Harley was of service to us every day, teaching us by his example to be satisfied with whatever came, not to complain or whine or cry, to be good-natured no matter what. In the motel, there was a delicious bath in a Jacuzzi tub, and leftover fish dinner with some orange juice. Early to bed that night, our alarms set for visiting the Siddha Yoga Ashram in Oakland early the next morning.

FROM ASHRAM TO WINE TASTING

Up at 4 a.m., we stood outside the ashram ringing the bell until someone came to let us in. Within the darkened, fragrant room, we poured ourselves into the velvety silence. It was heaven to be there, like coming home, feeling my mother, my Siddha Yoga companion through so many years before, sensing her presence right nearby, very close. An hour of meditation flew by, then we were directed into the hall for chanting the *Guru Gita*. "Offer a handful of flowers, humming with bees," my favorite verse instructed. I chanted for my mother, and for an old friend whose father had just passed away. At the end of the chant, we entered the sacred atmosphere of Nityananda's Temple, where the sounds of a fountain, water splashing, the scent of flowers in the air, all were bathed in a celestial vibration. I remembered my nephew, Jud, who had lived for a while at the ashram in New York State, and sent him goodwill wishes from this special place. Then, breakfast in the Amrit Cafe, for Baba's sour cereal, an ashram favorite, and some chai, their flavors redolent with memories of so many ashram visits with my mother in years past. We were greeted and welcomed by the regulars there, and we felt like regulars too, all one together in this extended family of meditators.

On to Napa Valley, wine country, with vineyard after vineyard spread out across the hillsides. We stopped first at Luna Winery, where we paid $15 for a tasting, and applied that toward a $40 bottle of Merlot. Then I conferred on the phone with Derek for his opinion, he suggested Silver Oak Winery. Derek was feeling low that day, having broken his ankle, thus unable to work his job as a bartender. I told him maybe this could be a good time to change direction and study for some kind of online certification, and he agreed. The apparent tragedy ended up being a valuable turning point in his life.

The grounds of the vineyard were magnificent, with rows of vines stretching out into the distance, rimmed by mountains along the horizon. They made only Cabernet Sauvignon at Silver Oak. We went on a tour with Zeke, an 86-year-old man who'd worked there for thirty years. "They treat us good here", he explained, refilling our glasses over and over with the Cab '06, as he led us around the machinery of wine making, the vats, and the barrels. He carried a bottle with him as we walked, and when one ran out, he'd open another, until all of six of us on the tour were beginning to fly high. In the expansiveness of the moment (maybe Zeke had counted on that), I ordered a bottle to be sent to Derek in Florida, along with two Silver Oak glasses. That ought to cheer him up!

A young couple on the tour, devotees of wine country and coming all the way here from Connecticut, recommended Saint Helena, so we went there to check it out. An elegant, upscale town in Napa Valley, it was evident there was a lot of wealth in the area. Gorgeous architecture, ubiquitous rows of grapevines, a verdant town park where Harley had a rollicking fun romp, chasing sticks, balls, even twigs. Whatever we threw, he was game. We found a delicious lunch at The Model Bakery, home of brick oven breads, and a fabulous cheese and veggie sandwich on crusty bread. And the El Bonita Motel, dog-friendly, absolutely lovely, a respite for the night in this idyllic Napa Valley. How fortunate could we be? It seemed our every move was enchanted, sprinkled with fairy dust.

But now reality struck, since rain was predicted along the coast every day that week.
OK, but our game plan would remain the same: up the coast, rain or not, we'd just see how it went. North on Route 128, we got lost, then found on seemingly endless

winding roads with rain and thick fog, through the red-wood forest and on past Mendocino. An *I Ching* reading was right on target with number 47: Oppression, Exhaustion. "The superior man remains cheerful in times of adversity". But this one changed to number 24: Return, Turning Point. "After darkness, the powerful light returns."

And indeed it did. The sun began to peek through, a window of opportunity provided at the Westport KOA, a superb campground by the beach. Good fortune had smiled upon us, a partly sunny day by the ocean, where Harley romped freely. Different rules seemed to apply here! Peter pulled out the awning during a brief shower. We played some music under the shelter. Then a cup of wine, some guacamole and chips, and a game of Scrabble at the picnic table. Peter almost always beat me at the game, he was remarkably lucky with picking letters, the high-number ones, like X, Z, and Q, whereas I often ended up with all vowels. I used to get all in a snit about it, but oh well, it was just a game. And actually, I did win that time!

The rain passed, the sun reappeared. Our firewood was brought to us by a guy named Jim, who worked at the KOA. He proceeded to split some and build a fire for us (above and beyond the call of duty) and then went on to tell us his story. Hard hit by the economy, he had lost his job and was living out of his van. He'd found work as a security guard at the Rite Aid in Fort Bragg, where apparently people were shoplifting during tough times.

Our fire finally got going despite the damp wood. We thanked Jim and wished him well. Playing music into the evening, we reveled in the window of opportunity we'd been given that day, a respite from the rain. Harley had a great day, with lots of fun, running and playing on the beach! It was a clear cold night, the moon on its way to full.

PERVASIVE RAIN

There were some blue sky holes in the pervasively gray sky. I took a hot shower, letting the water beat down on my back. You could really depend on KOA for a civilized bathroom experience! Another romp for Harley, and we were off, heading north on Route 1 along winding, hairpin turns as the road veered away from the beach. Immersed once again in fog and steady rain, the Redwoods were all covered in lush moss, ferns thriving here, wet rhododendron drinking up the moisture. Just like in a book we loved, *The Heart of the World* about the hidden lands of Tibet, where it was raining so frequently and was so moist that leaches had to be pulled off your legs repeatedly as you hiked. At least we didn't have to deal with that!

At the juncture of Route 101, there was a deciding point, should we go north or south? But first, we went to Leggett, nearly getting stuck on a rain-rutted road, and finally paying our five dollars at the Chandelier Tree, a giant redwood with a huge hole cut in the bottom so vehicles could drive through. It's estimated that the tree is around 2,400 years old, from around the time of Buddha. I apologized to the old giant, I felt sorry for the insult of carving a tunnel right though this ancient being.

By the time we made our way out the other side of the tree, our decision had been made. We were heading south where we hoped there would be some warmth and sun to dry everything out. But the rain continued, relentless. All the streams were swollen, gushing, overflowing their banks from all the rain. After days of pervasive rain, everything in the camper was wet, a leak somewhere.

It was a good night for a motel. We found one right in Berkeley, a TraveLodge where I smuggled Harley in. It's not always so easy to find a pet-friendly motel when on the road. One block down from the motel was a store, Bazaar of India Imports, now that was for us! A store of many delights, statues of Ganesh and Shiva Nataraja were in abundance, plus all kinds of chanting CDs, Indian clothing, and a multicolored embroidered jacket. But most of all what drew us was a small travel harmonium for me, and a Shruti box for Peter. He used the little bellows box as an accompaniment for his fiddle, it provided a drone backup sound which enabled him to be a kind of one-man band. After oohing and aahing, a deal was made, 10% off if we payed in cash. The owners directed us to an ATM four blocks down and awaited our return. "We'll stay open until you get back!". We recognized that we were over the top here, but really, these were special instruments. Peter wavered a bit on the way back from getting the cash, but in the end, we returned to seal the deal, and please throw in a tambourine, a bag of dhal lentils, and two boxes of Yogi Indian Spice tea (my very favorite). We bid goodbye to the Indian couple, who asked, "Would you like us to drive you?" But no, thank you, it was just one block.

Both the harmonium and the Shruti box were traveling in handsome red zippered bags. We entered our room and tried them out on quiet mode, not wanting to draw attention to our contraband dog. One skulking walk after dark in the back of the parking lot by the dumpster, and I hustled him back in for the night. Alarms were set for 4:30 a.m. for our return to the Oakland Ashram in the morning.

216

HOHO

Smuggling Harley out to the van in the dark of morning, we drove to the ashram and parked near a grassy area, where our faithful four-legged friend ate his breakfast and did his business. We drew the curtains in the camper and kissed him, saying, "Go back to sleep now. We'll be back in a little while."

They opened the door for us right away this morning, "Oh, you're back! Welcome!". And right away, we seated ourselves in the velvety darkness of the meditation hall. Down, down, I plummeted, into a silken land, leaving body and mind behind in the deep stillness. I felt so relaxed, all tension and lines melted from my face. I had the feeling that being there was removing any hard karma from our journey, lightening our load.

At breakfast, Robert, a resident, joined us and told his story of working construction there, and also at the ashrams in Ganeshpuri India, and South Fallsburg, New York. I asked about the guru. "She's in seclusion right now", he stated. "Lots of people are not very happy about that."

We bowed, saying goodbye to Oakland Ashram, goodbye to sour cereal, chai, the meditation hall, Nityananda Temple. We planned to head for Half Moon Bay and take our chances there again. But at the campground, the ranger told us he'd seen a spout, a tornado, out over the water. There were some die-hards camped in the heavy rain, but it wouldn't include us. Peter wanted to stay in a fancy motel, but they wanted $150 plus pet fee and I couldn't go for that. We stopped at the Mayan Cafe for some seafood chowder, and weighed our options.

How was it possible to go from so relaxed and at peace this morning, to so constricted and tense this afternoon? My emotions were swinging like a pendulum. Finally, in Marina, we found a wonderful Best Western, overlooking the ocean. The RV had leaked fiercely that day. All the covers on the bed were wet, as well as Peter's clothes. We hauled them all into the motel and spread them out on the chairs and little sofa, hoping they'd dry . A low energy dinner at a sad little Chinese restaurant called the HoHo, where the cook wore a grimy stained apron and carried a fly swatter, put the finishing touch on our day.

We loaded up all our semi-dry things the next morning. Harley needed some prompting, actually pushing, to get him back into the camper. We spread out a towel for him as he jumped on the bed and just quietly sucked it up, resigned to his fate, no complaining. The heavy rain returned, but we were headed south and east where we hoped for drier lands. We stopped in Tehachapi at a great little Thai place, the King of Siam Restaurant, for some Tum Yum soup and pad Thai, the spicy food somehow lifting our moods.

Leaving in the nick of time as a huge dark rain cloud moved in from the west, we found that just a few miles outside of town, suddenly the landscape dramatically changed from super-green lush hillsides to dry desert land. As we drove on, Yogananda sang to us on the CD player, "In the Temple of Samadhi, in the Temple of Bliss." His heartfelt chants saw us all the way to a Days Inn in

Barstow, at the cusp of Routes 15 and 40. Again, all our damp sheets and clothes came into the room to be spread out to dry. We had chips and salsa on the motel bed, while Chris Mathews stirred up the political fervor on TV. We slept for ten and a half hours. We must have needed it.

CHAPATIS FOR HARLEY

A stellar meditation in the morning before hitting the road made all the difference, transforming all the emotional wrangling of the past few days. We called Peter's mother, Inge, who was very relieved to hear that we were okay. She followed the weather and had been worried to hear that a storm had caused part of Highway 101 to collapse right near Big Sur. We'd seen it on the news a couple of days earlier. A whole portion of the road had cracked open and fallen down the cliff, closing 101 entirely. And we had just driven that road three days before it happened. Divine providence. Big gypsy bad luck averted.

Across the desert we went, as endless trains stretched out along the tracks as far as we could see, carting their goods across the country. Still, the skies were mostly gray, it was getting hard to imagine a real sunny day. At a Denny's in Needles, California, Peter said, "Let's see what's going on in Sedona". And lo and behold, Karuna-mayi, who we'd met once before and loved, would be coming to Sedona that coming Tuesday. She was an Indian holy person, a spiritual leader who visited the States to offer meditation programs promoting global peace. "Let's go!" we said in unison.

We stopped at a station to get gas, and a guy who worked there noticed our front tire was low. Then he showed us how our two front tires had cracks. They were cheap ones to begin with, and he'd sell us two new tires for eighty dollars off and no labor charge. Peter was doubtful, but I gave the go-ahead. And while they were at it, the oil had to be changed too. Meanwhile, I checked online and found the same tires for a much higher price, so it felt providential to discover this place and have things taken care of right then. Perhaps we'd dodged some gypsy bad luck once again.

Before long, we were back on the road and over the bridge with the emerald green Colorado River below, into Arizona. Down the scenic 89A into Oak Canyon, descending 3,000 feet in elevation to the magical red rock area. Back to our Oak Creek Canyon Campground where Harley was delighted to submerge himself in the creek. After his dip, we told him, "See you in a little bit" and we walked to a restaurant tailor-made for us, A Taste of India, where the food was excellent. The walls were painted with murals, scenes of India, the Taj Mahal, tigers, Indian women in their saris. "All done by a local artist", said the owners sitting nearby. "If you'd like to meet him, he's here almost every day. He loves Indian food!"

Peter wrapped a piece of chapati in paper for Harley, and the owner came by with a little bag to put it in. We thanked him for the superb food, and he brought us an even larger bag of chapatis for our lucky doggy. We took Harley to a local park for a romp, but he did something to hurt his eye. We weren't sure what. Thankfully, we had some of his eye antibiotic from a past injury, but the trick was to get it into his eye. It was a two person job, and even then, most of it went on the fur around his eye. We hoped at least some of it got in. Harley wasn't the most cooperative patient.

There was more rain that evening, we just couldn't seem

to shake it. Peter had refused an umbrella, his hair was all wet and water was dripping off his nose. I grabbed a towel and rubbed him down, just like we did with Harley. The constant gray skies were beginning to wear us down emotionally, and with dampened spirits, we took refuge in the camper for the night. It was hard to sleep, so Tylenol PM was the only recourse.

DARSHAN

OK, a tiny opening of blue appeared that morning, as we went for the darshan of Karunamayi. Darshan, or being in the presence of a holy person, carries a special quality of silence, reverence, a hushed atmosphere. One last walk for Harley, and I entered the center with a group of elderly spiritual ladies who were all dressed in white. Inside, the sevites, or workers, were busily putting it all together. Peter and I sat meditating, but as the hall filled up, it became chattier and chattier in there. We relocated to a back row. Someone came to tell us, "Karunamayi will be coming here in 10 minutes, if you'd like to go out and welcome her."

I stood outside the hall to wait with the others, when a woman beside me asked, "Have you been here to this center before?"

"Yes", I answered. "I came here to meet her once before, a few years ago."

"What did it feel like to be hugged? I read online that she hugs each person. I can't wait for my hug!" she exclaimed.

"Oh, that's another guru, a different Amma, this one doesn't give hugs."

The woman looked confused, as though she wasn't sure if she should believe me. She was certain she'd come to the right guru, the hugging one.

The darshan line went on and on, waves of shakti,

heavenly energy, filling the hall. Timeless and powerful, I felt like I was swimming in a sea of ethereal love.

Eventually, I visited the bookstore, bought two chanting tapes, and went outside to get Prasad, or blessed food. But there were only two cups left to dish it out with. Just then, the guy from the Indian restaurant came by and suggested to try pouring it into the mouth with the cup not touching your lips, so that others could use it too. And so we did it that way.

Peter and I had reached the saturation point. It was time to leave. Amma had said, "Meditation, mantra, chanting, these are our offerings to the world." She stressed the importance of work, and told a story about Lakshmi, the Hindu goddess of wealth. She said if Lakshmi gave everyone wealth, no one would do any work. She recommended three hours of chanting and meditation a day as our way of contributing to the earth. I didn't know if we were quite up to that and I wasn't so sure that enlightenment would be mine this go round. Wasn't the most important thing to simply appreciate whatever comes our way and not look ahead? Pretty much like we were learning from our dear Harleydog, just to be satisfied and make the best of this moment right here and now.

UTAH

Bidding goodbye to Sedona, then onto 89A to Freedonia, down 2,000 feet in elevation, our ears were popping all the way. And there before us, a sprawling length of vermillion cliffs, so grand in scale no photo could have captured them. We were under a cloud which dumped a brief rain shower, but ahead the cliffs were bathed in glorious sunlight.

Ah, and then we entered Utah! It was so good to be in Kanab, Utah, a nice little town, where Bob had hoped to get help for his migraine some weeks ago. Grocery shopping, washing and cleaning the RV, these were the day's tasks. Hanging out at the Subway sandwich shop picnic table, I called Mom's Tuesday group and they actually answered. It was unusual for someone to pick up the phone during their session, and I was so happy they did. I thanked them for the gift card they'd given me as a goodbye present and told them we'd used it for a wonderful dinner in Sedona. But mainly, I wanted to tell them about the dream I'd had of Mom last night. Her presence had been so real. She'd been concerned about someone and had wanted me to communicate to the group that she'd be sending love and healing. So when I said this on speaker phone, Nancy, one of the members, let us know she'd just been found to have a recurrence of her cancer, and was to have surgery and chemo. Nancy said she'd been feeling my mother's presence lately and that this message really spoke to her. "Love and help from unseen realms are with you." So this confirmed it for me also; I'd been wondering what Mom had been up to. She was still around and doing healing work!

We stopped for the night at a KOA, actually quite a nice place. It slowly filled up a little as the evening progressed. Having just visited Sedona, we were reminded of the psychic counselor we'd met who recommended Peter change his eating habits. So we reconstituted our eating regime, which we'd begun briefly and then had forgotten about. Peter would have mainly rice and beans, raw salads for me. I found a nice German couple who were happy to take the brie and Laughing Cow cheese that were not on our program. Some beautiful horses were grazing in the pasture next to the campground, I patted them and fed them some carrots. Harley was only vaguely interested in the horses, but he had his eyes on the carrots, so he got some to crunch on too. We were plugged in, so we watched Babel, a movie about miscommunication, and I fell asleep that night thinking about my mother, how I'd love to be able to communicate even more clearly with her.

GOD ON LSD

Indulgently, I let the hot water wash down my back for a long time. It was utter heaven, the shower in the KOA ladies room that morning. But meditation that morning was not so heavenly. It was thinking, thinking, thinking.

There were other ways to meditate, I guessed, and later on, gazing at the hoodoos, or rock formations, of Bryce Canyon might have been one of them. It was a vast magical fairyland of crimson spires and the unbelievable sight stopped the mind in its tracks. No campsites were available, though, so after witnessing and drinking in the grandeur of the canyon, we continued on the utterly scenic route 89 North past rough, rugged rock formations, with sage growing everywhere. I insisted on stopping to pick some, which I'd later tie into bundles and leave on the dashboard to dry and perfume the camper. Peter said they looked suspiciously like bundles of marijuana.

We checked out Piute State Park. Out guidebook said camping, but no, it was tent only. We were already pooped, but Salinas had nothing to offer us as the sign said, "No Bull - No Services for 110 Miles". And it was true.

We drove on Route 70 East to Green River, astounding vistas unfolding before us. Peter remarked, "God on LSD created this!" Around every curve in the road was a whole new mind-blowing grandiose landscape. Huge rock mesas and giant slabs of rock looking like massive sinking ships going down at an angle. Utterly magnificent.

There was no thinking now, only mouths agape in awe.

Green River State Park was just the ticket, restful, with shady green cottonwoods and Russian olive trees. A swim for Harley in the muddy brown water of the Green River, wide, with a strong current, so Harley stayed on his long lead to keep from washing away downstream. He swam out for sticks, which the current carried swiftly away. I hauled him in some on the lead and tossed a closer stick so he could feel he was doing his retriever job successfully.

There was good reception here, so we set up an office at the picnic table, and we were in business. With a wet, happy dog at our feet, we emailed, wrote letters, and phoned until the stars came out. Over the trestle bridge spanning the river, a lonely train sounded its passage, the first of many to come during the night.

DEAD HORSE POINT STATE PARK

Yoga on top of the picnic table this morning under an overcast sky, since the ground was too rocky. The old hippie couple we'd seen while doing laundry in Kanab said a brief hello as I finished my sun salutation and got down from the table. Tent camping out of their Mercedes SUV, they'd be going to Dinosaur National Monument, then heading home to Steamboat Springs in Colorado. "Yeah, we were in Moab yesterday, it's like a madhouse there. Beautiful views, a great restaurant, but we didn't want to stay. It was too crazy." Later, Peter said he'd seen them going down to the river last night to smoke a joint. Old hippies, his long white hair sticking out from his hip-hop cap, she, in a long tie-dye skirt. We loved their style!

It was 70 East past Moab for us. We'd take our chances at Dead Horse Point State Park. The landscape looked like what you'd see on Mars, totally barren, mounds of rippling sand, no vegetation in sight. All was brown. There was an open site for us at number 14, overlooking some of the awesome canyon. But there was a bit of an upset this morning. I'd lost one of my hiking shoes. This triggered the inner critic and I could hear my father saying to me as a kid, "You and your slapdash way of doing things." I told myself, "OK, I need to be more careful, I'm just moving too fast and not paying attention. I've lost my shoe with the orthotic in it no less. How will I hike now?" I pitched a fit, mixing in plenty of expletives, and putting on a pair of rubber slides, said, "I'm going on that four mile

even if I get blisters", and stomped off with Harley in tow.
   The trail started at the visitor's center, so we went there
first and admired the views. Well, it couldn't hurt to ask if
anyone had found a shoe. Maybe it had fallen out of the
RV when I'd gone to register. I asked the ranger who said
he'd go in and ask for me, since I couldn't take the dog in
the office. He called out, "No one has found the shoe!"
And just then, a guy who'd heard that shouted out, "Hey, I
found a shoe. It's over there on that curb!" And sure
enough, it was my missing shoe! I thanked him profusely.
He had no idea how happy I was on the one hand, and
how embarrassed I was on the other hand about what a
stink I'd raised over this earlier. And I also felt badly that
Harley had to witness my big drama, remembering the
saying, "Be the person your dog thinks you are." In perspective, it was just a shoe. No one had been injured or in
an accident, or lost a wallet or died or anything. But the
message for me was to wake up. You could really feel
more vulnerable on the road and needed to keep your
wits about you. And of course to trust that everything is
fundamentally OK no matter what.
   I walked back to camp holding up the errant shoe for
Peter to see, my tail between my legs. I put both shoes on
and he and I got on our bikes and rode out to lookout
point, instead of me hiking by myself. Harley waited in the
camper, so it didn't work out as well for him this time.

The story was that at one time there'd been wild mus-
tangs in this area, and the cowboys would corral them out
on a point by laying juniper branches across the path.
Then the ponies would be trapped on the point, unable to
get away down the steep cliffs overlooking the canyon.

Legend had it that once, they'd left the horses too long without water, and the horses had jumped off the cliff to their death, trying to get down to the Colorado River to drink.

We followed a trail back into the desert, going off trail at one point and sitting on a rock to admire the view. Red sand, the green of piñon pines and junipers, prickly pear cactus blooming in a brilliant red, the entire scene was a desert work of art. The sage growing here only had enough oomph to muster up a faint scent. All around were the carcasses of fallen trees, weathered by the elements in this arid climate, their wood splitting apart at the seams, ravaged by the desert. It was a long lingering sunset that night at the lonely, exquisite outpost. Silence pervaded.

CHO

The EklectiCafe was the happening place in Moab, where at the next table over, they were discussing art, yoga, and music. We felt right at home here with this crowd. Ordering up two coffees and some breakfast, we agreed to take the morning off from the austerities of our "program". And what a breakfast. I got the huevos with green chili, and Peter went for the breakfast burrito. It was really good, well worth the debauching involved! A stop at the Moonflower Health Store to stock up, and we were back on track with our regimen.

There was to be a Desert Rock Concert going on all weekend just outside Moab, but the forecasted rain and the rutted access road were both deal breakers for us. Not to mention the fact that it'd probably be all teenyboppers and disaffected hip-hoppers. Did we sound just like old geezers? Oh well, we wished them all a great time at the concert, and drove on by.

Route 46 took us switch-backing on a winding road into Colorado past awesomely huge rocky mountains, jumbled every which way along the horizon. I drove from the town of Paradox, onwards through rain, hairpin turns up and down the mountains' ribs. Was there a Paradox here, a hidden irony? Wasn't life itself a paradox, a mystery beyond our control, so full of love and suffering, and try as we might to understand, we could never really put our finger on it. I contemplated all this while driving on through verdant valleys, with horses grazing despite the down-pour. Streaks of lightening in the distance and rolling thunder caused Harley to tremble with anxiety under the bed in the back. The only help for him was to wait it out for the storm to move through. Passing by small towns which some people called home, the road curved beside the San Miguel River, which was gushing with the strength of the rainfall. The sky was heavy, dark, low to the earth, a very different feeling from the wide-open blue sky and big-hearted sun we'd enjoyed since heading back from California.

Coasting into Ridgway State Park, we found only two sites open. Like an *I Ching* hexagram, one was above on the mountain and one below by the lake. Keeping Harley's interests in mind, I chose down near the water, where we'd have electric and water hook-ups. It was a big family scene, Memorial Day, and even though it rained off and on, people seemed undaunted, determined to do their holiday thing. Campfires were blazing, baseballs being tossed back and forth, children laughing, dogs barking, everywhere the sounds of a celebration.

Then we both spotted him, an unusual looking guy lop-ing up the hill with a strange little hat on, clipped back with laundry pins. Peter went up and befriended him, inviting him to our campsite. We both really took to some-one like him, who didn't quite fit in and didn't seem to care what anyone thought of him. Peter regaled him with food, making rice, offering dried apricots, a banana, an apple, some nuts, some juice. Cho ate it all, holding a bowl of rice in one hand, shoveling the food in with chop-sticks with the other. It became clear that he knew very little English, but had managed somehow to communicate to us that he was here from Korea, bicycling from LA to Chicago and on to NYC. "Home August 2." It sounded like he might also be hitchhiking some as well, it was hard to tell.

Since a campfire was going, we gathered around. Peter played the guitar and sang while Cho, at least we thought that was his name, recorded the whole thing on his camera. We took photos, then exchanged gifts. A penknife for Cho from us, and Cho gave us an exotic paper bill from Korea. It had picture of an ancient sage-looking guy on one side. "Who?" we asked, but he couldn't think of his name. A picture of an ancient temple was on the other side of the bill. It was worth 1,000 "won" in Korea. "Is like one dollar", Cho let us know. And it was worth a lot more to us, this sweet feeling of a special kind of bond together. How brave he was to come explore this country on a bicycle without even really knowing English. Goodnight you courageous adventurer, Cho. Sleep well in your tent under the shelter. We've been honored to meet you!

HARLEY'S REBELLION

We bid goodbye and good luck to Cho, and he was off on his bike with four yellow saddlebags, two attached to each side of the bike. He pointed to his jacket with the flag of Korea sewn on the shoulder and said, "Army, strong, good." And he was strong and good. What could it be like for him as he pedaled off through those mountains in bad weather, not even really knowing English? Peter wondered if maybe we should have given him some money, but it was too late.

Pulling up stakes ourselves, we were in search of higher ground, and just a few miles farther on lay Ouray, a beautiful little mountain town of hot springs, supported by the tourist trade. At the town park, Harley went for a romp, chasing balls and meeting Missy, a fellow golden retriever of a more relaxed nature. She was content to let Harley do the chasing, which he did with great dedication and focus. Standing by with tail wagging, Missy deferred to his intensity. Missy's people were Ron in a wheelchair with an oxygen cannula, his daughter Toni, and her husband Tom. Really nice people. It turned out that Ron and Toni had lived in Jemez Springs and had run the cafe in nearby La Cueva called the Ridgeback. "We owned land along the Jemez River and built a house there. It was a good life for many years. But now it's so busy. People come roaring through on their motorcycles and big SUV's. They just pour through the valley on Highway 4, stop at Los Ojos, the cowboy bar, then turn around and roar back out." We knew what they meant, but loved the little village anyway.

I recommended the book about the history of Jemez Springs. "It's by the authors who are the editors of the local newspaper, *The Jemez Thunder* and has lots of photos of the area. You'd love it!" I considered giving them our copy. But just then Harley made a dash for the river, the Uncompahgre River, a gushing torrent, all white-water tumbling down from the mountains with spring run-off from melting snow. It was a muscular river with steep banks, and fearing for Harley's safety, we all ran over to try to grab him. In this strong current, he could have been washed away down river and out of our sight in no time. We tried various ways of getting him out of the water, but Harley was staging a rebellion. After too many hours spent riding in the RV, he was having it his own way now. Cleverly having found a little spot on the side of the river protected from the onrush of water, he was not about to move. A branch had been lodged there and had formed a small pool of water just big enough for him to rest in safely. Gumming his ball and looking up at us from time to time, he remained unmoved by our calls for him to come. Harley was claiming this little bit of bliss for himself and there was no luring him out. Finally, we gave up and figured he'd follow us if we left. The old trick of attracting him by rattling dog food in his bowl wasn't working. The sound of the rushing river was probably all he could hear.

We sat on a bench and waited, feeling a little embarrassed for Missy's people to see the reality of how our dog called the shots and had his people trained. But sure enough in a while, Harley emerged dripping, lured finally by the dog food and was safely leashed once again. Everyone simultaneously breathed a group sigh of relief. We felt really touched by how engaged these dog-lovers had become in our little drama. At one point Ron had tried to get up out of his wheelchair to help rescue Harley, but his daughter had made him listen to reason. "No Dad, there's nothing we can do." But they all had done plenty by supporting us with love and caring. Once again, we felt so close to people we'd never met before, our extended family on the road.

They asked where we'd be staying that night, and we told them we hadn't found a place yet.

"Go to the 4-J RV Park, two blocks down from here, right on the river."

And we did, bidding them goodbye for now, "Thanks so much. We hope to see you again somewhere down the road!"

On our way into the campground, a guy came up to our window. He introduced himself as Jim, and told us he was camping here in his tent. Riding his bicycle along beside us, Jim talked to us in a conspiratorial tone through our open RV window. His shaggy hair was tucked under an orange bandana with peace signs printed on it, and he was decorated from head to toe with colorful woven belts, leather pouches, scarves, and beads.

"Yeah man, I'm biking along, I like to let people know you don't have to get the whole package, you know, you can put it all together yourself. Like I got my bike baskets from a yard sale, hitched them up with rope and put this little rug around it all, then hung up my flags from the side." And then, switching topics with hardly a breath between, "Like you know man, I've been studying mining, I got my master's in mining. I worked in New Zealand doing something for the government. That's where my eyes got burned out. You know what I mean? That's what they do to you there. Like I can't even see anymore. Like I'm legally blind."

Jim's eyes were blue and kind of glassy with no depth, but it looked like he was able to see us, and it seemed as if he was able to see well enough to get around on his bike. He had a perpetual smile, like nothing was really going to get him down, though there was a little paranoid flavor to some of what he was saying.

"You know man, like you just have to be careful out there, what with the way things are and all. Know what I mean? Like I saw this guy, I thought he was from Japan or something, but he's coming here from Korea on his bike."

"Yes, we met him. His name is Cho," I offered.

"Yeah, so he's outfitted pretty good with those yellow packs on his bike and all. But, like, he can't really speak any English. I gave him a granola bar when I met him along the road. But anyway, this is a pretty good scene here and all, but you have to watch out for some of these people, you know what I'm talking about. I mean, I have some money now, but for a while, I didn't."

It seemed like Jim could go on forever, and we had yet to pick out a campsite. We aimed to camp somewhere away from his site. If we were nearby, there might be no stopping him. Jim didn't seem to be too big on boundaries.

So Peter said, "OK man, we're going to get going now, we'll see you later!"

As we drove by Jim's site number 2, we saw his picnic table, laid out with plastic cloth and all kinds of bottles of condiments, plastic containers, cups, bottles, and some assorted flags and banners. We wondered, how did he fit all this stuff on his bike? It looked like maybe he was planning to be here a while.

238

The campground at 4-J was perfect. We joined the line-up of RV's by the river. There was one slot left for us under a tree, with a huge rock to sit on and gaze out at the wild Uncompahgre, which would be roaring to us all night in its big rough voice.

But first, the hot springs at the Wiesbaden Inn, where a beautiful hot pool awaited us. Nearby, cherry trees were just beginning to shed their blossoms in the breeze. The occasional delicate pink blossom found its way over to the pool and drifted silently onto the hot water, one landing in Peter's hair. All around were steep mountains with dark clouds sitting heavily on top of them. And the stone bell tower of the Catholic Church across the street would wait for the next morning, Sunday, to sound its call.

The hot water lulled us into a dreamy state, and at each corner of the pool, couples whispered languidly to each other. When we couldn't stand to soak anymore, we ventured down into the vapor cave, a dark rock enclosure where the hot water oozed from the walls, creating a natural steam room. We emerged, limp and washed clean, renewed.

A thunderstorm was underway, so we ran right back to the RV and administered to Harley who was shivering and panting. Umbrella in hand, I took him out on the leash to do his business, with him eyeing the river longingly. I told our doggy he'd had enough for one day. We all holed in very cozily on that rainy night, curled up together on the bed, while I read aloud a story from the ancient Hindu epic, the *Ramayana*.
And the river raged on through the night.

THE RAMAYANA

Peter loved for me to read aloud to him, and he particularly enjoyed the story of the *Ramayana*. This ancient epic tale was about the Hindu characters, Ram and Sita, and how she was captured by a demon and was eventually rescued. The main theme was the importance of following your dharma, or or true purpose.

Peter also loved me to tell him the story of when I was at an ashram in India and had been part of a stage production of the *Ramayana*. While my mother and I were there, we were given a seva, or job, to do. She was part of the team that sewed the costumes; I was on the makeup committee. The play would be given one night up on a nearby mountaintop overlooking the ashram.

Every day, we climbed up the 108 steps carved into the side of the mountain to practice for long hours in the hot Indian sun. Big urns of water laced with electrolytes had been provided to keep us from becoming faint in the heat. The colorful stage was painted in celestial tones of lavender and blue, and three large, billowing white tents had been set up for makeup, costumes, and one for the cast, some of whom were monks at the ashram. In the makeup tent was Tod, who would be gluing the beards on the characters, Sally, who'd be doing the hair, and me. I'd be putting on the makeup. Day after day, there were numerous changes made in the script, the costumes, the makeup, and we all felt pushed to our limits.

240

Finally on the night of the play, under a vast sea of stars, the stage was lit, surrealistic against the backdrop of darkness in the valley below. There was an atmosphere of intensity and magnificence that permeated everything, like some archetypal drama. But we, who'd been practicing everyday in the heat, we were all completely exhausted. I had to dig deep into my reserve of energy and patience. Yet after all, weren't we all at the ashram to train ourselves, to refine the spiritual qualities of tolerance, perseverance, and detachment? At one point, Tod, looking gray and drained, turned to me and said, "You're in charge now. I don't feel well. I'm going to go lie down outside."

Just then, a monk entered the tent to have his beard applied. Tod was the one who'd practiced with him. I hadn't put on fake hair since my days of high school plays. Gamely, I began, but the glue and hair were all getting stuck to my fingers, not his face. I was thoroughly exhausted, at the end of my tolerance, at the very edge of what I thought I could possibly do. "Excuse me," I said to the monk. "I'll be back in just a moment."

I went outside to check on Tod, but he was out cold on his back in the grass. I just wanted to run and hide somewhere. All my self-doubt, insecurity, and fear came rushing up, choking in my throat. I saw in living color all the issues I'd been limping along with in my life, the issues that I'd come to the ashram hoping to transform.

But then I heard someone say, "What happened to Susan?"

The monk answered, "I think she got cold feet."

There was a pause. From somewhere deep inside me, a fierce resolve welled up, and I thought, "Oh *NO,* that will *NOT* be me!" I marched back in and put that beard on with determination, sending the monk out to play his role onstage. It was more than just a beard; it was a transcendence of limitation. That was what I'd come to the ashram to experience.

Later that evening, I saw my mother, and we compared notes. She'd also been up against her own barriers, and believed that she could do no more. And then she experienced a wonderful sense of freedom, breaking through from self-limiting beliefs. And wasn't that the kind of transformation that this open-ended journey in our RV was also about for me? I aimed to live outside my self-created box, to liberate myself from small self-concepts and live in the spaciousness of not knowing.

BLUE SKIES

Waking, slowly rising up to consciousness, I wondered, where are we? Oh yes, by the Uncompahgre, its insistent music continually playing. Mists hung low over the mountains, and rain drizzled steadily, as if we'd been immersed in a cloud. I remembered what Teri had said yesterday. "Sometimes it gets a little claustrophobic here if it's snowing or raining a frog-choking rain, with the mountains all around and the clouds thick overhead. Then I just want to hop in the car and drive to Montrose, where it's a little more wide open".

And that was just what we did. There were a few breaks in the clouds, and the sky began to open up as we drove on past Montrose toward Grand Junction. Back in desert country again where it was dry, and it sure felt good. "A witch's apron" - that's what Peter called the low-hanging dark curtain of rain that was over just one section of a distant mountain.

We pulled up to number 58 at Island Acres State Park, the only site left, fortunately, right beside the muddy Colorado River, high and wide, rolling smoothly along. Massive walls of rock curved around the horizon, the sky big and open, clouds clearing away. The delicious sun was shining once again, and I drank in its warmth. Harley and I went hiking up a trail around the canyon, right beside the river. I let Harley submerge in the water, but was sure he was well-leashed. No rebellions would be staged this day!

When he was good and tired, we put him in the RV, and Peter and I went for a bike ride on the trail. It so happened that this campground was the closest one to the town where the bluegrass festival would be held in a couple of weeks. We reserved number 58 for that weekend and it was set. We'd be coming back for the event, and we'd see how things would unfold until then. Each day was a little lifetime.

It was a beautiful afternoon, just what everyone had in mind for Memorial Day weekend when rain had apparently been widespread. But as our campground host pointed out, "This area rarely gets any rain, so actually it was a blessing." I gave her a bag of Science Diet dog food for her little dog, Angel, who ate that brand. We'd bought it for Harley when his brand of food hadn't been available. But it didn't agree with him, and I said, "We're going to find someone who's really happy to get this, so let's not throw it away". And sure enough, Angel's owner was really happy, "Thank you so much. This is just great!"

Everything worked out. A brief thunderstorm, and Harley hunkered down between the front seats, his place of shelter during anxious times. I covered it over with towels to make a little protective tent for him.

CAUTION AND SPONTANEITY

We left for Moab. The main issue would be finding an
empty campsite anywhere today, as the area was really
crowded with tourists. Calling Dead Horse Point State
Park, they informed us that yes, there was still one site
open for tonight. I didn't get that it would be ours that
night, but I kept that to myself. And sure enough, when
we arrived, the site was gone. The same thing happened
at Canyonlands. No open site. So it was all the way back

to Moab to the River Oasis RV Park, where all the big rigs were lined up, and we fell in at the end of the row.

Harley and I went for a walk by the river. Remembering how he'd slipped out of his halter in the river recently, I attached his leash directly to his collar and wrapped the end of the leash around my wrist. There would be no goldie insurrection staged here today. I threw some sticks close to the shore so he could get wet, yet not go too far out. But he saw something that caught his eye in the water, and leaping to get it, he hauled me with him, knees first into the muddy water. Soaked up to my neck, my favorite pants ripped, and my knee was bruised, along with my ego. Sigh. How could this have happened so fast when I'd been trying so hard to be more careful? The bruised knee was the same one that had been injured a few years ago when the meniscus was torn. It had remained perpetually swollen and sore, and fearing that the knee was really screwed up now, I thought, "OMG. Now I've really done it". I walked around with Harley while my clothes dried a bit and I had a chance to test the knee. I didn't want Peter to worry about me every time I went out for a walk, so I waited a while before returning.

Finally back at the RV, Peter was sympathetic and supportive. "We'll buy you a new pair of pants. Your knee will heal. It's all okay." But still, I was sobered, and I figured the day called for an earnest look at things. This was something I needed to do for myself, in silence.

And somehow nature responded synchronistically. Winds whipped around, and huge dark thunderclouds moved in across the sky. Rain started to let loose, cracks of thunder going kaboom! Harley burrowed his way between the front seats of the RV, panting and in a panic.

The electricity went out, just when I was looking for some diversion by watching PBS. And then I was face to face with my own fear. It all seemed a pretty grim picture that evening, a low ebb. I felt so vulnerable. Falling asleep to the sound of rain on the roof, I contemplated how to balance caution and spontaneity.

DREAMY DAYS

The air was clear, the sky blue, a good day to let my soggy sneakers dry out in the sun. At the EclectiCafe for breakfast, some scrambled tofu with wakame seaweed and a cup of strong black coffee were good medicine for me. We bought the last of our supplies, some tofu and DVD movies, had the hubcap fixed, and then were on our way back to Dead Horse for one more try at a campsite. And it was a yes. Site 11, a no-reservation walk-in site, and that meant we'd have squatter's rights to stay as long as we liked to, up to two weeks. In astrology, the eleventh house has to do with hopes and dreams realized, so this site was auspicious for those who were ready for a more hopeful outlook, and that was me. In no time, we were all set up, the awning down, the rugs spread out to dry, my favorite chair situated in the sun perfectly for optimum basking. Harley was tied to the picnic table where he would, as usual, get himself completely tangled up within a short while, but we'd deal with that later.

Deliciously quiet, this was a desert outpost far from the teeming crowds in Moab. The green of the piñon pines and junipers against the red of the sand, the dried out carcasses of old trees, weathered by the elements over time, all suggested the austere harshness of this environment. It had a beauty all its own. A perfect place to come to terms with life, though that wasn't something that happened on a conscious level. It wasn't something that could be figured out rationally, more like something that needed to be digested and assimilated on some deeper level within. "Desert Solitaire", my own version.

This was the most relaxed I'd felt in a while, sitting in my chair, feet up on a rock, drinking in the sun, with a delicious cool breeze stirring. I dreamily read a book, while Peter whittled a fetish out of a piece of wood. We were lost in the beauty of the place, the afternoon stretching out into a long, slow sunset, purple lingering along the edges of clouds and fading into dusk. Peace pervaded.

The next day passed as in a dream. I finished my book and was so relieved to get back to my life, much as I'd enjoyed being with May Dodd and the Cheyennes. The three of us took a leisurely hike, my knee still healing. Peter in his white dress shirt and Italian pants looked like an elegant Mormon going out to proselytize. We stood together in awe before a grand view of the canyon below. There was a big silence here, profound.

Toward sunset, a young woman wearing a necklace reading "Kate" approached us with her chocolate lab in tow. "Do you know if there are any open campsites or any other campgrounds around? The sign said 'campground full'. The ranger's office is closed and it's been a long day on the road." Kate needed a place to set up her tent for the night, and it was to us she came with this problem. So together, we examined the options and ended up offering to let her put her tent up on our site. No problem.

While Kate got her little backpacking tent up, she let her wild child puppy off the leash. "I can't believe how easy it is to put it up. Come here, puppy. And look, there's a nice inflatable pillow. I love a pillow. Can't sleep without it. Come here, Bella. Get out of the cactus."

Harley watched Bella's antics, looking ever so mature and well-behaved in comparison. Though he did continually get himself tangled up in his tie-out as he wandered around a big rock, under the picnic table, and out the other side. Before long, he was throttled with no slack left on the leash. Then we'd have to untangle him and begin the process all over again. But there was a law on every campground that you needed to keep your pet on a leash at all times. Except, of course, if you're young and unfettered by rules!

"Would you like a beer?" Kate called out as she rummaged through the back of her Honda Civic hatchback. "They're really good. From a brewery in Oregon. Oh, but they're warm. I don't have a cooler." That was a real deal-breaker for me, but Peter took one, and we all gathered at the picnic table as Kate told us of her life.

"I was raised in Portland, Oregon, where everyone is all the same: all young people, all white, into ecology, same politics, all voted for Obama. It was too homogeneous, and I needed a change so I moved to San Antonio, Texas after the Peace Corps. Yes, I spent one year in South Guinea, but had to leave. They were having a civil war. Do you mind if I smoke? My boyfriend and I just broke up, and I rationalized that this is OK for now. So now I'm moving to Austin Texas. It's very laid back there. Bella, come here, baby." And she went trotting off after her dog who was busily gnawing away on a fellow camper's hand in true puppy fashion. The ranger must have been taking the night off.

Peter and I bid her goodnight, sleep well, and we trundled off to our RV with Harley to watch one of our DVD's, "Frost-Nixon". We really got into it, and when it was over, we asked ourselves, "Yikes, now where are we...?" And gazed out the window from our bed at a brilliant sky full of stars. The vast silence all around spoke louder to us than any DVD.

PAGOSA SPRINGS

We gave it our best shot at meditating that morning, amidst much thinking. Then we packed up and got ready to leave, saying good-bye to Kate and Bella. We gave her our extra dog bowl and the book I'd just finished. "Thanks so much for your generosity. I love to read. And thanks for the bowl. I've been meaning to get one. Now I can stop feeding her out of this cottage cheese container."

Waving to her as we drove off, we headed down to Moab to do some laundry, secure a few supplies, and after an exhaustive search at the dollar store, we finally emerged with the right containers for our water hose and Harley's dog food. I discovered that Peter did have a bit of an obsessive streak, and this was fully on parade as he hit the local Ace Hardware store. An hour later, he'd collected all the supplies necessary for wood carving, saying "These won't take up that much room." Then he loaded a toolbox full of gadgets, files, sandpaper, a Dremel tool, and a vise. "These will fit just fine into this cabinet". Good thing we'd given away the extra bowl and the book that morning!

One more breakfast at the Eklectic, and our "program" seemed to fade into distant memory. We agreed we'd return to Moab in the fall when it'd be cooler, but now we were off to Colorado.

Right away the landscape changed. Good-bye to the massive rock structures of Utah, and hello to snow-covered mountains on the distant horizon of Colorado. Past fields and fields of sage, I resisted the urge to collect still more of it to line our already full dashboard. Transient showers from low-hanging curtains of rain, this was the land of water, rivers for Harley and hot springs for us.

We stayed the night outside of Dolores, beside the Dolores River. No place to walk with Harley but on the main road, where we saw a field of cattle and went over to say hi. A whole bunch of cows came over to the fence, and seemed to be listening intently as I spoke to them. Harley eventually lost interest in the whole affair, so we walked on.

This was a nice place, but we really didn't want to spend the weekend here. So often, we'd had to drive around a lot before finding an open campground on the weekend. And because many parks got packed on the weekends, we aimed to position ourselves somewhere good for Friday and Saturday nights. By Sunday, many campers would leave to get back to work on Monday, so then the coast was clear for us to move on. Which is all to say, it was time to get hunkered in somewhere.

And that was Pagosa Riverside Campground in Pagosa Springs, Colorado, a beautiful, peaceful place, with campsites both beside the river and also beside the small lake. The choice between the two ended up being a little problem for Peter who seemed to have gotten himself into a bit of a funk. Now I myself preferred the site beside the melodious river, but I left the ball in his court since it looked as if he might be snagged up in some sort of personal tangle. At this point, I just wanted for him to feel settled and at home. We registered for the riverside site, but soon enough, he changed his mind and asked me if I'd mind moving to the lakeside site. No problem. Both sites were good! He went off to the office to tell them we were changing, but as he walked back, I could see that hadn't really done the trick. The mood may have had some other origin and might take a while for him to unravel.

Meanwhile, Peter dropped me off at the hot springs, and I assured him I could walk back, it was just two miles. So I left him to do his sorting out. Sometimes you just needed some space and time.

The Springs Resort, that was the name of the hot springs. About 12 different pools of varying degrees of hot mineral water were sprinkled across the hillside, all overlooking the beautiful San Juan River. So you'd sit and soak in water as hot as you could stand it while gazing at the river, tumbling down all frilly with whitewater splashing. When you got too hot, you could go down some steps for a cool off in the river, but yikes, that was really cold! Then you'd be glad for the 108-degree pool. And so it went, until you were reduced to a limp, well-cooked noodle.

I somehow got it together after soaking and being reconstituted by a large iced tea, to walk back to the campground. Peter called on the cell phone and offered to pick me up, but I was quite happy to be walking. Then, out of nowhere, a thunderstorm came over the mountain, and I got back just in time for it to let loose. I could see Peter hadn't quite kicked the mood. He played some guitar outside under the awning, then we ate mostly in silence. Just give it some more time, I thought. It'd blow over just like the weather did around here. He didn't seem to want to talk about it, saying talking would just stir the water up and make it muddy. Better to let it sift and settle. Emotions could come up while on the road, especially in close quarters in a tiny home on wheels, day after day. And sometimes, we just needed some space to work it out on our own.

"I'm taking some knock-out drops tonight", he said, and I handed him the bottle of Tylenol PM. They really did the trick when you needed to get a good night's sleep. Tomorrow would be another day. We could let this one go.

RINGO AND THE FIBER FESTIVAL

We were a little hung over and foggy from the Benedryl, but the feeling wasn't anything that a strong cup of coffee couldn't handle. A glorious sunny morning, and Peter suggested that we go to the hot springs together. We soaked in the hillside pool overlooking the frisky San Juan and watched the rafters as they careened over one little waterfall near us, yelling with chilly delight as they were splashed by the cold water, then disappearing downriver into the distance. Peter was friendly to the older couple soaking next to us, laughing and joking with them, his little gray cloud gone today.

I soaked a while longer while he went to the RV to rescue Harley. Peter took him to the park on other side of the river where I could see them at a distance from the pools. They looked so sweet together, Harley chasing the sticks thrown for him, Peter sitting on a blanket on the ground. I met a mother and daughter who were researching all the hot springs of the Southwest. "This is the best one by far!", they exclaimed with delight, and I agreed, though my sampling hadn't been as extensive. Lying out on the stone wall of the spring and letting the sun bake me, it was so delicious I could have stayed all day. But I knew Peter was there with Harley, so I got dressed and went to meet them.

We walked Harley beside the river and along the path, meeting a couple of guys who'd just gotten two 6-week-old yellow lab puppies, Roxy and Ranger. Harley checked them out, sniffing and tails wagging all the while. I was feeling a sense of timelessness, like the day could last forever. We watched the bathers on the other side of the river, the whole scene looking as if it were happening in a dream.

There was a fiber festival going on in the park, and I had to go check it out because some livestock was there, and I was crazy about livestock! One dollar to enter and there they were: llamas, alpacas, sheep, a Scottish Highland bull who was totally darling, and some longhaired goats. I loved them all! The people tending them told me all about the care and feeding of the animals. "They eat some alfalfa, graze on pastures, and need shearing every one or two years. They're easy to care for," the caretaker said. I adored the alpacas and the sheep, and we watched as they were being shorn. They baa'd as they stood in the pen waiting their turn. With one big guy holding them down, and the other doing the shearing, the animals submitted and surrendered to being denuded. After their ordeal, they nuzzled up to their owner, Ellen, who told me how she and her daughter had rescued some alpacas and sheep.

"Now little Ringo here," she explained, "he came to us half starved and sick, but he's doin' real good now. We put him in the pasture right next to the alpacas, but he cried something fierce til we put him in the same pasture. And he's been happy as a clam ever since." Ringo had one blue eye and one brown eye, horns, and a really goofy look about him. But he was as sweet as anything and obviously a lover. He'd stolen my heart! Probably understanding that I was captivated, Ellen continued, "Alpacas are related to the camel family, with soft pads on the bottom of their feet, and only lower teeth, no uppers. They never over-graze in the pasture. They just know when to move on."

Then we spoke with a weaver, Nancy from Arizona, and I bought a skein of her wool and told her I'd learned to make baskets from a woman on Easter Day in Tennessee. "Oh, would you like to lead a workshop next year at this event?"

"Sure, I guess so." And I gave her my email address. Who knew where we'd be next year, or even if I'd be good enough at basket-making by that time to actually teach it? Though, so far, I hadn't actually made even one! Still, I might as well keep an open mind. Anything was possible. Our journey was certainly teaching us that.

"I see you're very comfortable in nature," Nancy told Peter as he walked out in the rain, not hurrying to get out of it. "You're just taking your time."

Yes, we were taking our time, and it felt like a great blessing to be able to do so. There was no rush, no real agenda other than paying attention in the moment. We felt so fortunate to be able to open ourselves to this new way of life, able to explore whatever and wherever we felt led.

One thing we were noticing in Colorado, rain could suddenly appear out of nowhere, and then disappear just as quickly. The sky could be clear and look quite optimistic, and suddenly clouds could blow in from the mountains and a thunderstorm of large proportions took over. Or the clouds could decide to veer over in another direction altogether. There was no predicting it.

Back at the campsite, the weather held out long enough for a nice campfire. We had to go ahead and make the fire while we could. A fellow camper stopped by to listen to Peter play his fiddle. "Clay's my name. I play some old time music, just learning. I don't read music, but maybe it's better to learn by ear. My fiddle has beginner frets marked on it. I'm not sounding too good and wouldn't be able to play with someone else at this point." Actually, he sounded pretty good on his fiddle, despite all his disclaimers.

When a big thunderstorm descended, I went in the RV and found Harley shivering in the bathtub. Poor baby. I wished I could help him relax. I pulled the shower curtain, so he could feel safely hunkered in a little den. Finally, I coaxed him out of the tub, placing a coveted dog biscuit outside the bathroom door. Then we three curled up in bed together, our pack all safe and sound, as we listened to the rain steadily beating down on the RV roof. `

*** PART FOUR ***

TAOS

Harley ran free at the campground, his ears flapping as he chased the object of his desire, the tennis ball. The two-ball method worked quite well, given that he never wanted to let go of one unless he could see the other right there in our hand. Since we always had one of the two balls, we could maintain some measure of control and power. But in the end, Harley had his say and staged a rebellion once again, lying down in the shallow river. He was in blissful oblivion, and for now we were content to let him have his way. Not his favorite thing, he had to tolerate endless hours in the RV as we drove along. And of course, there were the thunderstorms, his personal traumatic nightmare. So we wanted to give him some slack, and besides which, we knew he wouldn't allow himself to be caught and leashed for a while anyway. This was the path of least resistance. But finally he did succumb to the dog biscuits laid out in a trail from the river bank to our feet, where the leash was in ready.

And then we were off to Taos, taking Route 64 East along a winding mountain road. That road was closed in winter, and there were still large patches of snow scattered in the shade of tall pines. New green leaves of aspen trees flickered in the sunny breezes, looking so pristine, it could have been a painting. We stopped at the Black Mesa Winery for a tasting, where a woman with her hair dyed in rainbow colors of red, blue, and purple, poured for us. She told us how she used to live in Taos, but found it all too busy there. And she was right about that.

Approaching Taos on the main road through town was a wild scene, kind of like a drag strip. Motors were gunning and tuned up high. This was a place to see and be seen. At the World Cup Cafe on the corner, there was always good people-watching, with a collection of eccentrics maybe not unlike ourselves. We hung out on the porch for

a while and watched it all happening. Today, a child-mother sat on the bench near us with her muddy cowboy boots and a dress that looked like a slip. She had her two young kids, wild ones, in tow, and she was telling some guy, "No, that's what you need to understand about children. They don't listen. Do you hear me? They just don't listen. That's the way children are." Meanwhile, her little ones were running around, totally out of control, loud and hyper. The guy with her tried to corral them, but she reminded him, "See? They just don't listen." I thought of our rebellious Harleydog who didn't listen to us some- times, and cut this young mother a break.

Today, we were splurging and staying at the El Pueblo Lodge, in our favorite room 247. We rested a while, then ventured out again to see who was playing at the Adobe Bar that night. Harley was totally content to stay in the motel room, making that perfectly clear by not budging from from his position on our king-size bed. There was a group playing at the bar, Middle Eastern music, and three belly dancers jingled the coin chains around their waists as they danced nearby. We ordered drinks and something to eat, sitting on comfy sofas among a really nice looking group of people in the bar. It was a warm-hearted at- mosphere, but eventually that king-size bed called to us, and Harley was asked to move onto the sofa for the night.

INSPIRED WANDERLUST

We made the eventful choice to stop in front of the Taos Prudential Realty office just to look at a couple of properties pictured in the window, and then out of curiosity entered to inquire about them. And we were off and running from there. Peter was looking quite bright-eyed and bushy-tailed, so the realtor, Tiva, took us around in her car to see the properties. I was feeling kind of sad, as though maybe he wanted our trip to be over now. Had the wind gone out of his sails? I would go with this escapade for now, but planned to let him know later where I stood: I wanted to continue our free lifestyle.

She showed us a piece of land with a stream, then a house up in El Salto. As we stood outside and talked, an amazing double rainbow materialized, one so low in the sky that we could see both ends right across the road. Buffalo and what looked like a yak grazed on a nearby meadow. These sights somehow inspired the wanderlust in me, and I felt pretty clear that I wasn't ready to stop traveling yet. The house was nice, but there wasn't enough land, and anyway, none of it felt right to me. But Peter seemed gung-ho about all of it. It was a low ebb, but I'd just give it some time to work itself out.

The next morning, we let Harley chase sticks at the park, then caught breakfast at Michael's. Happily, Peter was not so interested in the Taos properties that morning. He was over it and wanted to move on. We devised a plan to go to Colorado, yet checking the weather app on my phone, discovered it'd be raining all weekend in Alamosa, but sunny all weekend in Jemez Springs, so our direction was set.

Campsite 8 at Vista Linda offered regeneration. A guy from the next site showed up to say hello. Andy, a computer megageek, was outfitted to the hilt with 550 DVD's, mostly sci-fi, his Mac desktop computer, six solar panels on the roof, and four batteries to cover it all. A self-proclaimed "full-timer", he had a year's pass to New Mexico State Parks, and went from one to the other, staying the maximum allowed at each. We offered him something to drink, but he said, "I hate to use up your stock." We dispelled him of that idea, and gave him an iced tea. He wrote a blog where he offered all kinds of information on the easiest way to RV, kind of like Helga's Helpful Hints of RV-ing. He had a Lazydaze RV, and he told us of its superior design, including a large glass back window that was really nice. We learned that there were Lazydaze enthusiasts all around the country, and apparently they would gather for large conventions a couple of times a year. Once Andy had delivered his information to a listening audience, us, he trundled back to his site, and we didn't see him again for days. Presumably, he was deep into his computer, his downloaded electronic reader, or any one of his 550 DVD's.

I thought of our occasional nights of watching TV or a movie, and was thankful that we did really enjoy nature where we camped, including playing music around a campfire and having meals at the picnic table. But there were all different approaches to camping and varying interpretations of how to enjoy the freedom of life on the road. And it was all good.

YES, NO, MAYBE

With breakfast at Deb's Deli, the day began innocently enough. But the The Jemez Thunder revealed some properties to look at, and before we knew it, we placed a call to Ron, a local realtor, and he'd be meeting us at the library at 9:30 that morning. I viewed this as an educational foray, just to investigate possibilities. No harm in that. On past trips to the West, we always researched properties out of a general interest and curiosity, but we'd had a home in Maryland at that time.

First on the list was some land in Canon on the Rio Guadalupe. We walked the land and made our way through the overgrowth down to the river. It was beautiful by the water, but this place didn't feel like it was for us, with old rusty trucks and a beat-up old trailer on the property and trash everywhere.

Next, a gorgeous home built by Mark Feldman, a local architect. Now this was a tempting home! The house was well-built and the views in every direction were astounding, but of the three acres, most of the land was too steep and unusable.

There was another of Mark Feldman's homes, but it was too big and conventional for our tastes. Next was an underground home on five acres, but the home wasn't anything we could actually live in comfortably. It was like an efficiency apartment open only on one side to light. And last, Ron took us to see a 15-acre parcel of land with great views in an area called the Red Rocks. But building a home just didn't appeal. Not to mention the squeaky windmill up the hill and the dogs that hadn't stopped barking the whole time we were there.

There was a lot to consider, such as was this really the right time and place to be thinking of settling down again? I loved the area and felt comfortable here, yet wasn't quite ready to end our time of freedom. But it seemed Peter was drawn to the idea. I suggested, "Why don't we just give it some time to sift and settle?"

Life on the road wasn't always easy and did take some stamina. There were ups and downs, like anything in life. Maybe we were seeking the respite of a home base when we simply could have used some down time and stayed at one campground for a while longer. We talked about the tendency to buy something new when a change of some sort was needed, but how it didn't always satisfy. Peter said, "Yeah, I bought my car back in Maryland when I just wanted something new and different, but it was impulsive, not a wise purchase."

We were in a strange place of yes, no, maybe. We'd move on the next day, and give it some space and time.

A GOOD NIGHT'S SLEEP HELPED EVERYTHING

We woke up with clarity, realizing that out of everything we'd seen so far, the one Mark Feldman home with great views was the only place that might work for us. Sometime.

A momentous morning, we went to open a post office box in our name. This much I could do happily. The woman behind the desk said, "Welcome to Jemez Springs!" Our friend, Jay, in Baltimore, had been collecting all our mail for us since we'd left, so getting our mail in Jemez Springs would take the onus off her. And this village had become a comfortable resting point for us on our travels. I called Ron the realtor to tell him we'd be giving it more time, but he got another call, asking me to call him back. Which I didn't plan to do. He seemed to be hot on our trail, and we didn't want any pressure.

We went on to visit Doc Minter, the neighborhood vet who lived on San Diego Drive. The signs on his door read, "A Fisherman Lives Here With The Catch of His Life", and "A Fisherman and a Normal Person Live Here". We'd heard that he took groups out fly fishing on the Jemez River, and that he was an expert at tying his own flies.

We dropped in without an appointment, but he seemed happy to see Harley on the spur of the moment. He was a diminutive man, wearing a T-shirt that read, "Doc Minter House Calls For Small Animals".

"I'm actually semi-retired," he explained. "I've had colitis and other health problems. But yeah, I'll check him out."

We all stepped into the camper parked out front that had been outfitted as a vet office.

"I used to travel in it, but now I just use it to make house calls." Lifting one of Harley's ears and peering in, he exclaimed, "Oh, a golden retriever, you can see right through to the other side! I know goldens, I used to breed them." We warmed to him right away.

He checked the injury on Harley's back paw where he'd cut himself swimming in the Dolores River. He shaved it, cleaned it with Betadine and water. Harley was tolerant and allowed Doc to put on some antibiotic ointment and a dressing. We'd see how long that bandage would last. The whole time in the vet's office, a bee had been buzzing around a light fixture above Doc's head. He told us he was allergic to beestings, and I when I pointed out how casual he appeared to be about it, he responded, "You don't bother them, they won't bother you." That seemed to sum up something about Doc, but I hoped he kept an EpiPen on hand, just in case.

After haircuts and a stop at Starbuck's in Bernalillo, we were Colorado bound. Peter told me he was thinking about flying to visit his elderly mother in Baltimore, then maybe driving his car back out to New Mexico. That was actually OK with me. It'd be fun for me and Harley to travel a bit by ourselves. Realizing that having his car out here would mean that Jemez Springs would be a kind of home base for us, I tucked that possibility away in the back of my mind for the time being.

Just before the border into Colorado, we stopped for the night at Sugarite Canyon State Park, where everyone seemed friendly. Mason, the campground host, came over to greet us. Around his neck, he wore a string of rawhide with an elk tooth hanging from it. "Did you know that the elk is the only animal in North America that bears ivory? Yep, just in their front eyeteeth. 'Course, elk are also some of the best eatin' around."

We set up camp at site 13 and before long, an old guy named Trey stopped by with his sheltie to say hello. Harley really liked smaller dogs, and after sniffing each other out with tails wagging, they both settled easily.

Trey, a big talker as we discovered, started in. "Yeah, me and my wife got a place in Louisiana. It's the last place we're ever going to buy. I'm gettin' too old for that now. I'm 76, and I don't want to move again in this life-time. But we're both in pretty good shape. We hike twice a day. This morning, it was five miles, this evening, four. Yep, you just go over that trail over yonder and keep on a goin'. Now, me and the wife would like to do what you two are doin'. Just take to the road and see where's you go. But you can get yourself some land cheap in Arkansas and Oklahoma. Five acres with 2,000 square foot of house for $150,000. You got yourself a computer? Well, just you look it up and you'll see. But take my word for it, check out your neighbors before you buy. Now my neighbor, he's a mean varmint. We were away and come back to find him sprayin' poison on my garden. So I says to him, 'You wanna take me on? Just stop all this sprayin' and meet me out back and we'll work it out.' Yes, ma'am. You be sure and check out your neighbors first."

After Trey said goodnight to us, he moved on down to the next campsite, where we saw him bending their ears for some time. Then, a nice young kid came by, maybe around 13 years old, and played some ragged riffs on Peter's guitar for us. Before long, his father came to look for him, saying, "I'll take him off your hands now. What do

you say, Josh, to the nice man for letting you play his guitar?"

Josh managed a weak "Thank you, sir" and his father
led him back to their site.

And with that, we were ready to take refuge in our
camper for the rest of the evening. Sometimes, it took a
lot of energy to listen to other people's realties. Sometimes we wanted to rest in our own space together and
just be. We lit a candle and a stick of incense and curled
up together on our comfy bed, Harley sprawled across by
our feet. It felt so cozy that night, together in our own tiny
refuge on wheels.

HARLEY AND THE CRESTONE BEAR

At the Shambala Cafe in Crestone, Colorado, right by the

base of a soaring mountain range, we ordered some chai and hummus, and sat to eat. It was a hippie cafe and all the offerings on the menu were organic, vegetarian, gluten free and dairy free if you wanted. The rustic wood tables and chairs lent a homey and pleasing simplicity to the place. Colorful prayer flags were strung around both inside and outside on the front porch. A bulletin board advertised various spiritual groups and local New Age happenings, like crystal healing and meditation classes. My old friend, Alan Abramson, originally had told me about Crestone and its history. He'd bought land here years ago when led to do so by the appearance of a butterfly that had followed him until he found the right acre. He and his wife said that a couple, Hanna and Maurice Strong, had set out in the 1970's to make a spiritual interfaith center here, and had donated land grants for that purpose on which there was now a Hindu Temple, a Zen Buddhist center, a Christian center, a Carmelite monastery, and a few Tibetan Buddhist centers. As you entered the village, there was a sign that read, "Welcome to Crestone, New Age Religious Capital of the World".

Crestone was a little village set at about 8,000 feet in elevation by the foot of the towering Sangre de Cristo Mountains. Making the turn off Route 17 to approach the village, we were face to face with the dramatic view of ethereal snow-topped mountains that actually formed the southern tail of the Rockies. There were lots of little New Age shops in town, some inns and restaurants, but we were headed for the Crestone Mountain Zen Center.

Up the steep mountain road to the center, the road was rutted and rocky so that we had to inch our way up in the camper. We arrived just in time to meet Baker Roshi, the teacher in residence there. An American Zen master, he

272

was a tall man, with an imposing presence, and bald head. Peter had heard him give a lecture years ago, and said he was an excellent speaker, giving a culturally rich talk. Baker Roshi let us know he'd be leaving for Denver in an hour, so he asked Dan to give us a tour of the gorgeous mountain top center. We entered a unique circular dome on the grounds, where in that amazing acoustic space, a woman played the violin for us, the notes resounding powerfully. In the Zendo, the meditation room, before a statue of Buddha, a profound outpouring let loose from the depths of Peter's heart.

Back down the mountain, we nestled in for the night at the North Crestone Creek Campground, site 9, right beside the muscular creek, where the water came gushing down from the mountain, roaring with great force over the huge rocks in its path. Harley eyed the water, but there was no way he could go anywhere near with his bandaged paw still healing. We set our alarm for 5 a.m. We'd rise early and join the zen group for morning meditation.

But sometime during the night, Harley began barking and snarling ferociously at the camper window, his spit foaming and dripping from his bared teeth. We'd never seen him react this viciously to anything before, and we were afraid to see what might be out there in the darkness. Finally with flashlight shining out the partially open window, we looked to see what was causing our dog to try to defend us so fiercely. We saw nothing, but Harley remained alert, growling, and he and Peter kept watch for many hours into the night.

Before I knew it, the alarm went off and I awakened with anticipation. It turned out that Peter hadn't been able to get much sleep, but he was still up for the adventure. With headlights on, our camper made it very slowly back up the difficult road to the Zendo. Japanese lanterns lit the way like beacons, and facing the wall, we sat with a few others in the field of the Buddha's mind.

Later, sunbeams stretched out across the mountains, as we descended back down to our number 9 for some coffee and a campfire breakfast. As we were eating, a guy walked by with his dog, looking pretty stunned. He told us how last night as he'd been camped a short way up the mountain under just a lean-to, his dog had bravely fought off an approaching and threatening bear. He said, "If it weren't for my courageous, faithful friend here, that bear might have gotten me." We shared our experience of last night, relating with new understanding what our resolutely devoted dog had been ready to do to defend us.

What a deep bond between our dogs and us humans, such an enduring loyalty. We felt deeply moved by Harley's valiant, noble nature. He deserved a special treat, in gratitude for his heroism. We'd go find a burger joint and get a big tasty one for him to enjoy. But it didn't look like we'd be finding that burger in this vegetarian town, so we'd have to hit the road!

Back onto 17 North to Salida, a beautiful little town, with just the right place, the 50 Burger restaurant, where we got one of those to-go, for our buddy who wolfed it down before he knew what had happened. Then, finding an RV park right on the Arkansas River, we settled in. What a river! White water tumbled down from the mountains with great force. Harley eyed the river longingly, but no swimming for him. He still had to keep his bandage on for a few more days to let that wound on his back foot heal. He'd have liked to chew the bandage off and lick the wound, but not wanting to subject him to the humiliation of wearing a cone, we just kept a close eye on him to prevent that.

BLUEGRASS FESTIVAL

On 24 North through Buena Vista, a feeling of freedom was in the air. I was singing Willie Nelson's great old song, "On the Road Again", "the life I love is making music with my friends". We were on our way to a music festival!

Onward we went through the old mining town of Leadville, the road riddled with switchbacks and cliffs with sheer drop-offs. Up there at 10,200 feet of elevation it was sleeting, the road getting pretty sketchy. Peter's full attention was on maneuvering the curves, especially by the Eagle River, which gushed by fearfully close to the road. The rivers were all feeling their oats, muscular and pumped up from the spring snowmelt. The mountain pass gave way to a spectacular, dramatic view of the rocky canyon below. Finally, the sleet stopped as 70 West took us to an overlook of Glenwood Canyon, where the Colorado River snaked by, and where we witnessed a monument of sheer, rocky cliffs with pine trees hanging on for dear life under impossible conditions.

As our RV coasted safely into Palisades, we went to check out the site of the weekend's Bluegrass & Roots Festival. The park was poised on the eve of a tidal wave of music and music lovers that would wash over it, starting the next day. Volunteers, wearing their Bluegrass Fest T-shirts, were looking all bright and shiny, ready to do their part to help provide an easy, comfortable space for the whole experience to unfold for everyone. There was a thorough tuning up of fiddle, guitar, and harp back at the campsite at Island Acres that evening, and anticipation was in the air.

Up early the next morning, we nestled our RV into an optimal spot on the festival parking lot, rolled out the awning, and we were in business. Peter was playing his fiddle outside, sitting on one of our gypsy rugs with Harley curled up beside him, while I was in the camper making some egg salad. Right away, a couple came up and introduced themselves, Judy and Ed. She was a fiddler with a classical music background; he was along for the ride. They were staying at a local B&B, Judy explaining, "My husband likes his creature comforts."

Judy returned in a while with her fiddle, and the three of us jammed together. It was clear, she was a bright light and used to performing center stage. She had a presence and confidence, was well-steeped in music, and it just poured forth from her.

We repositioned the camper in a shady spot behind the stage, where what looked like a huge ancient encampment seemed to go on and on. All along the way, musicians were jamming in informal circles, and as I walked Harley by the river, I saw all kinds of campers, some makeshift, some bigger RV's, gypsy tents, and colorful cloths spread out for shade. A sleepy, kind of hung-over atmosphere was in the air, and we discovered that many had been up all night jamming together, playing music until the early morning hours, the beer and wine flowing. There was the music you came to listen to, the professional groups hired to perform during the weekend. Then there was the informal music you played in small enclaves after the big name groups were done. I was still shy on my harp and needed to practice more, but this festival was a real inspiration for me to do so. We joined a jamming circle in which Judy and a guy named Joel were the obvious stars. And there in the circle was a lean, muscular guy looking very familiar. Peter put his finger on it, saying, "Were you camped at the North Rim of the Grand Canyon and played music with us briefly one night? And you were hiking the South Rim the next morning?

"Yep, that was me," answered this taciturn fellow. It was a small world in the camping culture, and we often felt like we'd meet up again with many of the characters that crossed our path.

The professional groups were beginning to play on stage, 45 minutes for each with time for an encore if people clapped long and loud enough. And we did. My favorite was April Verch, a Canadian fiddler with a sweet voice, who did it all: sang, fiddled, clog danced. Peter and I agreed, "This is what we came for", as we headed back to the campground and fell asleep to the sound of the Colorado River flowing on by.

FAIRY DUST OF LOVE

Up early the next morning to go to the workshops that were offered during off times of day, Peter went to April's workshop while I joined a harp workshop. Then there was a long session back at our RV with Judy, her playing, us listening, her talking, us listening. Her husband, Ed, seemed to have made himself scarce today. This was really her scene. Aiming to record Judy's music, Peter caught it all by mistake, as Judy went on about the death of her parents, giving the long, unabridged version. And once again, it was our job to listen, to lend our ears and our hearts.

Returning in time for April's second session, we listened for a while, but Peter had had enough, so we left to return to the campground. I was feeling low energy, kind of done with the whole festival scene, so I walked and walked with Harley along the river path. Hearing a guy playing the banjo, I stopped and we talked about the festival, and he said, "You have to go back tonight and hear the K Brothers. They're something special. You can't miss them."

I roused Peter and insisted we go back. He reluctantly agreed, and was he ever happy he did! The K Brothers were on stage when we returned, looking like monks, the three of them playing their music and exuding love. Their music coming out of their elevated state of consciousness had shifted the energy there that night. Everyone and everything had become imbued with a magical fairy dust of love that these musicians had created. We were deeply touched by the quality of their offering from the heart.

Some children were running and playing in a field of pure enchantment. All the people seemed to be bathed in a soft, entrancing glow. Cottonwood fluffs floated on the breezes, one landing in my cup, one in Peter's hair.

A PEACEFUL EASY FEELING

Peter asked, "Are these eggs cooked in butter?" At Kate's Cafe in Ridgeway, Colorado, was the best breakfast, actually one of many best breakfasts we'd enjoyed at different cafes on our journey across the country. Of course they were, eggs fried in butter just as his mother, Inge, used to make for us on a Sunday morning in her kitchen back in Baltimore, while "Saint Paul Sunday" played classical music on the radio. It was Kate's second anniversary of being open at this restaurant, and we were given slips of paper to write our feedback. We raved, giving our congratulations!

On we drove through Ouray, and then up, up impossible mountain passes to 11,000 feet elevation on snow-topped mountains. Switchbacks, hairpin turns with sheer drop-offs, and then down, down with no guardrails. I couldn't look. Peter was focussed and determined, continuing past Silverton, an old mining town. How on earth was it ever possible to get supplies up to this old town so many years ago? And how were supplies transported there now? Waterfalls were everywhere, streams pouring down from rocky slopes and into the river far below.

Then on the other side of the pass on the steep decline, the RV began to shimmy and shake and we smelled the scent of burning brakes. Fear set in, and we pulled off onto a turn-out. We figured emptying the water that we were carrying in the onboard tank might help to lighten our load and thus be a little easier on the brakes. Peter put the RV into third gear, downshifting as we crept the rest of the descent down the mountain. We were through the worst we hoped, and breathed a sigh of relief. Pulling into Trimble RV Park, we saw right across the road a sign for Trimble Hot Springs. Since on Sunday all service stations were closed, we'd have to take care of our vehicle tomorrow. But for now, it was time to relax and go soak in those hot springs. It felt heavenly, as all the tension and miles soaked away. We loved this restful place where families came for the day, picnicked, and then soaked together. Even the little ones got in the springs. This was all part of the culture here.

Gentle, cool breezes smelled so fresh on this lovely evening at the campground. The Silverton-Durango narrow-gauge train chugged by our campsite, three different times actually. This was the tourist season. I heated up some prepared Indian food in their pouches, and then went to soak again. Later, the campground host came over to schmooze for a while and dropped off a phonebook so we could research the local auto repair shops, the old fashioned way in the yellow pages. Back for one more soak, and I had a peaceful, easy feeling.

HOME BASE

At Bob's Trucks in Durango, we hung out while they
checked our brakes. Peter sat on a log and played his
guitar with the end of Harley's leash looped around his
foot. I walked down the road for two coffees from the gas
station convenience store. It turned out our brakes were
all right -a relief- but they'd overheated. The manager
recommended downshifting when coming down a big
mountain, a pretty basic thing we really might have already known to do, but somehow hadn't done. The walls
in the manager's office were covered with girlie posters,
naked breasts and women in suggestive poses, legs
spread. I felt for the women working there, subjected to
this sexist environment, needing their jobs so tolerating it
anyway.

We got on our way, south on 550 through Aztec, and
back into New Mexico again. Ron the realtor gave a call
and we arranged an appointment to meet next Wednes-
day at 9 a.m. by the Jemez Springs library. Oh dear, here
we were going again! Peter would be flying to Baltimore
on Thursday, so there wouldn't be enough time to get into
serious trouble with Ron. As beautiful as this area was, I
was still on the fence about pursuing a home here, not
even sure that I was ready to end our travels. And if I
were, was this really the right place for us? How would I
know?

Just as we were pulling into Vista Linda, we saw a guy registering, pulling all kinds of stuff out of his car's trunk and one item caught our eye: a guitar case. We made a mental note to visit him later. Getting to know us by now, the campground host told us, "Number 7 was just taken. But no matter, site 8 is good too." As I went to fill our water jugs from the pump, a guy came up and introduced himself as Jack. He and his buddy, Bob, looked like commandos, ready to do whatever it would take to defend whomever. Jack was lean, bare-chested, with tattoos scattered across his arms and shoulders, several silver bracelets lined up on his wrist. He wore a wide choker of Cherokee beads around his neck and from that hung a heavy cross with a snake coiled around it. He explained, "I'm one sixteenth Cherokee, and that snake symbolizes that Christianity has been all screwed up." Jack had a tough, intense look about him, "I was seven years in the Marines. We're the security force and medic for this year's Rainbow Gathering in Cuba, New Mexico, just an hour up the road."

I told them how recently, Peter and I had gone to our first Rainbow Gathering in Cape Hatteras, South Carolina. I didn't tell them how at the end of the day, when the others we'd spent the day cooking and playing music with were camping in the rain, we'd driven our camper out and snuck off to be by ourselves. The ideal behind Rainbow Gatherings was to be together with a diverse group from all over the country, and share resources like a family during the week or two of the gathering, with no capitalistic exchange of money. When new people arrived, you'd always say, "Welcome home".

But Jack told it like it was. "Yeah, it's crazy. Those kids are totally unprepared for the mountains. Some of them don't even have blankets or sleeping bags. They're constantly asking to bum cigarettes and dope. And the no alcohol or narcotics allowed rule, forget it. That's a joke. Some of these kids are always partying, and constantly drunk. Then if they hurt themselves, I have to patch them up or send them out if it's bad enough. I'm an LPN and proud of it, but it's a crazy scene there. Bob and I had to get away for some peace and quiet. We're totally burned out. We'll get some much needed R&R here in this spiritual place, then we'll go get our women and head on back for round two."

Jack's buddy, Bob, was of the Hunter Thompson genre. He was looking pretty grisly and overdue for a shower, the scent of alcohol wafting off his pores. Wearing a crumpled canvas hat and mumbling words under his breath, Bob looked distracted. Every once in a while, I caught part of his commentary. "Yeah, fuckin' crazy, man. Hadda get outta there. Made me nuts." He stopped long enough to light his pipe again and pass it on, absentmindedly thumbing through some New Mexico travel brochures all the while.

Jack informed me, "He reads all about things, but never actually does any of them." Bob, silent, continued to turn the pages, in his own little stoned-out world.

Later, we were drawn over to meet Tony at #7, where he was playing his guitar, sitting on a stool facing the river. Peter asked, "Hey, man, can I bring my guitar over and jam with you a while?"

"Yeah man, sure. Cool. Gotta tell you, though, I just saw "Across the Universe" with the Beatles and all, and I was so moved, I got tears over it. But since I'm from California, it's OK to cry."

Peter and Tony looked for some common musical ground, Tony definitely taking the lead with some Beatles songs, then blues and some slide guitar. They finally got in the groove and began to sound good, but I was content to simply listen this time.

We could see that Tony had only a canvas cot with blankets spread out to sleep on that night. "Yeah, man, my wife split. I got suicidal, went for psychotherapy. She called later and asked if she could come back. But my therapist said, 'Hell no, don't take her back. You can't trust her anymore.' So now I'm just looking to find some women. I mean I'd always like to have sex. I just want to have fun. I'm going up to the hot springs now, see if I can meet some honey there tonight."

And so it went at Vista Linda Campground that evening, our temporary home base in the red rock valley under a sky full of stars. There was something I really loved about this place, a quality of feeling at home, a growing familiarity and restfulness. Harley gave a deep sigh. Maybe he felt it too. After six months on the road, we could do worse than to settle here.

JOHN AND PHYLOS

The Highway 4 Cafe delivered some good chai and quiche in the morning, informing us, "We make all our own pastries right here." We sat at an outside table with Harley who was happily crunching away on one of the free dog biscuits they offered while we ate. There was a community dog bowl of water also, but really, he was most interested in what was on our plates, and was alert for any stray crumbs that fell. And of course, we saw to it that some did!

On our way back to the campground, an old van parked nearby caught our eye. Messages were painted all over the van, as well as an *I Ching* hexagram, #13 Fellowship with Men. The van read: "In the year 2012 the Mississippi River will split leaving a gorge 2 miles deep and 20-30 miles wide. Vietnam Nam War Veteran 1964-1967." This got our attention and Peter called out, "You throw the *I Ching?* So do we!"

A man's face appeared at the van window, with a long white beard, long white hair pulled into a ponytail, and the sweetest eyes. A gentle soul, we could tell. "Yes I have, for many years", and he held up a well-worn yellow book bound together with duct tape.

Peter called out, "Let's throw it together now, want to?"

And out from the van emerged what looked like a visionary man, John, and his son Phylos. I thought Phylos was a girl at first, until I saw the peach fuzz on his sweet young face. "I've gotten the same messages over and over again lately," John said. "The *I Ching* tells me to be peaceful and cheerful, and even though satanic forces are after me, I'm just remaining peaceful and cheerful." I let that part about the satanic forces just pass on by, without asking.

We all gathered, sitting on the ground at the park and took turns throwing the three pennies. John told us, "We've been on the road living in this van for so many years now. It's a hard path sometimes. Sleeping in different places, you never know who might come by in the middle of the night and ask you to move on. But Mrs. Minter has been so kind. She gives out food at the church. And then I'll go down and meditate at the Zen Center, and Hosen is so sweet".

It turned out that the hexagram we'd thrown was "Providing Nourishment", and it seemed like that was right on target. These people could use some food. I got two cans of beans, some rice and some grapes from our RV and brought that out to give to them.

"Oh thank you! This is so wonderful, so good." We all shared some of the grapes, and John said, "I really want to clean my body out and raise my vibration."

We told them to come to campsite 8 at Vista Linda that evening, and we'd all sit around the campfire together. When they arrived, I realized that there was a nice piece of salmon in our fridge, enough for all of us. That, with some couscous and broccoli, and it was a good dinner. Tony wandered over, and joined us, and then Jack and Bob also. Somehow, like the fishes and the bread in the Bible, it was enough for everyone. There was a wonderful spirit of camaraderie among this odd collection of people gathered together around the campfire there that night at number 8. I thought of the Rainbow Gathering and realized we were providing nourishment to this very diverse and wonderful family who had come here from all around the country. Welcome home, brothers.

The next morning on the way to meet with Ron, we saw John and Phylos parked by the library. When we went by to say hello, they said they'd be moving on that day. Phylos pulled us aside, saying, "I have a little something I want to give you two. You've been so kind." He opened a small box, and inside were three tiny jewels of different colors. "My mother gave these to me before she died, and I want you guys to have one of them."

We felt so touched and told him, "These are very special and have so much meaning for you. We're really moved that you'd want to give us one, but these belong with you. Your mother gave them to you."

He insisted, it seemed very important to him, so we finally agreed to take one. He gave us the amethyst wrapped in a piece of cotton, and I took it in my hand, "until we find a proper place to keep it safe." We hugged them both good-bye, this beautiful, courageous, big-hearted father and son on the road of life together in their van.

ON MY OWN WITH HARLEYDOG

The *I Ching* advised us with hexagram 43, Breakthrough, Resoluteness."Serenely cheerful, remain calm and resolute." Over breakfast at the Frontier Restaurant, we examined the options of the Mark Feldman house on Madrid Road, and the earth ship house on Vista Hermosa that we'd seen with Ron. We flip-flopped back and forth, but there was nothing else to do right then. This decision wasn't urgent. I'd be driving Peter to the airport that morning, and the sadness of saying good-bye enveloped me, as well as some vague anxiety over driving the RV and managing it all. We'd been acting as a team on the journey together all day, every day for all those months. And now for around a week or so, I'd be on my own with my buddy Harley for company. Remaining cheerful, calm, and resolute, I said good-bye, hugged Peter close, and telling him "I love you so much", dropped him off at the Albuquerque airport.

Driving on to Santa Fe, I tried to stop at Trader Joe's, but the parking lot was too full, with no spot where I could easily pull through and not have to back up after shopping. So forget shopping. I went to park the RV on the lot we'd parked in once before in Santa Fe, a perfect place, pull-through when leaving so I could relax about that. Backing up in the RV could be tricky as it wasn't always possible to have a clear view of what was behind. The lot was right across from the Santa Fe River, actually just a trickling stream, with a nice path where I could walk Harley later. But right then, we walked down to the plaza, where there was a free bench for me to sit and call my friend Jenny. Dog-lovers stopped to pat Harley, and one guy even wanted to take his picture, so Harley posed, looking very perky for him.

The afternoon stretched out, and with Harley back in the RV and curtains closed, I stopped for an early dinner at the Plaza Cafe, then bought a bottle of wine from a near-by shop. With some of it poured into an incognito to-go cup, Harley and I relaxed in the breezes at the park across the street. It actually felt good to be on my own, with only myself to please, and Harley too, of course. I decided to sleep there, right there in the RV parking lot. Why not? I was making my own choices with no one else to consider for now. How luxurious! And by the way, who was I? What did I really want? What did I really enjoy? I hadn't been alone like this to take stock of things for many months. I felt really thankful for the opportunity to kind of tune back in to myself and my own needs.

Sleeping in the parking lot was a little weird at first, though. Like John and Phylos, I wasn't sure if someone would come by in the middle of the night, knock on my door and say to clear out. But as the night wore on and I got up to go to the bathroom, I had confidence that this was working out fine. Derek called in the middle of the night, early morning his time. I was too groggy to talk much, but still it was so sweet to hear his voice, and knowing that he was thinking of me helped me feel less alone. I loved him always.

As the light from the street lamp snuck in past the RV window shade, I moved my pillow to shade my eyes until morning. My buddy Harley was curled up beside me, trusting completely, never wondering why or how.

HARLEY'S FAN CLUB

I woke up knowing that yes, the Feldman house on
Madrid Road was a gift and we would receive it gracious-
ly. Leave it in the hands of the angels. No worries, mate.
Maybe it was time to settle. Meditation was good that
morning, even while the road crew worked on the parking
lot outside the RV. Harley and I remained hidden inside
until it was time to emerge from our secret overnight there
and into the light of day. No one was the wiser.

   We walked down on Alameda for a cup of coffee to go,
and I tied Harley to a tree outside while I went in to get it.
He barked for me like a big old baby, and a guy offered to
sit with him until I came back out. Harley got a good
scratch behind the ears from the guy, and when I returned
I could see a fan club had gathered around him and he'd
been drinking up all the attention and love.

   Down near the Plaza, I sat on a bench in a courtyard
and talked with my sister, Janie, for a long time. People
passed by, dog lovers would pat Harley and ask to take
his picture. All the while I talked on with my sister, Harley's
adoring public lavished attention on him. Then I took him
back to the shady RV to rest on his laurels. I went to roam
the stores, buy some wine cups, stop in my favorite little
import store with all the textiles and statues from Asia,
and say hello to the friendly Guatemalan guy who worked
there. He always brought his big white Great Pyrenees

dog to spend the day with him. A gentle soul, the dog lay peacefully on his bed in the shop and gazed benevolently on all who entered. It was a dreamy day in Santa Fe, heavenly and slow-paced.

I had a long talk on the phone with my friend Vicki as I drove on into Bernalillo, Harley lying on the bed in the back. At the Coronado Campground, I dumped the RV's gray and black water and added some more water to the onboard tank. When Peter called, he was proud of me. Those maintenance tasks had always been his job to take care of. Pulling into Vista Linda just in time to get the last good site, number 9, the single woman, who was me, camping with her dog. It was a lazy afternoon, Harley cavorting in the water while I sat on a big rock right in the middle of the river and caught sight of a Native American family upstream. Three young children squealed with delight in the water as their parents sat nearby in lawn chairs, the river washing over their feet. The red rock mesas stood by and bore witness to it all.

The Griswold family was camping next to me that evening. I could hear every word they said in their loud voices. It was kind of humorous to listen, though they did seem to be having lots of problems. Everything was an issue: putting up the tents, building the campfire, roasting the marshmallows. All of it sparked discussion and great controversy. Straight out of *National Lampoon*, this family had it all down.

The single woman camping with her dog built a campfire, and ate some tofu and salad at the picnic table. With some wine in one of the new cups, she lingered by the fire until the moon rose over the mesa and bathed all in the encampment with its silvery light.

FEELING RIGHT AT HOME

Waking up at Vista Linda Campground once again, I got a little tangled up in real estate decision/indecision. It would be a big leap to move here, and making that commitment felt kind of scary right then. I consulted the oracles, but the *I Ching* never really gives definitive advice, and neither do the tarot cards. They both advised me to give it time, and so be it. No decision needed to be made right then. There was a light rain on the RV roof, and I was feeling a little lonely, but it was all OK.

I drove to the base of Madrid Road, parked, and walking up near the house, I took some pictures, but did no intensive snooping. Still a question: was this the right time and place? Did we need this right now? What would the future repercussions be?

Leaving these mental wranglings behind, I went onward to the library for some emailing and who should be there but John and Phylos. They'd lost their dog, Noble, and I offered to help them look. But they were exuding equanimity, saying, "We've looked and now if it's God's will..." I wished them well and hoped for the best.

Big dark clouds were hanging heavy in the sky, releasing a few drops of rain from time to time. "The whole village is wondering," remarked the librarian. "It's the talk of the town. Will it clear in time for the music festival tonight?"

Harley and I walked to the post office, where our first

piece of mail awaited us in the PO Box. I'd tied him up outside while I got the mail, but he began barking for me to come back. What was it like for him, having to wait for me, not knowing when I'd be back? We walked together back to the library, and there in the painted van, Noble the dog was at the window. It *was* God's will!

Harley romped on the grass in the park with a chocolate lab, Kelly, and a herder, Glory. Kelly and Harley, both retrievers, were all about chasing sticks, while Glory reeled around them trying her best to corral them. They spoke different dog languages, but it seemed to work out well for all of them anyway. Harley, panting, lapped up water from a bowl and lay down, spent. Now I'd be able to leave him with a clear mind while at the festival. He'd sleep on the bed in the RV, feeling secure there and ready for a rest.

The festival was small but still had a good enough turnout, and thankfully the sun made an appearance and the sky was clearing. Kelly's owners turned to go. They didn't have the cash with them. I offered to pay for them, but they said "That's OK. We really should get going anyway."

"I'm sorry," I offered, but they seemed decided.

A cup of local wine in hand, I talked with the proud parents of the festival's emcee, and then with a drummer who'd spent 12 years on the road touring and was happy to be living now in Santa Fe. He was teaching at the Hummingbird Music Camp up the road, where children from all around the country could come to learn to play a musical instrument or to further their skill. Mark and Dede Feldman called me over to their table and invited me to join them. They were natural, easy to be with, and kindly asked me to come to their home for breakfast the next morning.

The sun went down behind the mesa, the air grew cool as dusk gradually settled in. One of the performers, Ricca, was pacing back and forth, becoming increasingly anxious as they'd changed the schedule and kept bumping her later and later. We all tried to reassure her, it'll be okay, but that was easy for us to say. I listened as the groups were sounding better and better; the crowd was enthusiastic. I joined in with the spirit of the little Jemez community, feeling right at home, just like a local myself. The crowd had thinned a bit, and at last I pulled away also, though still no Ricca. My heart went out to her. I walked back in the dark to where I'd parked my lonely RV and to Harley, waiting faithfully inside.

We drove back to the campsite and what a surprise. Someone else had camped there in my spot, a young couple with their tent and their car. I decided there was no point in making a big deal out of it. I got the blankets and the leash from the picnic table, telling them it was all right while they apologized defensively. "The girls said you'd left..." I pulled in behind them and closed the curtains for the night. I felt so thankful for the companionship of Harley, stretched out right beside me on the bed.

golds, and to witness the 50 million stars
ly appeared in the vast sky above. Lister
of the water washing on by, my angst an
dissolve into the darkness of the night.

MARK AND DEDE

I gathered my forces to dispel the clouds of loneliness
and fear. The tarot cards had a message of strength for
me that morning:
The Emperor: indicates a fearless visionary, strength tem-
pered with compassion.
Seven of Wands: represents courage, standing your
ground, inner strength and conviction.
Two of Wands: standing for independence and dominion.
Many possible futures.

That was so true, at this point there were many possible
futures for Peter and me. We really didn't know how
things would play out. But I had plenty of inner strength,
courage, independence, and compassion to help along
the way.

The tarot cards had spoken to me, and I took their wisdom along with me to breakfast at Mark and Dede's
home. First off, courage was required just to drive the RV
up the impossibly steep and rutted dirt road and then find
a place to park near their home. Yikes, I breathed deep,
and gave it my best shot, arriving at their home wiping the
sweat from my forehead. Pulling the shades and leaving
the fan on for Harley, I could see the couple standing on
their front porch, and wondered if they'd witnessed my
tortuous parking job.

Mark seemed a little quiet at first and I didn't know if

maybe he'd have preferred a more so
Dede's ebullience more than made up
them with some campground stories
family and the commandos from the I
We discussed politics, the *New Yorke*
we loved it, and I asked them about tl
Dede was a New Mexico State Senat
of stories to tell. And Mark had been i
for many years. In fact, he designed a
we were considering. We went for a s
relaxed and congenial together; I enjc
them. We had found some fun comm(
shared some laughter. Thanking them
inviting me, I departed, saying a mant
down the rough, bumpy road.

Back at the campground, Fred, the
had saved number 7 for me, even mo
and leash from last night's site. So sw
really looking out for me, plus he migh
responsible for the campsite confusio
went for a swim, chasing sticks I threv
enough, though he continued to nose
It was a lonely evening. I made a cam
friend Harley curled up beside me on '

And then who should drop by but M
vited them to stay, but they were on tr
and kindly handed me a stack of *New*
of oranges. As they drove away, I won
pretty sad, kind of grimy and road wor
dog. I was filled with questions, wond(
ing with my life, asking myself if this w
road was worthwhile or meaningful. O
was still amazing to be feeling free, to
clouds painted with glorious sunset co

DENITA

I spread out my purple yoga mat on the picnic table and
practiced up there while Harley splashed around in the
river on his long leash. The *I Ching* gave its counsel to
burn through obstacles with joy. OK, I'd take it on faith
and was ready to get going. Down at the village park, I
threw balls for Harley on the nice grassy lawn, then made
a stop at the Forest Service office for a good topo-
graphical map of the Jemez area.

Driving north on Highway 4 to La Cueva, I found a place
to do a surreptitious dump of gray water in the overgrowth
by the side of the road. I was sorry, but it seemed there
was no where else to do it. In Los Alamos, I was stopped
at the gate while they conducted a search of the RV.

"Please step out of the vehicle and take the dog. Do
you have any firearms or explosives on board?"

I assured them I didn't, but they conducted a ten minute
search anyway. The Los Alamos National Laboratory was
where nuclear warheads were produced, where nuclear
waste was stored. Many people strongly objected to
these activities and over the past years, antinuclear protestors had often demonstrated against LANL. So I could
have been one of those protestors or even a terrorist,
coming here with my vicious golden retriever to plant a
bomb or blow up a lab with explosives. Which wouldn't
have been too smart given that nuclear materials were
stored here. What else wasn't too smart was storing

nuclear waste anywhere on the fault line of geothermal instability here, where an earthquake could happen at any time. While waiting for the search to be done, I got a call from Peter who was just passing across Tennessee. His nephew, Winston, was riding with him, having never had the chance to visit the southwest before. I'd be so happy to see them whenever they arrived!

I was finally given the go-ahead and was so glad to get out of this kind of creepy place. I headed into Bandelier National Monument's Juniper Campground, site 90, next to a woman named Denita who approached me right away as I drove in.

"Are you going to be running your generator? I had to leave the campsite I was at yesterday, the generators were driving me crazy. I'm here working on a project, a change of life course kind of thing, and I just need some peace and quiet so I can concentrate on my life choices."

I assured her I didn't plan to run my generator, I liked peace and quiet too.

When I returned from registering at the ranger's office, Denita had left me a note on the table apologizing and re-stating her case, signing it "from the campground witch". I went over to reassure her that I knew what it was like to have to listen to other people's generators all evening. The loud sound was intrusive.

"I'm from Santa Fe," she began, "and I'm going through a life crisis. I've had a lot of them so far, and this is always my haven; I've always come here to connect with myself and nature. I'll spare you the details, but there was a messy divorce." She actually did not spare me many de-tails. She must have somehow known that I'd been a psychiatric nurse and had a compassionate listening ear. "My husband and I used to always come here together.

We had a '74 Airstream, and I made it beautiful inside. We brought our children here. I was a campground host for two summers. And then there was a big fire, the Cerro Grande, in 2000, when 43,000 acres were destroyed around here. It was heartbreaking. I just don't understand this world. There's so much that's beautiful, and then everything goes screwy. Who can figure it? Just when you think you have a handle on things, everything changes. It's so tricky to navigate." Denita paused a moment to take a sip from what I assumed was her water bottle, but no. "I'm so embarrassed. I'm drinking white wine in the middle of the afternoon. Honestly, I don't usually do this, but I felt like a character in *Out of Africa*. I promise I won't drink all day..."

"I'll come back and join you for a glass," I said, "but first I'll just get settled in and then I'll stop back over." But when I returned later, she was nowhere around. So I took Harley for a walk on the overlook trail, through the ponderosa pine forest, and up to see a view of the ruins. It ended up being a longer hike than I'd thought, and I just had some little rubber shoes on, but oh well. Dogs weren't allowed on the trails down by the ruins, but I could see well enough from up on the path. There was a circular village of ruins, and caves in the wall of rock where the Ancestral Pueblo people had lived around 500 years ago. It's thought that they'd exhausted the resources around the area and had had to move on, leaving behind their dwellings. Now these archaeological ruins were clues to what their culture and life had been like.

Later, I made a great supper of shrimp salad, which I'd have loved to share, but still no Denita. After dark, she finally emerged, saying, "I got a terrible sinus headache from drinking in the heat of the day. I had to lie down in my tent, but it was like a sauna in there."

"I'm so sorry, Denita. You would've been welcome to lie down in my RV. We could have turned the generator on with the A/C!" The humor appeared to be lost on Denita, but she seemed to be operating at a deficit so I just let it go. We made a plan to hike together the next day.

"First," she said, "I'll have to go into Los Alamos for a cup of coffee. Then I'll see you when I get back". She crawled back into her tent, and I into my RV to curl up beside Harleydog, my faithful pal. Even though we'd only been able to connect briefly, I still felt comforted just knowing that another lone woman was camped beside me that night.

REPAIRING MY NETS

Feeling so alone and missing Peter, I was really thankful
for the companionship of my four-legged friend Harley. I
spoke out loud to him, saying, "When they can't fish, fish-
ermen repair their nets." The philosophical subtlety of this
might have been lost on him, since Harley pretty much
only knew a few words that were particularly salient in his
life. They included: go for a walk, wanna go swimming,
how about some dog food, want a tasty, and sit. He
perked up his ears at most all those words, but usually
chose to ignore that last one. Anyway, I was using this
alone time to repair my emotional nets. It was okay to
travel by myself for a while, but I often had to make an effort to burn through a feeling of low-grade anxiety that was
there in the background. What was it about? Just some
sort of existential thing about separation, feeling separate? The only thing I could identify that felt really meaningful in life was love, the experience of love. Love is all
there is, as the Beatles sang it. To live a life of loving service. To just *be* love, and let life manifest as it would from
there. Harley looked up at me just then; I was pretty sure
he got it.

Okay, so it was 11 a.m. and Denita had been gone for
coffee almost two hours. Should I wait for her, or say
"swaha", as the Brahmin priests used to chant when

sacrificing ghee or sacred herbs into the ceremonial fire. OK, question answered. She was returning with coffee stains all down her T-shirt. "I'm so embarrassed!" We talked and talked for a couple of hours, all about spirituality and the unfolding of our lives. Harley heaved a big sigh, and I offered him a biscuit to see him through. "We're soul sisters," we exclaimed. It was so comforting to connect with another woman, to feel simpatico, like we spoke a little of the same kind of language and understood each other. Denita gave me a jug of spring water, saying, "Remember me when you drink and say a prayer for me." I gave her the Peruvian noise maker I'd gotten from the import store in Santa Fe. "To scare off evil spirits," I told her.

She gave me a sage stick to smudge with, "Someone gave this to me, but I want you to have it." We exchanged email and phone info and hugged each other, and then pulling up her tent, she took off for her counseling session in Santa Fe. I waved to her goodbye for now. Who knew? Maybe we'd meet up in Santa Fe for dinner sometime.

OK, now what? Intuition told me to turn left on Highway 4, but whoops, I turned right instead toward White Rock. Searching there for a laundromat proved fruitless. Looked like I was going to have to go back to Los Alamos. And back to the security guards at the gates, but thankfully they didn't pull me over for a search this time. Still, there was such a strange feeling in Los Alamos, since the place had been so steeped in military secrets and covert goings on. During the time of the Manhattan Project, the scientists working on the bomb couldn't even tell their wives or families what their jobs were really all about.

At the visitor's center, they were unable to tell me where a laundromat was. Must have been top secret. I Googled and finally found one nearby. Dark clouds were moving in across the sky, and I was tempted to just forget the whole laundry thing. What was it about this place? Los Alamos was advertised as a great place to visit, with museums and restaurants, but it was all I could do just to get my laundry done. I couldn't wait to leave! Driving around the parking lot I finally found a user-friendly pull-though spot, and hauled my laundry on in.

When at last it was done, I was so happy to get out of there and back to site 90 at Bandolier. I ate a little something and went for a hike with Harley under threatening skies. I was actually happy for those dark clouds, which somehow felt just right that day. Later, I played my harp as the storm approached, then took cover inside with a good book. My faithful dog curled up beside me on the bed. The candle flickered, then died out for the night.

POT OF GOLD

The *I Ching* counseled, "Have faith. You are not alone. You are not forgotten." Wow, that sounded really good to me on that lonely morning. I pulled up stakes and went down the road to the Ponderosa Trail, where Harley and I started out for a hike. The parking lot by the trail was empty, and no one else was around on the path. We walked for just around 30 minutes, then a chill went down my spine and I had the thought, what if a bear would approach us, or a mountain lion? Or what if I fell and twisted an ankle? Who would even have known we were here? I did have faith that I was not alone or forgotten, but that didn't mean I should venture out on this trail alone. No. I turned back around, Harley in tow.

We went on down the mountain back to our familiar homey Vista Linda. My favorite number 7 wasn't available, but site 10 would do just fine. I went into the village, no mail was waiting at the post office, and the library informed me I couldn't get a card without a local address. I had wanted to take out a book of Tony Hillerman's, the New Mexican author who'd written many fun detective novels about the Navajo Tribal Police. But it was a no-go there. My campground address didn't convince the Jemez Springs Public Library. Picking up some supplies from the Trail Store, a nearby convenience store catering to campers and locals, I settled in at site number 10. Fred, the campground host, stopped by to say hi. He'd dropped his wife off at the Albuquerque Airport and was also a loner for a while. He let me know that once the couple picnicking at number 12 left, I could pull into that site which was a little nicer. It felt good that he knew me and was looking out for me. And this place was beginning to feel like home.

I tried to get my two options in mind, either buy the house and declare a new life or let it go and travel some more. Was I afraid of making the wrong choice? Afraid of taking a leap into the unknown? It was clear to me that trying to figure it out, or making lists of pro's and con's would not deliver a satisfying answer. Maybe that process was a necessary step along the way, but making a big life choice did not come from only the rational mind. I knew that for myself, the choice must come from a deeper place within, of certainty. I trusted that when the time came, I'd know.

I took Harley with me to dinner on the porch outside the Laughing Lizard. It seemed the owner of the restaurant was a dog lover and allowed them on the porch, a dog bowl of water nearby. A family joined me. The father had been a pilot with United, the mother very friendly, and their son seemed like a nice kid. Dad kept saying, "Son, when I went to Wyoming...," and "Son, there's a book about..." and "Son, would you go inside and ask them for some coffee?" Son would be going into the eighth grade in the fall and wanted to be a wildlife manager. "We're considering home schooling our son in the fall," the father explained. "There's so much homework we have to help him with already. Right, Son? We figure we might as well do the whole thing." I asked Son what he'd think of that plan, and he looked at his father a moment before answering. "Yeah, I guess maybe that'd be OK." They told me they were out for a drive today, would stop by the

Valles Caldera, then go back to their home in Albuquerque.

"I'm out for lunch and going back to my home at Vista Linda Campground," I answered.

The air became cooler. Dark storm clouds threatened rain. Back at the campground, after relocating to number 12, I lit the sage stick that Denita had given me. It burned away on a plate, purifying the atmosphere in the RV according to Native American tradition, and, I hoped, purifying my busy mind as well. And then, the storm clouds let loose. Harley crawled under the RV to hide from the thunder and got soaked. I played my harp under the shelter while the wind moved through the strings, creating what's called an Aeolian Harp, with all the strings playing at once and sounding like the voice of heaven. And then a perfect double rainbow appeared, spreading out huge across the mesa in all its splendor. Hmm...maybe our pot of gold lay right here in Jemez Springs.

MORE THAN ENOUGH

Oh yay! Peter would be getting back to New Mexico that day and would meet me there at number 12. Of course, I still didn't know what to do, what really felt right to me. We were at a crossroads, and somehow I felt the ball was in my court. The Madrid Road house could be a burden or a gift. It just depended on how I looked at it. What I was really looking for was a feeling of freedom and that would only come from inside, not necessarily from our outer circumstances. Could I feel free while buying a house? That'd take some work, as making a major monetary commitment doesn't always feel so freeing. In the end, I still trusted that I'd know what to do when the time came.

I went for coffee at the Highway 4 Cafe, and sat out on the porch, talking with some locals. There was Judy, who lived on Madrid Road, Emma and Joe who rented nearby, and Glo who lived across the road from the earth ship house. And Randy, the dog. He and Harley met and sniffed each other, then settled. We talked about land, who lived where, the different qualities of the various areas around the village. I let them know we were considering buying on Madrid Road. Emma suggested, "Maybe you should rent first." Judy said, "I've noticed when people are attracted to this place, they do eventually move here." Joe commented, "This place has so many artists, musicians, sculptors. I'm just a regular guy; I have no special talents. I don't know what I'm doing here." Judy let me know there was a good parcel of land for sale right now.

Just then, I looked up and there came Peter with his nephew, Winston! I hadn't expected to see him until later in the day. What a great surprise! It had been a golden morning, and I felt shot-through with good energy. I'd felt so wonderful and relaxed, sitting and talking with the group of locals. And now Peter was here!

We embraced. I introduced him and Winston to the group, and then we left for Vista Linda to get them settled in. Peter was remarkably energetic, given the long hours of driving that he'd been doing to get back as soon as possible. It felt great to be together again! We both had lots of stories to tell. And Harley was so happy to see Peter again. He wiggled and waggled and brought his prize tennis ball over to Peter, but of course, wouldn't let go of it. I made some dinner. We ate around the campfire. I was just going with it for now, forgetting all about the question of what would be next. This right here was more than enough!

THE JOY OF THE WEEKEND

We were kind of treading water, which was fine with me. I was able to buy some time while I was trying to see what'd be called for next. Derek had told me "Do what you need to to make yourself happy, Mom" and that sounded like great advice.

And what made me happy that day was the beautiful walk we all took together on the Las Conchas trail. The scenery was idyllic, with ponderosa pines and open grassy meadows, butterflies fluttering by in the sunlight, and huge rock walls looking as if they'd been poured like sandcastles or molded roughly out of clay. Harley was off-leash, tail held high, running in and out of the stream that ran by the length of the trail, romping free in his own version of heaven, as were we. Peter said, "I could just die here. This is a place you could just let go and transcend in." We followed the trail as it wound along over wooden bridges beautifully built over the stream, then past forested areas, and back again over the stream. Harley was hesitant to walk across the bridges, but quite contentedly splashed across the stream each time we crossed above. Winston was so happy to be there with us and thanked us again and again for bringing him to this magical place where we all became lost in time. I had the feeling that bobcats, mountain lions, and bears could be hovering up on the rocky cliffs, maybe looking over us silently from their perch above. But I didn't say anything about this to

Winston. He wasn't used to the wilderness areas out west.

And then, somehow it was time to turn around and come back, back to the world of time and thought. Back to the campground for beans and rice with sour cream and hot sauce, some salad, a cup of red wine, a campfire, a game of Scrabble. Winston ventured out to talk with the commandos at their campsite. He returned sometime later, all enthused about the Rainbow Gathering, which they'd told him about. He admitted to us that he'd smoked a little pipe with them, and we accepted this without making a big deal out of it, although we were pretty sure he was being exposed to influences that his parents might not have been so happy about. Perhaps he'd been kind of protected during his life, or maybe he just had a natural kind of innocence or sense of caution. The campground was alive that night with the sounds of laughter, and the joy of the weekend.

WINSTON'S GREAT ADVENTURE

This was to be the day for Winston's Great Adventure: Peter would take him to the Rainbow Gathering in Cuba, New Mexico, about an hour's drive north of Vista Linda. Winston had been inspired to venture forth for this new experience by his conversation with Bob and Jack, the commandos who worked as security team at the gathering. The content of this conversation we didn't exactly know, just that it had been laced with a liberal smoking of weed and had left Winston convinced to go experience it for himself. This was really pushing the envelope for Winston. I guessed that he'd usually been in pretty homogeneous company in his life up until then. He'd be bound to get an education at the gathering, but Peter was fearful it'd be too much of an education. Peter had visions of having to call his brother, Winston's father, and having to explain to him how his son came to have had a bad acid trip while at a gathering with a bunch of Rastafarians and hippies. But Winston was intent on going and his uncle had promised to get him there. And back. In one coherent piece, we hoped.

They gathered together all the necessary supplies, sleeping bag, tent, some food, change of clothes, sunscreen, and bug spray, in case. I hugged Winston and wished him a wonderful adventure and please be careful, won't you? And don't take anything strange or unknown, OK? Waving good-bye as they took off, I figured it might be a few days until I'd see them again, and as there might not be any cell reception, I wouldn't know how safely things were going for a while.

I gathered Harley into the camper, and we headed over to the village park for some ball throwing, two ball method of course, and then over to the cafe for a cup of chai. It was a quiet scene there, so getting the chai to go, my four-legged friend and I returned back to the campsite.

Thoughts of house or no house began to wrestle around in my mind, as I sat on the picnic table and tried to quiet down. And just then, my mother's presence began to wash over me, so real, bringing a feeling of peace and well-being that permeated everything. It was as if she was telling me, "All is well. Just relax and trust." Those comforting words felt so good to me, I drank them in deeply. I felt so thankful to be able feel her calming presence nearby.

I was hoping those words of reassurance would also apply to Peter and Winston and the rainbow event. One of the big fears in this extremely dry desert area was the very real possibility of a forest fire being started by the unconscious flick of a live cigarette butt or the careless campfire built during windy conditions. Things that were more likely to happen at a large gathering of young people who maybe would not be used to taking precautions and who might not be having all their wits about them. I'd go with the feelings of peace and well-being and trust, that'd be what my mind would focus on.

It was a quiet afternoon at the campground. I got to talking with Frank and Paul, two guys who'd been traveling together in their trailer for three years. They loved life on the road, and it turned out that they knew Andy, the guy we'd met with 550 DVD's in his Lazydaze camper. Small world. Just then, I looked up and who should be driving up to the campsite but Peter and Winston.

"Back so soon? What happened?" I asked. They looked happy enough, so it couldn't have been too bad.

"Come on, I'll make some tea and you can tell me all about it."

We gathered at the picnic table and they proceeded to tell the saga of the Rainbow Gathering. As they'd approached the gathering, the only way in had been on a one-way, 23-mile dirt road that was totally muddy due to lots of recent rain in that area. Peter related, "Thankfully, there was no danger of forest fire. Everyone and everything was soaked. As we kept driving along with the windows down, small bands of people would wave, and smiling, greeted us with 'Welcome home, brother'".

"Yeah, I loved that part," added Winston. "It was so cool! But it was raining and all and I didn't feel like getting soaked and having to spend the night like that. But it was so great to see everyone, so many people there!"

Apparently, everyone had been looking a bit bedraggled, as they'd walked along in the drizzle, with their dreadlocks, face piercings, tattoos, and tie-dye T-shirts. They all had seemed friendly and in good spirits though, and Peter said that a decided scent of weed had wafted in through the open car windows.

"But we just couldn't seem to find a good place to pull over and park," Peter continued. "All along the road were steep, muddy hillsides, where cars were precariously parked, with no room for another to safely squeeze in the lineup. We thought maybe we'd find a spot up ahead. So we just had to keep driving slowly along, taking in the whole flavor of the gathering from the road."

Mile after mile they drove, and Peter later told me he'd asked Winston if he'd like to be dropped off, but no,

316

he seemed quite happy just to keep on driving, viewing the scene from the safety of the car. Peter thought maybe there'd been an academic quality to his contentment with not getting too up close and personal, like he'd really only wanted to observe and learn. A kind of sociological study.

"Anyway, all of a sudden, there we were at the end of the 23-mile road with no way to turn around and go back. I asked Winston if he'd like to give it another try, but we were both ready to just come on back here."

"How are you feeling about it, Winston? Are you at all disappointed?" I asked.

"Oh no, Aunt Susan, I really had a good time. It was so much fun! And interesting, too. I loved it!"

"OK great. Are you guys hungry, how about some dinner?"

We ate at the picnic table, and then played a couple of games of Scrabble into the evening until it was too dark to see anymore. We all turned in early, so satisfied with this educational day of Winston's Excellent Adventure.

IN THE DARK OF THE NIGHT

We woke up to a beautiful sunny morning. The air was cool and smelled fresh with a hint of fall. Gentle breezes moved through the cottonwoods, their leaves flickering in the sunlight. A huge blue sky was dashed lightly with some wisps of clouds. Peter was playing his guitar. Winston was showering in our RV, the sound of his flip-flops slapping around in the bathroom somehow felt so comforting to me. I loved having Winston here with us for a while. I really enjoyed being around his youthful openness.

Harley was on his leash, tangled as usual around the picnic table, but not complaining. I asked for a sign from the angels, or the universe, or some benevolent part of my own self. "Please give me a sign about this house. I'm on the alert for some sense of certainty. Thank you, dear angels, we are in limbo here, waiting on some clarity." I discovered a beautiful message from Derek on my phone, sending love, so sweet, it warmed my fearful heart and helped me relax. OK, thank you, that was a sign, right there. Fear not. All is well.

Some lovely people were camped next to us. Regina, the grandmother of three dear children, was a lover of Eagles' songs and karaoke. And Frank, a modest soul who played guitar with Peter until late. Winston was fearful in his tent, as someone had told him that a mountain lion had been spotted recently on the mesa up from this campground. Winston wasn't used to being in the wilds of the West, and he had a cautious nature. Peter and I felt protective of him, and of course wanted to help him feel safe. I tried to calm his fears, but wasn't sure it helped. In the end, all of us are alone with our fears in the dark of the night.

And high in the sky, a quarter moon shone, playing hide-and-seek behind some clouds as I headed for bed.

HARSH YET SOFT

At Santa Fe for the day, Peter set up in the plaza with his fiddle and Shruti box. With Harley at his feet under the bench, Peter opened his fiddle case for donations, and he was in business. There were lots of tourists and we hoped they'd appreciate the music and be generous.

Winston and I walked to the Georgia O'Keeffe Museum and really got in to her paintings there. She never realized that she'd been looking for her spiritual home until she came to New Mexico where the land really spoke to her. She wrote, "It's harsh, the desert, but it's also soft." I could really see the truth of that. The sun was strong at this elevation, and cactus, junipers and cedars were about the some of the only plants that could make it in the high desert at 6,600 feet. But there was also the softness of the chamisa and apache plume bushes that could survive here as well. Would I be able to survive and thrive here in this desert land, so dry and distant from the ocean? Would I find New Mexico to be harsh as well as soft with me? Would I be content to settle here or would I always need to roam free around this country?

Winston and I parted ways for a while. He wanted to be free to explore this special environment in his own way. He later told us that this afternoon on his own had been inspiring, a real turning point in his life. Something inside him had shifted. After a while, we all met up again when it started to sprinkle. We let Harley rest in the RV while we went out for lunch at the Plaza Cafe. It was Sunday, a big day for tourists to visit, and the restaurant had a waiting list. We put our name in and went out to see the artists' displays at their booths in the plaza. One of those artists had once paid Peter $20 to play the fiddle in front of his booth to attract more business. There were also the local Native American artists lining the wall along the Palace of the Governors opposite the plaza, displaying their hand-made jewelry and pottery on blankets spread on the ground in front of them. They'd patiently sit there all day as a steady stream of tourists passed by, some stopping to talk, some to buy.

When our name was called, we entered to eat some typical New Mexican food, which Winston was really enthusiastic about. Enchiladas, tamales, empanadas, chimichangas, sopapillas and so on. He'd like to try them all! We shared tastes of what we'd ordered, enjoying those unique New Mexican foods. Winston's youth and inexperience with travel increased his sense of wonder and appreciation at the newness of it all, and that spirit infected Peter and me as well. I was inspired to see things with new eyes, to always be a beginner, to greet the unknown without thinking I already knew. Hit the refresh button on my mind's computer, and be new!

A CRACK IN OUR PLANS

The *I Ching* gave us hexagram 42 Increase. "It furthers
one to undertake something. It furthers one to cross the
great water, to make the best use of the time."
   Peter and I, armed with this timely wisdom, went out to
meet Ron at the Madrid Road house. We were ready to
do business. I'd finally gotten a clear go-ahead about
buying the house and settling here. I was ready to take
the leap. But fate turned the tables, and Ron pointed out
the cracks along the cement floor inside the house, and
suggested that this would be a real big problem struc-
turally. Was he catastrophizing? Was he actually trying to
talk us out of buying this house? He recommended we
get a consultation with a structural engineer, saying that
would probably convince us of the dangers of buying this
house. He then proceeded to tell us of all the houses he'd
seen where the cracks couldn't be fixed, and the house
had begun to split apart at the foundation. Oh merde. Well
if this was so, then we wouldn't want to sign on for all the
troubles this place could entail. Our balloon of hopefulness had lost its oomph, but we agreed that we should at
least make an appointment to consult with a structural
engineer and hear the advice.
   Back at the campground, we got the camper settled in
at site number 6 for the July 4th holiday weekend, and
there found a book, "Good-bye Martians", which the

322

previous camper must have left behind. At least it didn't read "Good-bye House", so maybe there was still some hope.

We decided to take off in Peter's car for Taos, figuring it'd be good to get some distance from the roller-coaster ride of buying or not buying, settling or not settling. Taos would also be an important part of Winston's continuing Southwest education. After checking in at the El Pueblo Inn, we all went to a park down the road. While Winston threw sticks for Harley, we made phone calls to a few structural engineers, and finally found one who'd be free to do the job soon.

Walking around town with Harley in tow, we ended up getting some Thai food at an outdoor food wagon. The chef told us, "Yeah, it's a trend. Many chefs have left the kitchens of restaurants and are now cooking out in the streets. People seem to love it, and it gives us chefs a lot more freedom." We found a nearby bench in the shade and ate there, while Harley lay down beside us. The food was really delicious and spicy, and we were happy to give this chef some business.

Later, Peter and I walked down the road to the Allsup's convenience store for some junk food. A Native American woman approached me while I waited outside with Harley. "Can I pat your dog?," she asked. "I had a poodle, but he got run over by a car two years ago." I told her how sorry I was, knowing that this was not going to be the end of our conversation. She seemed quite ready to spill her story. So I listened as she continued, "See, I have seizures. It's from having had spinal meningitis. A friend of mine has a grandmother who has seizures, and she got a dog specially trained to help her. He'll bark if she's about to have a seizure, or if she's had one, he'll bark for help. I'd like to get one of those dogs, I could ask my doctor for a prescription for one. Can my husband pat your dog? He had one as a kid that he says looked just like your dog. Hey John, get out of the car and come pat this dog." John, a large Native American man, got out of the car with some difficulty. "Yes, my dog looked just like him. My parents both worked. My dog was my babysitter. If I got sleepy, I'd just lay my head right down on him and fall asleep. I always felt safe with him around."

His wife told me, "This is what we do." She reached into the back of their car that was overflowing with a tangle of all their stuff, clothes, cans of food, some boxes, and pulled out a DVD. "We want you to have it. It's his flute music and my photos. I used to go to my grandmother's in the Pueblo and listen to all the men play Native tunes on their flutes, and it got into my bones. So this is our gift to you."

I offered to pay her, but she insisted she wanted to give it to us. So I told them, "Thank you so much, and may you find a special dog to be of service to you."

And I thought how Harley's presence had just been of service to them. Our dogs just naturally serve us by their unconditionally loving natures. They love us faithfully no matter what. Even though Harley had to withstand long hours riding in the camper, he always loved us despite any hardship or discomfort. And a good swim and a few biscuits didn't hurt either.

MAKING THE LEAP

We woke early to the beeping of Peter's alarm. He'd take our camper for service that morning, and I'd drive Winston to the airport in the pouring rain.

"Do you think they'll still fly in this weather? I've never flown by myself before."

I reassured Winston, and when we got to the airport, he hugged me three times, thanking me and his uncle for having had him. It seemed like this had been an educational trip in so many ways for him. He'd experienced some freedom, enjoyed learning about a new place, a new way of being. Putting it into words, I told him, "Travel has opened our eyes to a new perspective, has loosened us from the ruts in our minds, and we've learned so much from others we've met along the way." He agreed, saying that had been his experience here with us. And then hugging me one more time, he turned to go into the airport. I felt so thankful that we could offer him this experience and could help open those doors for our nephew.

I drove over to meet Peter at the RV service department, and together, we went to Albuquerque Old Town, the historic part of town. We asked an old hippie guy sitting in the central park with his cronies, "Where's a good place for breakfast?" He told us to go to the Church Street Cafe right behind the historic adobe catholic church. We wandered around, got kind of lost, then decided to stop at an outdoor cafe that seemed inviting. Looking up, we saw the sign and sure enough, it read "Church Street Cafe." Harley was brought an ice bucket of water by the waiter, and he also lucked out and got some tortilla and egg bits, but not the ones smothered in red chili sauce, slipped to him under the table.

Back at number 6 Vista Linda, now was the time to make the leap. After all this thinking and doubting, all this going back and forth in my mind, it turned out to actually be very simple. It really felt like home in this gorgeous desert outpost of Jemez Springs. I made a call to Ron, and we set a date for 5:30 that evening to sign a contract on our Madrid Road house. We insisted on an escape clause that if the structural engineer were to report a faulty foundation, the contract would be void.

Today was the day! And at just the right time, we signed the papers and were given our copies. Pretty shocking. My mind had stopped and there was no more inner dialog about it. What a relief to finally have made this choice. Everything felt right! We celebrated with margaritas and guacamole at our picnic table, while pouring over the photos of the house that I'd downloaded onto the laptop.

The moon was growing full that night, shining bright and clear in the vast sky above.

FOURTH OF JULY

It was the Fourth of July. A parade would go right down the main street through the village. Peter took off to go fiddle, while Harley and I went to the Highway 4 Cafe to watch the parade from their porch. Judy and Don who lived up Madrid Road were there, Mark and Dede arrived along with their friend, Dottie, and another friend named Raymond, and then Peter joined us. It was a party! When I told everyone about our offer on the Madrid Road house, they said, "We have our fingers crossed for you!" Judy told us, "It'd be so great to have you as neighbors!" We felt welcomed. This felt like a real community, as we never really had before in any neighborhood where we'd lived. Dottie invited us to dinner that night, and we happily accepted. I had seen a table in the closet when we'd toured our Madrid house, and I had dreamed about having a dinner party after we moved in, but wondered who we'd invite. And now I knew. Our new Jemez Springs neighbors, at a nice big dinner party in our new home!

Well, spirits were running high, and a celebration was going on at the cafe. We stayed while the parade marched on by, complete with plenty of floats, marching bands, drum majorettes, fire engines with their sirens sounding, and some old geezers on motorcycles bringing up the rear. It was a small village atmosphere, everyone in the parade throwing out candy into the crowds, just like at Mardi Gras. After the parade, I walked down to the town park and signed up for the duck race to benefit the Jemez

Valley Association. Yellow plastic ducks were numbered and set afloat in the river; the first one to get to the bridge by the library would win. Booths and tents were set up in the park, vendors selling colorful tie-dye clothing, hand-made soaps and lotions, fiber arts from the alpaca farm up the road, snow cones, and Native American fry bread. It was a real small town Fourth of July, all so sweet. This would be our town now!

Gathering stamina for all the activities we'd join in that day, we went over to a grand opening at the local art gallery. More people from the community were there, a real party atmosphere and everyone so friendly. From there, we continued on to Dottie's dinner party, up, up the mountainous Ponderosa Drive, first to Raymond's house to pick him up. His wife, Shefa, was in Ohio at a Jewish convention, but Raymond took obvious delight in showing us around their home. It had also been built by Mark Feldman, different from any we'd seen so far, and maybe a little more traditional. It was chock full of the richness of their lives, a scatter of books, artwork, treasures, all that they'd created together. Raymond showed us their mar-riage poems, the song of love CD and book to go with it that he wanted us to have. He rummaged around in a file cabinet, and finally pulled out a little plastic bag. "It's lo-cally grown weed. Dottie likes to drink wine, but Mark and Dede like to smoke with me, so I'll bring some over to Dottie's for us. But first, I want to show you our meditation room." Raymond's heart seemed so open. We felt like we'd known him for ages.

Finally we drove on to Dottie's which was just the next house up, but it took a while to get there, up this winding mountain dirt road and down her treacherous driveway. We were glad it wasn't raining! We all had drinks out on her porch where the atmosphere was rarefied up in the ponderosa pine tree tops, and where you could see way across to Redondo Peak at the Valles Caldera. We'd now viewed Jemez Springs from three unique perspectives. Down by the river, the mesa looked quite immediate, but up by Madrid Road, you could see from a greater distance the mesas and the line of cottonwood trees as they followed along by the path of the river. And finally up in the treetops at Dottie's, the expansive view felt more philosophical and contemplative, with the whole valley spread out below.

Moving inside for dinner, we learned that Dottie's home had also built by Mark Feldman. Dottie remarked, "It's Mark's dynasty here in this valley!" We sat at the table, with the huge windows offering views 360 degrees all around, just as the windows in our new home would offer. We touched on a variety of subjects, the arts and music in Santa Fe, hand-held blenders, chronic pain, the nomadic life on the road in the RV, and the broken health care system here in the U.S. Everyone felt compatible, easy to be with, as we shared lots of easy laughter. Harley and Dottie's dog, Annie, were both asleep under the dining table, and all was well. But then a huge thunderstorm began brewing and rumbling, although surprisingly it didn't seem to freak Harley out too much. He'd already committed himself to the space under the table. When it was time to go, Harley didn't want to leave the safety of his protected place. Maybe he was preferring the home life as opposed to life on the road. Maybe he was giving us a message it was time to settle.

The rain came pouring down in buckets as we bid everyone goodnight, and began the scary drive back down the winding, steep, and now muddy road in the dark. We inched our way back down into the village, just in time for the rain to stop and the fireworks to begin. We pulled off to the side of the road and watched the explosions of red and blue and white lights in the sky. We felt so thankful for this magical night in this sweet little town on this beautiful Fourth of July in Jemez Springs, our new home to be!

DIVE IN

A heat wave was on, and there being no electric hookups at Vista Linda, the only help for it was to plug in down at Coronado Campground, pull down the shades, and crank up the A/C.

There was some back and forth on the bid for our house; we offered, they countered. The process was all a little tense like a tennis match played for high stakes. And then, the waiting game, we'd see how the contract would all pan out.

Reading Andrew Harvey's *Journey to Ladakh* about his spiritual journey in remote India was my only salvation. That and Chinese food to go, watching movies (even second-rate would do!), emailing, talking on the phone, and PBS nature shows. We put ourselves in a certain mindless zone in order to maintain life with a minimum of angst.

We finally got a call from Ron, and they'd accepted our offer. We had a contract. But of course, contingent on the structural appraisal that was scheduled for the next day. Yikes, this was a happening thing, and though it hadn't happened yet, I was already feeling a sense of buyer's remorse. I'd gone through it with every house I'd ever bought, the sinking feeling that maybe I should just stay put and avoid this leap into the unknown. Like hesitating on the edge of a pool and wondering if the cold water would be a shock to my system. I told myself, "Just dive in already and start swimming!"

COLLISION OF TWO WORLDS

I dreamed I was in a small group, chanting the *Guru Gita*. The atmosphere became still. The teacher entered and sat opposite me. In silence, we looked at each other. I knew that my teacher, the very soul of me, my highest consciousness, was right there with me, every step of the way. I'd been blessed this day with an auspicious dream.

And on that note, we went for our appointment with the structural engineer. The *I Ching* we'd thrown had advised us with hexagram number 62, Preponderance of the Small, a time of non-action, when it would be best to conserve energy and keep a low profile. So we went with a very sober and conscientious attitude, ready to listen to the engineer's professional assessment, unattached to the results. Either way it would go, we'd be fine. We were ready to let go of it all if need be.

But you know what? Victor Chavez stormed through 1240 Madrid Road, fearless, victorious, like a conqueror with a sword of discrimination. Checking every angle, every doorway, every window, every inch of the outside perimeter, every ceiling and every seam where wall met ceiling and floor, he proclaimed, "This house is in better shape than mine! This home is solid. Its foundation is solid. Have you paid for it yet? Do it! You'd do very well to live here!"

The whole thing happened so fast. We asked a barrage

of questions, then schmoozed a little with Victor's wife. All the while Ron was standing on the periphery, silently observing, perhaps disapproving.

So it looked like 1240 was a happening thing. We'd had ourselves all prepared to let it go, but now this home would be ours! Our lives had taken a new direction. We were, once again, taking a leap into the unknown. A new way of life. When we later walked the land with Ron, he seemed somehow sober, not happy as we might have expected a realtor to be when anticipating a sale. It was clear that for whatever reason, he didn't approve of this house or of us buying it. But oh well, that was his problem.

We took Harley down to the village park for a celebratory romp and ran into John and Phylos there. They told us how they'd also been to the Rainbow Gathering. John related, "I counseled and uplifted the people. They needed this, and I was there to spread light and peace."

Just then, Dottie drove by and rolled down her window, saying "Did you get the house?"

A collision of two worlds, Dottie, cultured and worldly, John and his son, living out of their van on the edges of society. We introduced them and then talked a little while with Dottie, telling her our good news. She was so sweet and happy for us. As she was driving off, John hugged me and I was sure Dottie could see this in her rearview mirror. I wondered, what might she making of this incongruous meeting of two different worlds?

Then Peter finally fessed up, telling John and Phylos "We've got to admit, we're doing something very capitalistic. We're going to be buying a home here."

John didn't skip a beat, "How wonderful! This is a special place. We love it here, and this will be so good for you. We'd like to find a place somewhere to hang our hats and settle." John was so dear, a true visionary. Some of what he talked about sounded outlandish to me, but what did I know? I loved him and his son. I loved their open hearts and their earnestness. As I absolutely loved and appreciated the diversity of all the people we'd met on the road.

CHANGES TO COME

New phones, new laptop, new internet service, new home, new friends, new lives…something inside was scared, or maybe excited! The life of traveling the past seven months would not be over for me. I wasn't ready to end it. I pledged to myself I would retain the delicious feeling of freedom, the joy of keeping an open mind, the pleasure of not knowing, of being in the flow of life where magic happened. Paying attention to this moment and letting that be my schedule. Twelve forty Madrid Road was a gift freely given, not a noose of ownership. It was light, open, and free. Light poured in through the windows from every direction. This home was a haven, a sanctuary of renewal for us. Rest easy, dear one, and trust that this new life opening up will reveal greater dimensions of love and wisdom to be lived.

Andrew Harvey in his book spoke of finding what breaks your heart in this world and doing something about it. I aimed to make my little place here in the world more full of love and kindness.

John and Phylos, parked in the library lot, were going to be on their way to Taos today. John told us, "You and Peter are good friends. Of all the people we've met, it's you we really love. You both *are* love. We will stay friends. If you need anything, I will be there for you. I could drive a vehicle across the country for you if you want. We're taking the gas money you gave us and are driving to Taos, leaving now. Go in peace. Blessings on your day." We hugged these dear people close, heart to heart. And then we each went our own ways.

Camped at our favorite site number 7, where the music of the river played on always, where Harley was let off his leash to abandon himself to the bliss of the river. We threw sticks for him amidst furious splashing and gnawing, then lured him back to the campsite with his bowl of dog food. We cooked our dinner in the generator-induced A/C, and ate at the picnic table overlooking the river. Then after dinner, I left Peter playing his guitar, and went out to the Jemez Springs Presbyterian Church to hear a speaker talk about the sustainable value of solar panels ("they pay for themselves in two years"), solar hot water, and greenhouses. Hmmm…these could all be valuable additions to our Madrid home. I loved being at the lecture with the good people from our new community, even recognizing a couple of them and saying mentally, hello, neighbor!

Back at number 7, Peter rolled a joint from the weed that Raymond had given us. The evening air was gentle, with cool breezes wafting through the valley of our desert home. The pared-down stark beauty of this land was going to be a perfect place to meditate. We would return to our local headquarters, number 7, to camp even after living at 1240 Madrid. We would always continue to be nomads, wandering the roads and campgrounds of this country, open to new experiences and people, then coming back to this red rock valley, to our home.
We lay on our backs on top of the picnic table, and

looking up at the staggering array of stars above, gave ourselves, heart and soul, to this desert land. The leaves of the cottonwoods were lit up occasionally by the head-lights passing cars.

Susan Dollenger lives in Jemez Springs, New Mexico, with her husband, Peter Harrington, their cat Meowser, and their new puppy, Violet. Harley crossed over the Rainbow Bridge in 2019, having lived a great life to the old age of 15.

Susan is a potter, selling her work locally. She continues to be a licensed massage therapist and was an RN for 40 years. Peter Harrington is a renowned artist who has shown his oil paintings at galleries in Santa Fe and Fort Worth.

Travels with Harley is her first book, but won't be the last. Susan and Peter and now, Violet, continue roaming the campgrounds across the country, from coast to coast.